To my children, and all the women still living in fear

Disclaimer

This book is a work of creative nonfiction based on real events. While it is inspired by true occurrences, certain characters, names, incidents, locations, and dialogues have been fictionalised or dramatised for narrative purposes. Any resemblance to actual persons, living or dead, is coincidental or used fictitiously. The author has made every effort to portray events truthfully while respecting the privacy and dignity of those involved. This book is not intended to harm, defame, or misrepresent any individual or entity.

Copyright 2024 by Caroline Orman

All rights reserved.

No portion of this book may be reproduced in any form without written permission from the publisher or author, except as permitted by U.K copyright law.

Contents

1. Bodrum Harbour, Bodrum, Turkey. May 2016. — 1
2. Kirazlı, Turkey. August 2014 (2 years earlier). — 7
3. Maralya, Turkey. September 2014 — 19
4. Kos, the Greek Islands, May 2016 — 28
5. Maralya, Turkey, October 2014 — 34
6. Maralya, Turkey. November 2014 — 42
7. Maralya, Turkey. January 2015 — 49
8. Athens, Greece. May 2016 — 56
9. Maralya, Turkey. February 2015 — 61
10. Maralya, Turkey. March 2015 — 66
11. Maralya, Turkey. April 2015 — 72
12. Kirazlı, Turkey. May 2015. — 76
13. Puglia, Italy. May 2016. — 79
14. Maralya, Turkey. May 2015. — 86
15. Maralya, Turkey. May 2015. — 91
16. Maralya, Turkey, June 2015 — 96
17. Maralya, Turkey. June 2015 — 100

18.	Maralya, Turkey. July 2015	109
19.	Somerset, England. July 2015.	115
20.	Maralya, Turkey. August 2015.	124
21.	Torre Mileto, Italy. June 2016.	131
22.	Maralya, Turkey. September 2015.	139
23.	Maralya, Turkey. October 2015.	145
24.	Maralya, Turkey. November 2015.	153
25.	Rome, Italy. June 2016.	162
26.	Maralya, Turkey. November 2015.	167
27.	Maralya, Turkey. November 2015.	171
28.	Maralya, Turkey. December 2015.	174
29.	Maralya, Turkey. New Year's Eve, 2015.	180
30.	Maralya, Turkey. New Year's Eve, 2015.	190
31.	Tuscany, Italy. June 2016.	194
32.	Maralya, Turkey. New Year's Day, 2016	199
33.	Maralya, Turkey. January 2016.	208
34.	Istanbul, Turkey. January 2016	212
35.	Kuşadası, Turkey. January 2016	221
36.	Kuşadası, Turkey. February 2016	228
37.	Bodrum, Turkey. February 2016.	239
38.	Maralya, Turkey. February 2016.	246
39.	Maralya, Turkey. February 2016.	251
40.	Venice, Italy. June 2016.	257

41.	Bodrum, Turkey. March 2016.	262
42.	Bodrum, Turkey. March 2016.	267
43.	Bodrum, Turkey. March 2016.	274
44.	Bodrum, Turkey. April 2016.	278
45.	Maralya, Turkey. April 2016	283
46.	St. Tropez, France. July 2016.	294
47.	Bodrum, Turkey. April 2016.	297
48.	Bodrum, Turkey. May 2016	300
49.	Bodrum, Turkey. May 2016.	308
50.	Bodrum, Turkey. May 2016.	313
51.	Spain. July 2016.	322
52.	Epilogue	325
	About the author	328

Chapter One

Bodrum Harbour, Bodrum, Turkey. May 2016.

"**M**ummy."

Her voice was tentative, quiet, as if afraid of interrupting something important.

I opened my eyes and closed them again as another wave of nausea rose from my stomach. Pressing my forehead back against the cool plastic of the steering wheel, I wrapped my arms around it a little tighter, as if holding on for dear life.

Breathe, said the voice in my head. *Just breathe.*

"Mummy?"

The voice again. More demanding this time, pulling me back to a reality I didn't want to face.

I had no idea how long I had been sitting here, face down in the driver's seat of my car. Clearly long enough for my daughter to be worried.

"Mummy, are you OK?"

I considered the question. The lead weight of fear pressed down on my chest. My stomach threatened to throw up the coffee I drank an hour ago with every twist and clench. My palms were sweating, and my mouth was dry. I opened my eyes and forced myself to sit up.

"I'm fine, sweetie," I said with as much conviction as I could muster.

The travel agent had said eight-thirty, but we were early. The only car parked in front of a ticket office that was still closed.

Around us, Bodrum Harbour slowly stirred into life. Fishermen, their leathery faces crinkling into warm smiles as they greeted each other, stirred cubes of sugar into tulip-shaped glasses of *çay*. A skinny tabby watched with a slow blink as her three kittens played amongst the discarded fishing nets. In the blue-green water, wooden boats creaked back and forth.

The air smelled of salt and diesel and fear.

A man and a woman had appeared in front of the ticket office. They were smartly dressed; her skirt a little too short, his tie flapping over his shoulder in the breeze. He unlocked the door, holding it open for her, smiling with a brief nod as she stepped inside. I watched as they sat behind their respective desks and switched on their computers.

A year ago, this had been my life. Atakan making coffee. Beyza filling me in on the details of her weekend.

I wondered if they were aware of how fragile it all was. How quickly it could be snatched away.

The clock on the dashboard said eight thirty-five. Ignoring the lurch in my stomach, I took a deep breath and unclipped my seatbelt.

It was time.

I twisted around to face her. Alone in the back seat surrounded by all our belongings, she looked so very small and young. The thought crossed my mind that quite literally everything I owned was in this car. Ten years of life folded, condensed, and packed into bags and suitcases.

"Ready?" I forced a smile.

She nodded.

"Let's go."

The woman smiled a red-lipsticked smile from behind her computer as we entered the air-conditioned office. I flashed a nervous smile back. *Act normal* chastised the voice in my head. I smiled again. Better.

"One adult, one child, and a car?" she said in heavily accented English as she scrutinized our tickets.

"Yes."

"You have insurance?" she said. "For the car?"

I reached into my bag for the crumpled green insurance document and passed it over.

Behind us, the door chimed open and an overweight couple with matching backpacks and sunglasses pushed high on their heads came into the office. The woman smiled at me, fanning herself with a rolled-up newspaper. The man nodded a greeting.

"You have one month's insurance for the car," said the lipsticked woman, scrutinizing the insurance document beneath unfeasibly long lashes. "How long you stay in Kos?"

"A few days. A week at the most." I swallowed heavily as Elif and I exchanged silent glances.

The woman held our documents towards me with a crimson smile.

"Enjoy your holiday!" She said.

If only she knew.

We headed towards passport control. I gripped Elif's hand as the sliding doors opened onto a vast empty hall. Suddenly my legs didn't want to move.

"*Turn around,*" said the voice in my head. "*It's not too late. You can still go back.*"

I took a deep breath and forced one leg in front of the other, clutching Elif's hand a little too tightly as I made my way across the hall towards the customs desk.

Through the glass doors at the other end of the hall, the red and white ferry gleamed in the sun; its bow doors open like an invitation.

I had played out this moment so many times over the past twenty-four hours that it almost felt like déjà vu. Different scenarios with different endings. Planning what I would do and what I would say.

"*Pasaport,*" said the man without looking up. He had round wire-rimmed spectacles and a neatly trimmed moustache.

I slid our passports towards him under the glass, my heart thudding in my chest as he gave my photograph a cursory glance and placed it under the scanner. There was an approving bleep.

The thudding got louder as he did the same with Elif's passport.

Another bleep.

I breathed a faint sigh of relief.

Stifling a yawn, the customs officer picked up my passport again and began flicking through the pages. His forehead creased into a frown. He leafed through the pages again, slowly this time. Pushing his glasses further up the bridge of his nose, he raised his head and looked at me through the glass.

"Visa?"

I gave a blank stare. Pretending not to understand.

He leafed through the pages again. No visa. No entry or exit stamp. One conclusion.

"You live here?" he said in accented English.

My mouth was suddenly bone dry.

I nodded.

Sighing heavily at my stupidity, he held out his hand. *"Kimlik,"* he said, asking for our Turkish identity cards.

The game was up.

I steadied myself on the counter as a rush of dizziness threatened to overwhelm me. When I had imagined this scene countless times in my head, this was the part where I feigned ignorance or rummaged in my bag with a look of panic on my face, pretending to have forgotten our ID cards before pleading with him to let us through. I had a wedding to go to, I would say. A funeral. A family member was critically ill. Maybe a bribe would work. This was Turkey, after all. How much would it take for him to look the other way? 100 lira? 500? 1000?

In reality, I reached into my bag for our ID cards and placed them on the counter.

He picked up my card first, tapping in the number slowly as he stared at the screen. Satisfied, he placed the card back on the counter and reached for Elif's ID card.

I gripped the counter with both hands, holding my breath as he tapped in the numbers one by one. The faintest lines of a frown began to form on his forehead, a barely perceptible hardening of his eyes.

It was taking too long.

The room around me began to blur.

I closed my eyes. It was over.

How could I have been so stupid?

Police, guns slung across their bodies, grabbing me on either side, pulling me away.

Elif's screams echoing around the hall, as she tried to wriggle free from a police officer's arms.

The couple with the matching backpacks. Staring.

"*Hanımefendi?*"

A male voice jerked me back to reality. Soft fingers curled around my hand.

I opened my eyes and gazed around the empty customs hall. Elif was smiling up at me, her hand in mine.

"Mummy?" she said. "Let's go!"

The customs surveyed me with a mixture of curiosity and pity as he slid our documents towards me under the glass.

"*İyi yolculuklar.*"

"Have a nice trip."

"Come on, mum, let's go!" Elif was tugging my arm.

Tightening her fingers around mine, my nine-year-old daughter led me across the hall, through the sliding glass doors, and towards the red and white ferry on the other side.

Chapter Two

Kirazlı, Turkey. August 2014 (2 years earlier).

The cicadas seemed to get louder the higher the temperature rose as if screeching in protest.

I held the fridge door open for a little longer than was necessary, enjoying a brief respite from the heat as I cast my eyes over its contents.

There were three different kinds of salads. *Çoban Salatası*; diced tomatoes and cucumber drizzled with olive oil and sprinkled with fresh parsley. *Piyaz*; white beans, tomato, and chopped onion, topped with black olives, and hard-boiled eggs, and finally *Kısır;* bulgur wheat mixed with diced cucumber, mint, and lemon juice.

Elinize sağlık- health to your hands, they say in Turkish when you make something good. As I hoped this would be. At least good enough.

On the shelf below, plates of homemade *köfte, sigara börek* and skewered *şiş kebap* competed for space amongst the bottles of beer and wine.

I closed the fridge door and turned my attention to the living room. The carpet, vacuumed an hour ago, was now strewn with toys and the television screen sticky with fingerprints. I stooped to pick up a Star Wars action figure as right on cue, there was a loud bang followed by a scream from upstairs.

I sprinted up the marble steps two at a time.

Five-year-old Cem was sitting on his bedroom floor, knee clutched in both hands, eyes squeezed shut in a moment of suspended silence before the inevitable howl.

Elif, seven, stood next to him, hands demurely on her hips.

"He was jumping on the bed," she informed me as I arrived breathless in the doorway.

"What have I told you?" I chastised gently, crouching on the floor and scooping him up.

"No more monkeys…"

"… jumping on the bed" finished Elif, wagging her finger at her brother, who laughed despite himself.

Burying his wet face in my neck, Cem curled his fingers around my hair as I carried him downstairs.

"I love you," I whispered in his ear as I lowered him onto the sofa and carefully detached his fingers one by one. His eyes lit up. "All the way…"

He scanned the room before settling his gaze on the window. "All the way to that tree and back?" he said, pointing to the towering pine tree that veered dangerously to the left at the bottom of the garden. I shook my head.

"All the way to the sea and back?" he said, his eyes playful as he tilted his head to the side.

I shook my head again.

"All the way to the stars and back!" I kissed his wet cheek and picked up the remote control.

"Wow!" he said, visibly impressed. "That's really far!"

Elif appeared in the doorway and gazed disdainfully at the TV as exaggerated cartoon cheeriness filled the room.

"I'm going to have a shower," I said, making a mental note to wipe the fingerprints from the TV before Gülşen arrived.

"Try not to kill yourselves or each other until I get back."

I stood under water as cold as I could stand, closing my eyes as it ran down my body, taking with it the heat, sweat, and stress of the day.

I had been up at six. Preparing food, vacuuming carpets, polishing furniture, and cleaning windows until they squeaked. I had swept and washed the veranda under the punishing midday sun.

Wrapping myself in a towel, I had air-dried by the time I reached the bedroom. I grabbed a red, cotton sundress from the wardrobe, struggling to pull it on over skin already sticky with sweat. I ran a comb through my damp hair and attempted to dab on make-up which immediately slid down my face.

Downstairs, the doorbell chimed.

"Elif!" I called, straining my ears for a response, but only the high-pitched tones of Mickey Mouse drifted back towards me up the stairs.

The doorbell chimed again.

Spraying liberal amounts of deodorant under my arms, I headed downstairs.

"*Merhaba!*"

Gülşen launched herself at me, encompassing me in a bear hug and planting wet kisses on each cheek. She smelled of fabric softener mixed with sweat and cigarettes.

Today my mother-in-law was wearing baggy floral trousers, a bright orange T-shirt, and, despite the heat, a crocheted purple cardigan, thick socks, and sandals. Her head was wrapped in a multi-coloured scarf from which her wild, black hair stuck out at odd angles.

"*Merhaba!*" I replied, forcing a smile as she pushed past me into the living room. Her eagle eyes immediately honed in on the toy-strewn carpet and fingerprinted TV.

"I was just about to..." I said in Turkish, but her attention had been diverted by an even bigger crime.

Alfie, our 12-year-old mongrel, lay welded to the cool floor tiles like an inebriated reveller. Clapping her hands frantically until he staggered to his feet, Gülşen herded the ageing dog out of the back door, where he collapsed onto the veranda in the blistering sun.

Disney channel forgotten, the children made themselves scarce as Gülşen, muttering under her breath about the depravity of allowing a dog in the house, stooped to pick up toys from the floor, clutching her back for full dramatic effect.

The doorbell chimed again.

It was Azra. Wild black curls framing her face. She grinned a mischievous grin as she thrust a bottle of red wine towards me.

A lawyer from Istanbul, Azra was something of an anomaly in a small, traditional town like Maralya. Steadfastly refusing to conform to the expectations of women as dutiful, subservient, and virtuous, Azra was a free spirit who did what she wanted. And what she wanted, most of the time, was to have fun.

"Gülşen is here," I whispered, kissing her on both cheeks as her eight-year-old son, Husain, dove past us in search of Elif and Cem.

"I'm going to need a glass of that!"

I followed Azra into the kitchen, where she took a corkscrew from the drawer, expertly opened the wine, and poured us both a glass.

On the veranda, Gülşen had squeezed herself into a wicker chair and was fanning herself with a magazine. I took a sip of wine, relaxing for the first time that day as I gazed out across the vast untamed garden towards the mountains and the sea.

The sun hovered above the horizon, bathing the sky in a tangerine light as she bade the day farewell. The air was still, heavy with the scent of honeysuckle and jasmine. The cicada's singing now calm and melodic. Fireflies danced like tiny fairy lights around the glow of a street lamp. High on the white wall, a pale orange gecko stared down with bulging black eyes.

"The grape vines need pruning," Gülşen's voice penetrated my hazy contentment like a barracuda through tranquil water.

To my relief, the doorbell rang again.

"Carr-iee!" Atakan's chirpy tone drifted towards me, "Where are you Carr-iee?".

We squealed in delight as I opened the door, throwing ourselves into each other's arms as if we hadn't seen each other for a year, though in reality, it had been barely forty-eight hours. Helping himself to a beer from the fridge, Atakan pushed his arm through mine, launching into an account of his latest internet date as we returned to the veranda.

"Mother-in-law is here," he whispered, stopping mid-sentence and eyeing Gülşen nervously. Gülşen surveyed us from behind her magazine, the cogs of her brain already turning as she prepared to deliver this tasty tidbit to anyone who would listen. Thankfully, the real gossip, that Atakan dated boys would never occur to her.

Guests continued to arrive. Kissing cheeks and filling glasses, I put some music on and directed them towards bowls of crisps and nuts as I wondered, not for the first time, where my husband was.

Amid the strains of Bruno Mars and the laughter-punctuated conversational hum, the doorbell chimed again.

Marie was wearing a white cotton dress embroidered with butterflies, her glowing skin a testament to a lifetime of art, vegetarianism, and yoga.

"Long time no see!" she smiled, passing me a bottle of organic wine.

"I'm so glad you could come!" I pressed my cheek to hers, "It's been ages!"

Marie followed me into the kitchen, where I rummaged in the drawer for the corkscrew.

"How long are you here for?" I said.

"Only until Friday." she replied, "Then I need to get back to..."

The rest of the sentence was lost, drowned out by the roar of the motorbike that flooded the room. I froze, corkscrew in my hand, listening until the engine cut out. Footsteps and male voices approached. The front door swung open.

The house was instantly filled with his presence. As large in personality as he was in size.

"Let's get this party started!!!" Serkan barged into the kitchen, closely followed by his best friend and constant companion Kadir. He did not look at me.

"Baba!"

Cem flew down the stairs, launching himself at his father, who picked him up with the ease of a bear lifting a mouse.

"My boy! I missed you!" said Serkan, plastering the child's face with kisses. From the doorway, unnoticed by her father, Elif watched silently.

Cem still clinging koala-like around his neck, Serkan opened the fridge and scanned the contents. I held my breath, watching as his eyes passed slowly over the salads, the *köfte*, the *börek* and the *kebabs*. Reaching for a beer, he slammed the door shut and walked wordlessly past me.

Slowly, I exhaled.

Marie was looking at me expectantly.

"Wine!" I remembered, glancing around for the corkscrew before realising it was in my hand.

On the veranda, the women and the men had drifted into separate groups. The women sat on chairs at one end. The men were gathered around Serkan at the other. Roars of laughter punctuated the night sky as, beer in hand, he kept them entertained with jokes and anecdotes. The proverbial life and soul.

It was at times like this that I got a glimpse of the old Serkan, the one I had fallen in love with, and I wondered what happened to him.

My eyes drifted back towards the garden. Cem lay on his back in the hammock strung between the lemon and plum trees as Elif and Huseyin swung him gently from side to side. The chickens headed past them, single file, back to the coop to roost. Alfie, rejuvenated by the party and the welcome drop in temperature, waddled arthritically from guest to guest pushing his muzzle into their hands with a wag of his tail.

I looked up with a jolt as Serkan sat down heavily opposite me, an amber bottle of *Efes* beer in one hand, a chunk of bread in the other. He took a swig of beer before tearing off a chunk of bread with his teeth.

"Someone's hungry," laughed Marie.

"My wife doesn't feed me," Serkan replied, patting his protruding belly.

Everyone laughed.

"You're lucky to have her," Azra smiled in my direction.

"I don't know about that." Serkan tore off another chunk of bread and turned to me. "Somebody has to put up with her, don't they, Carrie?"

I smiled faintly as everyone roared with laughter. His sense of humour was one of the things that had most attracted me to him. Before I became the butt of every joke.

"Maybe if she learned to cook like my mum," he continued, pinching his thumb and forefinger together and kissing them to emphasise the point. For a fraction of a second, his eyes locked with mine, long enough for him to acknowledge my misery, his longed-for reward. A flicker of satisfaction passed across his face as he took another swig of beer.

"Never mind Carrie, you'll learn," he said with a sigh.

The laughter was more subdued this time. A few of the guests glanced at each other, seeking reassurance that he was still joking. I gripped my wine glass hard, wondering how hard I could squeeze it before it broke. From her wicker chair, Gülşen smiled a self-satisfied smile.

At around one, the party started to wind down, and the guests began to leave.

Serkan was deep in conversation with Kadir and two other men, a half-empty bottle of *rakı* on the table between them.

In the living room, Gülşen lay collapsed on the sofa, snoring loudly. A fine line of saliva trickled from the corner of her mouth.

Collecting the plates, glasses, and cutlery, I piled them onto the already cluttered kitchen worktops, scraped the leftovers into the bin, and scrubbed them clean before stacking them on the drainer to dry. I wiped the worktops and swept the floor. It was almost two by the time I dragged myself up the stairs, creeping silently into the children's bedrooms, to kiss their sleeping forms before washing my face with water, brushing my teeth, and collapsing into bed in an instant and dreamless sleep.

***

Something was pulling me from the depths of sleep. I tried to cling to it, but it was slipping through my fingers like sand. A strong smell of rakı and stale sweat hit me, hands pulling at my top, heavy breathing in my ear. I winced in pain as he squeezed my breast hard.

"Let me sleep," I murmured.

"Come on, Carrie," he grunted, squeezing harder.

I opened my eyes. Outlined in the orange glow of the streetlamp that shone in through the bedroom window, his vast, Buddha-esque belly hung over the top of his shorts, eyes protruding and bloodshot, chin thick with three days' worth of stubble.

He hasn't even cleaned his teeth, I thought to myself as the aniseed stench of rakı and barbequed chicken wafted towards me. I knew there would be consequences, but I was too tired to care. I turned away from him.

"I'm tired Serkan."

The light snapped on. A searing pain sliced through my brain. He glared at me.

"Tired?" He spat the word out in disgust.

"What do you have to be tired about? Sitting all evening drinking wine like the queen, while I do all the work!"

I squeezed my eyes shut, covering my face with my hands in an attempt to block out the excruciating light. Sometimes when I refused him, he would sit at the end of the bed until morning, jabbing my feet, refusing to let me sleep.

I hoped tonight wasn't going to be one of those nights.

There was a sudden crash, followed by the sound of breaking glass.

I opened my eyes. The lamp from the bedside table lay in pieces on the floor. Serkan stood over me. Pure hatred oozed from his eyes.

"You're a waste of space, Carrie," he snarled. "What kind of wife are you?"

"Please Serkan," I said, my heart sinking as the sound of Cem crying drifted into the room.

"You're spoilt that's your problem," Serkan continued, "I treat you too well. You need to learn to behave like a proper wife. I need to teach you some manners."

"I know," I placated. "I'll learn. I'm sorry."

Seemingly satisfied, he turned, igniting a flicker of hope in me as he began to walk towards the door.

"Mummy! Cem's crying!" Elif's voice.

"Coming honey!"

I sat up, swung my legs out of bed, and pressed my bare feet to the wooden floor. Serkan had reached the door. I willed him to keep walking, to turn the handle and leave. He stopped.

"Mummy!" Elif's voice again.

"Coming sweetie!"

I stood slowly; keeping my eyes fixed on Serkan's back as I took careful, tentative steps towards the door. Still, he did not move.

"I need to check the children," I said, as calmly as I could muster.

He turned to face me.

"So, check the children." Amusement flickered in his eyes.

"I can't get past," I said quietly. "Can you let me pass, please?"

"And if I don't?" he sneered. "What are you going to do, Carrie?"

He said it like a dare, a chilling smile playing around his lips as he savoured the power he had over me.

"Please, Serkan..." I began as his hand shot out, grasping my throat, and slamming me back against the wall.

"You can't do anything, and you know it!"

His other hand flew up, fingers curled into a fist. I closed my eyes, bracing myself for the impact as his fist collided with the wall next to my head.

I kept my eyes closed, staying completely still until I felt his hands around my throat relax their grip. When I opened them, his face was inches from mine, so close I could smell his breath. My stomach heaved.

"You can NEVER get away from me," he hissed. "I'll destroy you, Carrie. I'll take the children and drive you out of Turkey. This is MY country! You are nothing here. NOTHING!"

Giving me a last shove, he opened the door. The room shook as it slammed behind him.

I stood, unable to move, barely daring to breathe, listening to his footsteps on the stairs until I heard the welcome slam of the front door.

"Mummy!"

They stood together on the landing. Bleary-eyed and blinking in the harsh light. Cem clutched his favourite teddy bear.

"It's OK," I said, crouching down and putting my arms around them. "Let's go back to bed."

Outside, I heard the car engine splutter into life, the squeal of brakes and the crunch of tyres on gravel as Serkan drove away.

"We wanna sleep wiz you," Cem rubbed his eyes.

"Yes, can we? Can we sleep with you?" There was fear in Elif's eyes, although I know she would never admit it. She must have heard everything.

We climbed into bed, the three of us, me in the middle, the children on either side.

The red digits of the clock on the bedside table glowed 3:42.

When I was sure they were asleep, I extracted myself from between their sleeping bodies and crept out onto the balcony.

The air was warm and still. The crescent moon glinted scythe-like in the night sky. Somewhere in the distance, an owl hooted softly.

I sat there for a long time. On the balcony of my beautiful home, wondering when it became a beautiful prison.

I sat until the mountains on the horizon changed from black to shades of purple, mauve and blue, the cicadas singing ceased and the wail of a distant minaret echoed across the empty sky. At some point, I must have drifted off to sleep because when I opened my eyes, Alfie had joined me, his head on my lap as we dozed.

The worst prisons, though, have no walls, and the most powerful jailers were the ones inside my head. They kept a running commentary of my failing marriage, arguing amongst themselves as they took turns trying to convince me to stay.

Hope promised that one day things would be different.

Pride refused to accept that it wasn't working.

Shame convinced me it was my fault.

Guilt whispered in my ear about the effects of breaking up the family on the children.

I talked to no one. Not Azra. Not even Atakan. I carried my unhappiness around like a secret, as heavy as lead and as invisible as the breeze.

My jailers were silent now. All but one.

My last remaining jailer barely said a word. Yet it was with me every day, in everything I did and everything I said. The sound of his key turning in the lock, the clench of his jaw, the flicker of a shadow across his face.

It was my last remaining jailer that now tightened its grip around my chest, seized the breath in my lungs, seeped into my bone marrow, and ran through my veins like blood.

Its name was Fear.

Chapter Three

Maralya, Turkey. September 2014

It was a long, straight road from Kirazlı to the nearby town of Maralya where I worked.

I often spent the journey deep in thought, trying to pinpoint the moment it had all started to go wrong. When did a bad mood become a bad patch and then a bad marriage?

It hadn't always been like this.

In the beginning, we were happy. A dangerous mix of first love and stubborn naivety were enough to paper over the glaring differences in outlook, educational background, culture, and expectations of what a marriage should be.

We spent twelve years in London where I qualified as a nurse and Serkan worked a series of jobs from waiter to kitchen porter to taxi driver. After Elif was born, a combination of the spiralling cost of living, grey skies and an absence of any real quality of life pushed us to sell the house and start again in Serkan's hometown of Maralya on the Turkish Mediterranean coast.

Within a year, I was pregnant again, and Cem arrived. We bought a villa in Kirazlı, a sleepy farming village about ten miles outside the resort town of Maralya, and I swapped my stethoscope and scrubs for life as a wife and mother. After four years, I was near fluent in Turkish and found a job in a private hospital as a translator. In summer, Maralya quadrupled in size as tourists in search of sunshine and cheap beer descended on the town in their droves. There was also a steadily growing community of mostly British expats who had made Maralya their home year-round.

There was no single moment when I realised it wasn't working. Like the proverbial frog in the cooking pot, the heat increased notch by notch, year by year and by the time I realised what was happening, it was too late.

As my marriage disintegrated around me, Serkan and I lived mostly separate lives. My attempts to talk were met with blank stares or increasingly aggressive outbursts until soon I was living in survival mode. I watched his body language intently, trying to predict a fit of rage before it happened. I became docile, compliant, and inoffensive, taking care to never say anything that might trigger his temper. I cooked, cleaned and took care of the children. Of the money from the sale of the house in London, nothing was left. The villa was in Serkan's name. We were in his country now. His power over me was absolute and he never let me forget it.

Sometimes I wondered what would happen if I missed the turning for Maralya and just kept on driving on the long, straight road.

***

"*Günaydın* Carrie!" the girls chorused from behind the desk as I entered the spotless reception.

"*Günaydın!*" I smiled, turning left and making my way down the long, gleaming corridor towards the translation office. The hospital smelled of disinfectant and iodine.

I reached the door marked **FOREIGN PATIENTS' ASSISTANCE** and pushed it open.

The translation office was a hub of ringing phones, tapping keyboards and babbling conversations in an array of languages.

From behind his computer, Atakan looked up and flashed a wave and a smile. In front of him, an elderly man leaned forward in his chair, eyes narrowed in concentration. He had a bushy moustache and watery eyes.

"Your wife needs to stay in, sir," said Atakan slowly over the din. "She's dehydrated. The nurses are taking care of her."

The man nodded. "I'll pick her up this evening," he said.

Atakan shook his head. "She needs to stay here tonight. We'll look after her, I promise. I'll call you a taxi. You can visit tomorrow."

"A taxi?" replied the old man, cupping his hand over his ear. "You drive a taxi, did you say?"

"Carrie, they need an English translator in Emergency," said Beyza as she rushed past me clutching a patient file.

On the sofa sat a tall blonde family wrapped in brightly coloured beach towels, their flip-flopped feet patchy with sand. The husband clutched their passports and insurance documents, a solemn expression on his face. The wife flashed me a bright smile from beneath her floppy hat, her arm strapped across her body in a sling. Twin girls with damp pigtailed hair sat between them, giggling at something on a screen. They looked German, I thought, as Beyza confirmed my suspicions by launching into a stream of rapid Deutsch.

I sat down at my desk and switched on my computer, glancing warily at the stack of patient files in my in-tray. They would all need medical reports translated from Turkish into English by the end of the day.

"This one came in last night," said Atakan, turning his attention from the old man and passing me a file.

"Broken wrist. She needs surgery. The insurance needs an urgent medical report."

The office door opened, and a familiar face appeared. Maralya resident and hospital regular Margaret Crosby entered the office in varying shades of grey, her long, silvery hair piled in a half-hearted bun on the top of her head. She forced what could barely be called a smile before sinking onto the sofa with a sigh.

"Oh Carrie," she said feebly. "I don't feel at all well."

Margaret visited the hospital at least twice a month with a variety of non-specific ailments, each one more vague than the last.

"I think I've got another water infection," she sighed.

"No problem, Margaret," I said. "I'll take you to the doctor."

***

Eight and a half hours, twelve patients and seven medical reports later, I said goodbye to my colleagues and stepped outside into the warm September sun. I got into my car and started the engine, glancing nervously at the petrol gauge as I made a rough calculation of how long I had before the arrow reached the bottom. Two more days, three at the most. There was still a week until payday.

In London, I had been the main breadwinner, covering the mortgage, food and bills, and this hadn't changed when we moved to Turkey.

When we first arrived, sky-high interest rates on the money from the sale of the house gave us a generous passive income, and by the time I bought the villa, I was working at the hospital and paying our monthly expenditures from my salary.

I never asked what Serkan did with his money. I knew better than to ask. When he was happy with my behaviour, Serkan would put a few lira notes in a book on the bookshelf in the living room. There had been no money in the book for a long time.

***

It was Serkan's favourite. White beans soaked overnight and slow-cooked with finely chopped onion, tomato and diced lamb until it melted in the mouth.

I needed to make amends. To try harder. Maybe if I cooked better, cleaned better, had sex better, we could be like we were again.

I added a little more black pepper and replaced the lid as an unwelcome memory flashed into my mind.

The pot large and heavy in his hands, his face like thunder as he kicked open the back door. Chunks of stew stuck to the wall as it dripped down onto the grass below. The chickens running, pecking hungrily at the beans and chunks of meat.

I pushed the thought aside as, right on cue, the roar of his motorbike filled the room. I took a deep breath, waiting for the sound of his key in the lock.

The door flew open. Serkan threw his keys on the counter and headed straight for the stove where he lifted the lid and shovelled a spoonful of stew into his mouth.

No comment. I exhaled slowly. No comment was good.

"Good day?" I enquired as he walked wordlessly past me into the living room, sank heavily onto the sofa, and reached for the remote control.

I laid the table and placed the pot of stew in the centre along with rice, fresh bread, salad, and a jug of lemonade made with lemons from the garden.

Homemade lemonade had been one of the things I had been most excited about when we bought the villa.

Silly really.

"Elif! Dinner's ready!" I called up the stairs.

Cem, who had joined Serkan on the sofa, climbed down and took a seat at the table.

"I'm hungwi," he announced, eyeing the pot of stew.

Serkan continued to stare at the evening news as Cem and I waited at the table. Eventually, he sighed and got to his feet. Sitting down next to Cem, he filled his plate and began shovelling forkfuls of food into his mouth, eyes still fixed on the TV.

"Elif!" I called again, trying to keep the urgency from my voice as the first flutters of panic started to build inside me.

"Coming!" came back the reply.

"Come on, dinner's ready!"

I spooned rice and stew onto Cem's plate and then my own, the knot in my stomach tightening as I willed my daughter to make an appearance. She was probably so absorbed in the picture she was drawing, or the book she was reading, that she had lost track of time. Finally, she appeared and pulled up a chair next to mine. To my relief, Serkan didn't appear to have noticed. The news, something about President Erdoğan, taking his full attention. We ate in silence until the news was over. With the spell broken, Serkan turned his attention to his daughter.

"How are you Elif?" he said.

She froze, a forkful of rice midway between her plate and her mouth.

"Are you not talking to me?" he continued. "Why aren't you talking to me, Elif?"

Elif put the fork down. "I am talking to you," she said, staring at her plate.

Serkan smiled and shook his head. The knot in my stomach tightened.

"My son," said Serkan calmly, gesturing towards Cem. "My son loves his Baba, don't you, Cem?"

Cem glanced from his sister to his father before nodding vehemently.

"My son," continued Serkan, "comes to see me when I get home from work. Says hello. Gives me kisses. Why don't you give me kisses, Elif?"

The little girl was silent. She looked at me, but my face was blank, impassive. I could not help her.

"I was drawing," she said finally.

"Drawing," repeated Serkan, pouring a glass of lemonade for himself and Cem. "You were drawing."

He took a gulp of the pale yellow liquid and spooned a few more forkfuls of food into his mouth. Elif was no longer eating.

"Tomorrow, I'm going out for ice cream," said Serkan, mopping up his sauce with a chunk of bread.

"Do you want ice cream, son?"

"Yay! Ice cream!" Cem clapped his hands with delight.

"I am going to take Cem for ice cream," continued Serkan. "Cem deserves ice cream. Cem loves Baba."

Elif's eyes filled with tears as Serkan and Cem exchanged smiles, the wobbling of her bottom lip barely noticeable as she tried not to cry.

"Serkan, come on..."

The words were barely out of my mouth as his fist crashed down on the table. Lemonade sloshed from the jug onto the freshly washed tablecloth.

"You stay out of it!" He lunged towards me. "This is between me and my daughter!"

He glared at me, inviting me to retaliate.

"I'm sorry," I said, lowering my gaze.

"You didn't put in enough salt again," he muttered, pushing his empty plate away before returning to the sofa, and sinking down with a sigh.

"I'll buy you ice cream," I mouthed silently to the little girl, making her smile.

After clearing the table and washing the plates, Elif and I took Alfie out for his evening stroll. I loved this time of day. The chickens were heading home to roost. The owl who had taken up residence in our roof arches perched on the electricity pylon surveying her kingdom before swooping silently off into the night. Gül, one of our neighbours, was sitting outside on a wooden stool, shelling peas. She waved and smiled.

"*Iyi akşamlar!*"

I waved back.

"He doesn't mean it," I said to Elif, hating myself for defending him. "He loves you. You know that."

"Will you buy me ice cream?" she stopped and looked up at me.

"I'll buy you the biggest ice cream ever!" I said, putting my arm around her shoulder and pulling her close as we walked.

***

The numbers on the clock glowed red in the darkened room. 11:43. It must be over soon, I told myself as the weight of him pushed down on me. I could feel the heat of his breath, smell his skin, and it was all I could do not to scream and push him off me. I needed to pretend to enjoy it. He got angry if I didn't enjoy it. Closing my eyes, I began to disconnect. Floating up and away. Away from my body, from this bed, from this bedroom, from this house. Higher over the houses and fields of Kirazlı, above the palm trees, beaches and hotels of Maralya. Higher still, above the clouds where the air was still and quiet. Where nothing could hurt me.

Finally, with a grunt, he collapsed on top of me, crushing me with his weight. Exhaling with relief, I opened my eyes as he rolled off me. The red numbers on the clock said 11:54.

Afterwards, I lay completely still in my marital bed. The one I had made and would continue to lie in, waiting for his breathing to change, to become regular and rhythmic, for the snores to catch in the back of his throat.

When I was sure he was asleep, I crept out of bed and made my way to the bathroom to wash away all traces of him. My debts paid for another day.

Chapter Four

Kos, the Greek Islands, May 2016

I pushed my bare feet deeper into the warm sand, hugging my knees and watching Elif as she paddled in the shallow surf. Behind her, across the wide, blue Aegean, the sugar-cube houses of Bodrum were just visible, nestled into the craggy Turkish coast.

Strange to think that just this morning I had been there, looking at this view in reverse, my body a mess of jangled nerves, barely daring to imagine this moment.

I took a deep breath.

I had done it.

I was free.

I cast my mind back to the beginning of this journey, seeing myself as I was then; trapped, afraid, searching for a way out.

Would I do the same again? I asked myself. Knowing what I knew now? That it would cost me everything.

I caught Elif's eye and smiled.

Well, almost everything.

***

After parking the car on the otherwise empty car deck, we had made our way up to the passenger cabin to await departure.

"Can we go up to the top deck?" said Elif as we sat at the end of a row of blue seats.

"A bit later," I said, pulling the curtain across the window.

Such was my paranoia that I half expected him to appear at the dock, run onto the ferry and drag us kicking and screaming off the boat. Serkan had friends everywhere. What if somebody recognised us and called him? Or the customs officer realised his mistake?

From inside my bag, my phone buzzed a message. It was from Serkan.

> Are you coming?

I glanced around the cabin. A steady stream of tourists chatted back and forth as they shrugged off their backpacks and swigged water from plastic bottles. The couple I had seen in the ticket office were among them, the woman fanning herself with a rolled-up newspaper as she grumbled about the heat.

I switched my phone off and dropped it into my bag, staring down at my lap, as I willed the ferry to move. After what felt like an age, the engines spluttered into life and the ferry began to pull out of the harbour. I pulled the curtain back an inch, watching the slowly expanding breadth of sea, as it took me further and further away from my old life.

For a fraction of a second, Cem's face flashed into my mind before the shutters came down. I wasn't strong enough to think about him yet.

"Can we go up to the top deck now?" said Elif. "We need to wave goodbye to Turkey."

I smiled at her, "of course."

The top deck was windy. Elif and I clung to the railings, laughing as our hair whipped around our faces.

"Bye-bye Turkey!" she cried, waving her arms. This was an adventure for her. A game. Only I was aware of the far-reaching consequences of the decision I had been forced to make. Hoping that one day she would understand.

And forgive me.

The ferry ploughed onwards, the noise and smells of the harbour giving way to an empty expanse of sea and foam. The steady chug of the engine punctuated only by snatches of conversation from our fellow passengers and the swooping calls of gulls.

I watched as Bodrum got smaller and smaller in the distance. How ironic it was that, as I had fallen out of love with my husband, I had fallen in love with this beautiful country. Not for the first time, I wondered; What if we had never come here?

***

"Let's move to Turkey."

Serkan, about to take a bite of his bacon sandwich, froze.

"What?"

"Well, we always said we would retire there," I said.

He nodded. "But that's years away."

I stared out of the window at the colourless London sky.

A grey squirrel sat on top of the bird feeder, his eyes darting guiltily about as he nibbled his ill-gotten gains. A familiar restlessness churned in my gut. The desire for something different. Something more. I had been up since five, working the early shift at the hospital before arriving home half an hour ago. Now it was Serkan's turn to go to work, driving a minicab until the early hours of the morning. He would arrive home around the time I awoke, if indeed I had slept at all. Between the drunken arguments of our next-door neighbours and a colicky baby, sleep had become an elusive luxury.

"Maybe we shouldn't wait," I said.

Serkan stared at me. "Are you serious?"

Exhaustion suddenly hit me with the force of a truck. The mortgage was due to go up next month. Even now, with both our salaries, we barely had enough. I turned to face him.

"Serkan, I want to enjoy life now, not when I'm old. I want a big family home with a garden. I want Elif to have a childhood. Play outside. Be free. We could sell the house and have a far better quality of life there than we could ever afford here."

He walked towards me, cupping my face in his hands, and kissing me on the nose.

"Imagine the garden!" I said. "With fruit trees! We can grow vegetables... and chickens, let's get chickens!"

"My crazy wife," said Serkan, stroking my cheek.

"This isn't living, Serkan, it's existing. I can't do this for another thirty years."

Serkan finished the last of his sandwich and put his plate in the sink.

"Think about it a bit more," he said. "If it's what you really want, you know I would love to go back. it's my home." He smiled at Elif, sleeping peacefully in her bouncy chair. "And I would love Elif to grow up there."

Grabbing his jacket from the back of the chair, he picked up the keys to his cab.

"I'd better go."

"Think about it," he said as we approached the front door. "Turkey is very different from the UK."

"Maybe I want different."

Placing a soft kiss on my lips, he stepped outside. Suddenly, I had the urge to pull him back.

"Wait!"

"What's wrong?"

I looked into his eyes, dark brown, kind, and honest. My best friend.

"I want different, but I don't want us to be different," I said. "Just promise me you'll never change."

Serkan laughed and ruffled my hair. "Don't be silly, Carrie, I think you know me by now."

He stepped out into our postage stamp-sized front garden. A light drizzle had begun to fall from the colourless sky. I watched as he walked down the path to the little wooden gate, turned, and waved. I waved back and closed the front door. The panic in my chest had begun to subside. Probably the thought of spending another night alone with a colicky baby, I thought to myself as, right on cue, Elif began to cry.

A year later, we sold the house and moved to Maralya. With the money from the sale of the London house, we bought four apartments that we rented out and the villa in Kirazlı. When Cem arrived, our family was complete, and life should have been perfect. But ten years later, here I was. Alone with my daughter on a beach in Kos, our worldly belongings packed into suitcases. Running from him.

I shivered as a chill breeze whispered across my shoulders. A short ferry ride away, Turkey was still too close for comfort.

"Elif, let's go!" I got to my feet. "We don't want to miss the ferry."

Elif splashed towards me, pushing her feet into her flip-flops as together we headed back up the beach towards the car.

Chapter Five

Maralya, Turkey, October 2014

A piercing scream jerked me back to reality, and I stared, startled for a second by my reflection in the windowpane. Hollow cheeks. Pale skin. Dark circles around my eyes. A thin, red trickle ran from the corner of my mouth.

Across the table, Azra was watching me with concern. Red sparkly horns protruded from her black curls. Her eyes were encircled by thick black liner. Her shoulders were cloaked in a red-lined cape.

"Are you OK, *canım*?"

"Sorry," I said. "I was miles away."

We were in a bar on the promenade that stretched the length of Maralya's Caretta beach, named after the turtles that laid their eggs there every summer.

The Halloween party was a hit every year, attracting a mixture of expats and curious Turks, as excitable kids (and a few adults) dressed up and enjoyed the fun.

I glanced around, searching for my children's faces amid the mob of diminutive vampires, ghouls, and witches. I saw Elif first. Dressed as a miniature witch, she was watching as her brother took his turn at apple bobbing. Although I suspected he may have been the source of the earlier scream, now he was laughing, head thrown back as he missed the apple for the second time. Never one to abide by convention or follow the crowd, Cem was dressed as Spiderman.

I looked back at Azra across the table. The feisty independent lawyer who refused to play by the rules of conservative Turkish society. Who drank and smoked and lived "in sin" with her partner, even having a child out of wedlock. Such things bear little relevance in Western society, but in a town like Maralya, home of twitching curtains and duplicitous gossip, it took courage not to follow the herd. Azra had always stayed true to herself.

I, on the other hand, was a fraud who had deceived everyone, myself included, with a performance worthy of an Oscar.

After every argument and violent outburst, I slid back into my role as the perfect wife and mother with the ease of putting on a favourite coat.

Until that night.

It had been about a week earlier. I had turned up at Azra's house at midnight, my face a mess of snot and tears, my clothes stained dark red.

I had sobbed for what felt like hours in her living room, Elif and Huseyin watching, pale-faced and silent until Azra had sent them upstairs.

I had told her everything. The fights. The violence. The threats. The fear.

When I had finished, she was silent for a long time.

"What are you going to do?" she said, eventually.

"I don't know," I replied.

That night, his temper had come from nowhere.

Serkan was in a good mood. Alfie was asleep on the floor in front of us, paws and muzzle twitching as he dreamed. There was a film on the television. The kind of thing Serkan liked, with guns and lots of swearing. We were talking about something. What were we talking about? I still can't remember.

I was normally so careful not to say anything to trigger his temper. Maybe I had become too relaxed by the wine, or by his good mood, but suddenly his face changed. The ominous knot of fear tightened in my gut. I froze mid-sentence, trying to remember what I had said so that I could backtrack and prevent what was coming.

Sensing the change in atmosphere, Alfie got to his feet and slunk away, head down, tail between his legs. He had seen this situation too many times before. Usually, Serkan kicked furniture, but mid-rage, the elderly dog would make an equally suitable target.

"I'm sorry, I didn't mean..." I said, trying to diffuse the situation with the skill of a hostage negotiator.

"We were having a nice night," he ranted. "And you have to go and ruin it, Carrie!"

"But I didn't mean..."

"You're a fucking bitch!" he yelled, hurling his glass of wine at the wall where it smashed, sending shards of glass flying and splashes of red down my white t-shirt.

I ducked as he lunged towards me, grabbing my wrist and twisting it hard as I cried out in pain.

"Where do you think you're going?"

"Serkan, please, you're hurting me!"

He pulled me back to the sofa and shoved me down hard.

"Serkan, please. Let's not wake the children. I'm sorry. I'll clean this up and get you another glass of wine. Let's get back to the film."

"Fuck the film!" He looked around the room, his eyes alighting on a statue on the shelf. It was a figurine of a man and a woman embracing as they cradled their newborn baby. A gift from my mum when Elif was born. Serkan turned and reached for the statue, his momentary distraction enough for me to make my escape.

I ran to the downstairs bathroom. My hands shook as I fumbled with the key in the lock, turning it just as the door handle began to rattle.

"Open this door!" he bellowed, his fists hammering against the wood.

"Open the door NOW, Carrie!"

I slid to the floor and sat on the cold tiles, hugging my knees as the hammering continued. *Leave*, whispered the voice in my head. *You can't stay here. Do whatever it takes, but take your children and leave.*

"Baba, stop it please!" came Elif's voice, as the hammering came to an abrupt stop.

"Go back to bed!" barked Serkan.

"Where's Mummy?" Cem's voice.

Swearing in Turkish, Serkan moved away from the door. There was the sound of something being kicked. The sound of snapping wood.

After a few minutes had passed, I got to my feet, turned the key slowly in the lock and stepped barefoot into the darkened hall. The house was silent except for the sound of police sirens blaring from the TV. Reaching for my car keys from the hook on the wall, I pressed them into my palm to prevent any telltale jangling and gently pushed open the living room door. The children sat crammed together in an armchair. They looked up in unison as I appeared in the doorway, their faces serious, their eyes large.

In the middle of the room, the coffee table lay on its back like an upturned beetle. Two of its legs had been snapped off. The carpet was stained a deep red and strewn with broken glass. In the middle lay the statue, broken in half.

Serkan sat on the sofa, staring at the TV. He didn't look at me.

"Come on kids, back to bed," I said.

Elif rushed towards me.

I motioned to Cem.

"Come," I said, trying to keep my voice light. "I'll read you a story."

The little boy swivelled his gaze towards his father as Serkan opened his arms wide. All traces of anger had vanished, replaced by a huge smile that spread across his face.

"Come, my son!"

Cem stood, walked towards his father's outstretched arms, and clambered onto his lap.

From the TV, the sound of machine gun fire filled the room. Serkan turned to me, a look of triumph on his face as he ruffled Cem's hair.

I drove to Azra's, Elif in the backseat. When I allowed the tears to come, they didn't stop.

***

Rapturous applause and laughter pulled me back to the present as Elif emerged from the bowl of water, the apple firmly lodged between her teeth. Around us, the party was in full swing as excited children jumped and danced to the beat of Michael Jackson's "Thriller."

In stark contrast, the conversation I was about to have with Azra was deadly serious.

"How are things?" she said gently. "With Serkan?"

It was the first time we had spoken about that night.

My eyes filled with tears as I shook my head. "I don't know what to do."

"How long has it been like this?"

"Too long."

Azra nodded. I took a large gulp of wine.

After that night, I had returned home the next morning to find the carpet cleaned up, the statue glued crookedly back together, and a scrawled note.

I'm sorry

But it wasn't enough. Not this time. Like a plate that's been smashed and glued back together too many times until there's nothing left to glue.

"I can't stay with him," I said. "I'm afraid of him, Azra."

She nodded.

"I have to leave."

It was the first time I had said the words out loud. Suddenly, I wanted it more than anything. Staying was no longer an option. I would take the children, leave Turkey, and start again.

I looked at Azra across the table.

"I don't want to go back to the UK, but..."

Azra stared at me. "Why would you have to go back to the UK?"

"I can't stay here," I said.

"But your job?"

"I'll get another job."

"And the villa? You love that house!"

"The villa is in Serkan's name," I said with a sigh.

"It was easier," I explained in response to Azra's confused stare. "To buy as a foreigner was expensive and the paperwork would have taken months."

"But you paid for it?" continued Azra.

"Yes."

"And the flats?"

"They're in my name," I said, silently thanking my former self for insisting on ownership of the four apartments.

"Then you can't just walk away…"

"Serkan says if I ever leave, he'll sell the villa, take my children and drive me out of Turkey."

Azra snorted a brief, involuntary laugh. She took a cigarette from a packet on the table and lit it. The tip glowed orange in the dark.

"Bloody men," she inhaled sharply and turned to me, blowing smoke out of her nose.

"Carrie, he can't do anything to you. You have rights. You are the children's mother. The courts will give you custody. You have a good job. You are entitled to the villa and at least two of the flats. You are in a far stronger position than he is."

She smiled. "He can't do anything to you," she said. "Trust me."

Azra had the kind of carefree confidence of a sports car with the top down. It was contagious, and I wanted nothing more than to join her in the passenger seat as she pressed her foot down on the accelerator. But my constant companion, Fear, refused to loosen its grip.

"He has a temper," I said. "It's getting worse. I'm afraid of what he'll do to me if I leave him."

"Carrie, I've dealt with hundreds of divorces," said Azra, flicking ash into the ashtray. "They are all the same, barking like little dogs. He won't do anything to you."

"And if he does?"

"There are laws to protect you. We'll go to the police."

Azra took a sip of her wine and grinned at me.

"Don't worry," she said with a wink. "You have a great lawyer!"

Chapter Six

Maralya, Turkey. November 2014

The above-named patient was admitted to the emergency department in the early hours of this morning with central crushing chest pain and shortness of breath.

I stared at my computer screen as I had been for the past ten minutes, reading and re-reading the same sentence.

Last week, the first rain of winter had fallen on Maralya, signifying the end of another hellishly hot, manically busy summer season. The last dregs of tourists were gradually disappearing from the bars, restaurants, and beaches and the town was returned to us, the locals, and the people who had made it their home.

After the rain, the air felt fresher and lighter. It was as if the town itself collectively exhaled.

Maralya was a town of two distinct personalities. In summer, pink-shouldered tourists traipsed the burning streets, western pop music blared from bars and bronzed men lured tourists into restaurants with well-rehearsed patter.

"Cheap as chips."

"Special price."

"Where are you from?"

In winter, the air was heavy with the smell of wood smoke from the wood-burning stoves or *sobas* that blanketed the town with smog. Most of the bars and restaurants closed, and those that remained open were occupied by those same men, less bronzed now, nursing glasses of *çay* as they whiled away the empty days with idle chat and games of backgammon.

Today was Serkan's last day before the restaurant where he worked closed for the winter. The prospect of him being home for the next six months loomed over me like the storm clouds that hung heavy in the air, leaving me unable to concentrate.

My computer bleeped the arrival of an email. It was from my sister, Rebecca.

Hi Carrie,

Sorry to ask again, but I really need your measurements for the bridesmaid's dress. Also, would you prefer salmon or beef for the main course? What about the children? I know it's over six months away, but there's so much to plan!

This wedding is taking over my life! Aaargh! Love you!

Making a mental note to myself to reply later, I closed the email and tried to focus my attention on the medical report in front of me.

On arrival, his vital signs were as follows: B/P 190/110, Pulse 120, Oxygen saturation 89%.

My attention was diverted again as my mobile buzzed into life. I was surprised to see Serkan's face staring from the screen. We had barely spoken in months. I lifted my phone to my ear.

"Hello?"

The office door opened and Atakan sashayed in, clutching a patient file, which he added to the pile in my inbox.

"The kid in emergency needs an urgent report," he said. "The doctor wants to transfer him to Antalya."

I nodded and picked up the file as Atakan disappeared into the little kitchen at the back of the office.

"I'm going to England," Serkan said flatly in my ear. "Murat needs help with the café."

In my chest, my heart sprouted wings and began to fly.

Atakan peered around the door, pointing meaningfully at an empty coffee cup in his hand.

"Coffee?" he mouthed silently.

I laughed and nodded my head.

"What are you laughing at?" snapped Serkan. "Is something funny to you?"

"Nothing! Just Atakan messing around, that's all," I said, praying that he would believe me. I dared not get on the wrong side of him now.

Serkan didn't say anything. I wondered when our conversations became so stilted. There was a time when they flowed so easily. Along with love, laughter, and respect, the words in our marriage, it seemed, had also died.

"It's up to you," I said, taking care to keep my voice neutral. "There's no work here in winter and we could use the money."

Another lengthy silence.

"Can you book me a flight?" he said, eventually.

Not for the first time, I wondered what Serkan did with his money. With his earnings and tips from the restaurant, his salary in summer was almost double mine, plus he pocketed the rent from the flats every month.

"Sure," I replied.

Atakan placed a steaming mug of coffee on the desk in front of me and sat down. I grinned at him.

"Is everything OK, babe?" he said.

"Everything is great!" I felt a sudden surge of happiness as I imagined months of blissful Serkan-free existence.

"What's happening with you?"

"I met someone," replied Atakan, looking around furtively although there was no one else in the room.

"Oh my God! Who is he?" I clasped my hands together in anticipation. I loved hearing about Atakan's romantic escapades.

He looked dreamily upwards. "He's a teacher!"

"Is he cute?"

"Oh, Carrie, he is soo cute!" Atakan picked up his phone, frowning slightly as he searched for the right photo before turning it to face me. The man in the picture was in his mid-twenties with a short beard and black, spiky hair. His hands were thrust into his jeans pockets as he gazed wistfully into the distance.

"What's his name?"

"Ali."

"Ali and Atakan," I said, "It has a nice ring to it."

"I'm just popping outside," I said, grabbing my phone.

"I'll be back in a minute."

When we first moved to Turkey, Serkan would return to London at the end of the summer season to work at his friend's café, leaving me alone. I used to dread those months, counting the days until his return. Now I couldn't wait for him to leave. For the past couple of years, he had stayed in Maralya, content to spend the winter supine on the sofa with a beer, staring at the TV as the housework built up around him.

Finding an empty table in the corner of the hospital cafeteria, I called Azra.

"Serkan's going to England," I said as soon as she answered.

"To work?" she replied.

"I don't care what he does," I said. "As long as he is not here."

Since the Halloween party, Azra and I hadn't spoken further about my plans to divorce. The decision, it seemed, was the easy part, but the logistics remained a mystery as I contemplated my next move. What did other women do in these situations? Sit down with their partner and explain that it wasn't working? Pack a suitcase and move out? Both options were unthinkable with Serkan in the house. But the universe may just have thrown me a bone.

"Can we still open a case if he's not here?" I asked Azra.

"Of course," she replied. "It may be safer for you if he's not. We can open the proceedings and break it to him before he gets back." She laughed. "Give him a chance to get used to the idea."

Somehow, I couldn't see it being that easy.

***

A week later, we stood on the veranda, Serkan, his best friend Kadir, Elif, Cem, Alfie, and me, in a circle around Serkan's large blue suitcase as if we were at a funeral.

In a way, we were, although nobody knew it but me. The last time we would all be together before…My stomach lurched at the thought of the months ahead. I had been on tenterhooks for days, watching his every word and movement, terrified he was going to change his mind about going.

"When will you be back?" I asked, trying to keep my voice casual.

"Murat needs help over Christmas," Serkan replied. "After that, we'll see."

He knelt down as Elif gave him a polite hug and kissed him on the cheek.

Throwing his arms around his father's neck, Cem clung on for dear life.

"I wanna come wiz you."

"I'll be back soon, I promise," Serkan prised the little boy loose and looked him straight in the eye.

"Be a good boy for mummy, OK?"

A pang of guilt hit me squarely in the chest. Serkan had no idea what he was going to come back to.

"We should go." Kadir looked at his watch. "You don't want to miss your flight."

Serkan bumped his suitcase down the veranda steps and along the drive to where Kadir's dark blue sedan was parked outside the gate. He heaved it into the boot and slammed it shut.

"I'll call you," said Serkan to no one in particular as he ducked into the passenger seat.

"OK," I said.

"*Görüşürüz Yenge,*" Kadir waved as he started the engine.

The children and I watched in silence as the car made its way to the end of the road, turned the corner, and disappeared from sight.

"Can we have pizza for dinner?" said Cem, squinting up at me.

"That's a great idea!" I smiled.

We went back inside; the kids laughing as they ran upstairs together, closely followed by Alfie, who let out an excited sneeze.

I closed the front door and leaned back against the polished wood. The villa felt immediately lighter, the knot in my chest looser, my heartbeat slower. Closing my eyes, I took a deep breath in and slowly exhaled.

Chapter Seven

Maralya, Turkey. January 2015

When I lived in London, I dreamed of this house, although I hadn't seen it yet.

A large white villa, its wide veranda encompassing the entire ground floor. A garden with fruit trees. A hammock strung between them. In the distance, the mountains and the sea.

I dreamed of hot summer days. Relaxing in the hammock with a book, listening to the chatter of the children as they played outside. Warm summer evenings. The heady scent of jasmine and honeysuckle. Serkan and I on the veranda with a glass of wine, talking long into the night.

After moving to Turkey, the change in Serkan was as immediate as it was insidious. Distracted by a mixture of Elif's teething, the inevitable culture shock, and hellish temperatures that scraped the late-forties, I didn't notice it right away. Then there was the day-to-day challenge of living with my mother-in-law.

Gülşen was as volatile as mercury. Her mood veered from tearfully declaring her undying love for all in the vicinity, to violent, wild-haired rages. We clashed almost immediately as she meddled in everything from how I boiled an egg for Elif's breakfast to how I dealt with her tantrums.

Serkan made himself scarce, leaving me alone with Gülşen and baby Elif from early morning until late at night. During the day, a steady stream of visitors descended on Gülşen's flat. Headscarved, baggy-trousered women who sat cross-legged on the floor, drinking the *çay* Gülşen brought out on a silver tray and peering at me as if I were a museum exhibit. I was sure they were discussing me, though at the time I had no idea what they were saying.

When Serkan was there, a wall seemed to have gone up between us. The loving husband and doting father had been replaced by a stranger who mumbled single-word responses and avoided my gaze. Suddenly, my opinions no longer mattered.

It was the stress, I told myself. The move. The heat. The clear animosity between myself and his mother. It would be better when we got our own place.

We searched Maralya for a home, but the soulless square houses on complexes full of other expats, with their perfect Astroturf lawns and rectangular swimming pools, left me cold.

As we slid into winter and the outside temperatures finally cooled, my relationship with my mother-in-law had reached boiling point. We moved into a rented apartment, a respite of sorts, albeit close enough for Gülşen to appear most mornings on the dot of seven, wild-haired and waving as I pulled back the bedroom curtains.

By the end of that first winter, I was pregnant again. The pregnancy was beset by problems, running the gauntlet of morning sickness, crippling fatigue and back pain, and putting our house hunting indefinitely on hold. The cracks in our marriage deepened as without work, Serkan spent his days sprawled on the sofa, eyes glued to the TV, and his nights out drinking with his buddies. Unlike in London, housework and childcare seemed beneath him. My pleas for help only resulted in him calling Gülşen, who scrubbed, polished, and mopped, clutching her back in protest, and mumbling under her breath before collapsing on the sofa to watch her favourite soap operas. It was marginally less stressful to do everything myself, so I stopped asking. By the time Cem was born, our marriage needed nothing short of a miracle.

***

It was a rare dry day in a month of torrential rain, and after spending days cooped up in the flat, we had driven out to a beach bar close to the pretty village of *Kirazlı*, about ten minutes outside of Maralya.

The bar was empty except for a British man reading a newspaper and nursing a bottle of *Efes*. Dressed in only a pair of khaki shorts and a sunhat, despite the cool February air, he had the kind of orange, leathery skin of someone who spent every day outside.

He looked up from his newspaper and smiled as we sat down.

"Alright, mate?" Serkan was in a jovial mood. "Where are you from?"

"Barnet. North London. You know it?"

"I used to be a cab driver," said Serkan. "I know everywhere."

"Pete."

The leather-skinned man smiled as they shook hands.

Pete, it turned out, had been in Turkey for fifteen years but had finally grown bored with sunshine and cheap beer and wanted to return to the UK.

"What's stopping you?" I said.

"I have a house up in the village," he replied, tilting his head towards Kirazlı. "Been trying to sell it for over a year. Beautiful place, huge garden, but a bit out in the sticks for most people."

Serkan and I glanced at each other.

A house. A garden. And far enough away for Gülşen not to appear before I had even had coffee.

"When can we see it?" I said.

I knew I was home from the moment I stepped out of the car. It was exactly as I had imagined. Whitewashed walls. A driveway draped in trailing grapevines. A banana tree swaying gently in the breeze. From the wide veranda, I gazed down at the large, untamed garden sloping gently towards the sea.

"What do you think?"

I spun around as Serkan appeared behind me. We had been fighting for so long that it caught me off guard as he slipped his hand into mine and gave it a gentle squeeze. He was smiling at me the way he used to.

"I'm sorry," he said.

I smiled back. It didn't matter anymore. Nothing mattered. We were home.

***

The cicadas were silent now, or maybe they were sleeping for the winter. I had no idea. I lifted the wooden hatch of the chicken coop to reveal Marilyn, my favourite hen, arranged like a tea cosy over the morning's batch of eggs.

"You broody again, girl?" I said, tickling her head as she cooed softly. There were six chickens in all, named after old movie stars, Grace, Rita, Betty, Joan, and Audrey being the other five. The cockerel, Marlon, had enjoyed a brief reign of terror, chasing Alfie, tail between his legs, around the garden and karate-chopping anyone who got too close, before ending his days prematurely in Gülşen's cooking pot. Despite the absence of a cockerel, Marilyn refused to let go of the hope that one day her eggs would hatch. Every morning she would position her fat, feathered body over the morning's yield and refuse to budge, much to the chagrin of the other hens waiting to lay.

I gently pushed my hand underneath her soft down and felt around for the warm brown eggs before placing them in my basket. On the way back towards the house, I stopped at the orange tree to twist six juicy oranges from their stems.

In the kitchen, Azra looked up from the goat cheese she was slicing and smiled. On the tray next to her were tiny glass bowls containing diced tomatoes and cucumber, black and green olives, local honey, and rose-petal jam along with a basket of thickly sliced still-warm bread.

"One each," I said, placing the five eggs into a saucepan and covering them with water. Next to them, the *çaydanlık,* a two-tier metal teapot, bubbled contentedly, steam flowing from its twin spouts.

"Have you heard anything?" she said. "From Serkan?"

I shook my head, reached for a knife, and sliced an orange in half.

"I've filed a petition for divorce with the family court," Azra continued. "There's a court order to prevent Serkan from selling the villa. We need to get him to transfer the deeds to your name as soon as possible."

"OK," I nodded, pressing and twisting the orange halves into the juicer.

Azra placed the plate of cheese on the tray and carried it out onto the veranda.

"kahvaltı!" she shouted towards the fallen pine tree at the bottom of the garden. "Breakfast!"

The tree had fallen last week as a ferocious storm unleashed its wrath on Maralya, ripping the awnings from the bars and restaurants, rattling the doors and windows, and plunging the town into darkness. Without electricity, the children and I had spent three nights bedded down on the living room floor. I had read them stories by candlelight until they fell asleep, the heat of the *soba* keeping us snug against the howling wind and rain.

The following morning revealed the pine tree's plight. Its fall saved by a power line that straddled the garden, it had languished precariously for several days until one of my neighbours appeared with a chainsaw and brought it crashing to the ground.

I poured the fresh orange juice into a jug and ran the boiled eggs under cold water, drying them with a tea towel before placing them in a bowl and carrying them outside.

The sound of wellies squelched towards us on the veranda.

"We made a camp!" announced Cem as he sat down.

"*Aferin sana,*" grinned Azra, picking up the *çaydanlık,* and pouring us each a glass of steaming *çay*. Strong brown liquid from the top, diluted with hot water from the bottom.

"*Ellerinize sağlık,*" she smiled as she piled sugar into her glass with a tiny spoon.

"*Afyiyet olsun,*" I gave the standard reply.

Having wolfed down their breakfasts in record time, the children disappeared, eager to get back to their pine tree home. Azra poured us each a second glass of *çay*.

"Do you know when he's coming back?" she said.

I leaned back in my chair and closed my eyes, enjoying the faint warmth of the winter sun on my face. After almost a week of rain, it felt good to be outside. I didn't want to think about Serkan or his return.

"He said after Christmas," I said eventually. Christmas was three weeks ago.

"You need to talk to him," continued Azra. "Before he gets back."

I sighed. If I told Serkan I had filed for divorce, he would be back on the next available flight. I wanted my fragile peace to last a little longer.

Since Christmas, the knot of anxiety in my gut had been slowly tightening its grip like strangleweed. At night I lay awake, listening for the sound of his key in the lock, jumping every time Alfie barked, my heart beating out of my chest every time a car pulled up outside.

I opened my eyes and stared out across the garden. The bare branches of the fruit trees were stark now in the pale sunlight. The banana tree's leaves ragged and torn after the storm like Cinderella's dress at midnight.

My dream house was as much a dream as it had always been.

"I don't want it," I heard myself say.

Azra stared at me.

"The villa," I said. "I don't want it. I want to buy a place of my own. A place that is mine. That has always been mine."

"But... you love this house..."

I shook my head. "I don't want it," I said again, taking a sip of *çay*.

When Serkan returned from the UK, the divorce petition would be waiting for him.

But I wouldn't be.

"I'm moving out," I said.

Chapter Eight

Athens, Greece. May 2016

The marble seats swept upwards in a semi-circle around the stage, the remaining window arches crumbling and roofless, as the city below bathed in the rose-gold glow of the setting sun.

Around us, tourists swarmed over the ancient ruins, gulping water from plastic bottles, and wiping sweat from their brows. A tall, skinny man balanced precariously on a jutting rock, trying to get the best angle for a photograph as his girlfriend voiced her concern in some indecipherable language.

We had spent the day exploring the Acropolis in a living, breathing history lesson far superior to anything Elif could have had at school.

The Parthenon. The Odeon of Herodes Atticus. The Temple of the goddess Athena.

As we wandered amongst the ruins, I imagined the ancient acoustics echoing with the tales of Oedipus, Medea, and Medusa, inevitably reminded of my own Turkish tragedy. The universal themes of love, loss, revenge, and betrayal running like a thread through the centuries.

"Are you hungry?" I said to Elif.

She grinned at me. "Starving."

We headed to the narrow, cobbled streets of the *Plaka* district, where delicatessens crammed with jars of honey, feta cheese, and fresh olives competed with souvenir shops selling T-shirts, plates, and miniature replicas of the Acropolis. Elif stopped in front of a display of fridge magnets.

"Shall we get one?" I asked.

"We should get one from every place we visit," she replied, "To remember our trip!"

"Great idea!" I said, picturing an unfamiliar fridge in some unknown apartment in the future covered with tiny magnetic memories of our travels.

The streets of the Plaka district were alive with restaurants, bars, and tavernas. The mouthwatering smell of Moussaka, Kleftiko, and Souvlaki mingled with the heady scent of perfume in the warm night air.

We found a table in the corner of a large terrace, crisscrossed overhead with trailing grape vines and twinkling fairy lights. Servers rushed past, balancing trays with glasses of wine and plates of food. I was suddenly voraciously hungry and reached for the menu.

"Can I have the lamb again?" Elif frowned as she searched for the right word. "Klafi..."

"Kleftiko," I smiled at her. "You can have anything you like."

As we waited to order, the static sound of a microphone crackled through the air. An elderly Greek man, his face lined and leathered by life and the sun's harsh rays, had positioned himself on a stool on the tiny stage in the corner of the terrace. He began to play the lute, slowly plucking the strings in a traditional Greek lament. The sound was melancholy, instantly snatching away my fragile happiness and replacing it with my old friend Guilt.

My thoughts drifted back to him. Towards the locked door in my mind, the one I had forbidden myself from opening lest it pull me inside. His face filled my mind, like ripples in water, the face of someone you haven't seen for a long time.

"Mum, are you OK?"

Elif was watching me.

"I'm fine, sweetie," I said, forcing myself to focus on the menu until the words were no longer blurred.

***

The hands were relentless, grabbing, intrusive. The breath, hot on my neck. I couldn't breathe. I needed to fight, but my body wouldn't move. A scream built in my throat as I managed to open my eyes, sucking air gratefully into my lungs as I sat up.

In the hotel room, a pale moonlight shone in through the window, casting the furniture in a ghostly glow. A wardrobe. A dresser. A chair. A luggage rack upon which my suitcase gaped open, revealing its hastily packed contents. Next to me, in the double bed, Elif slept soundly.

In the darkness and silence, the questions I had been avoiding since we left Turkey forced themselves into my mind. Insistant. Accusing. Demanding an answer.

What have I done?

Where am I going?

What am I going to do?

With sleep out of the question, I considered turning on the TV. Anything to drown the questions out. But I didn't want to wake Elif.

There was a book somewhere. A paperback I had found in the hotel in Bodrum. I vaguely remembered putting it in my case before we left. I got out of bed and rummaged through my suitcase in the dark, stopping as my fingers closed around something cold, hard, and metallic. My phone. I had kept it switched off since we left Bodrum. Afraid of what lay in wait.

He can't hurt you, I told myself as I held down the power key and watched as the device glowed into life. Immediately his voice shouted, in furious capitals, from the screen.

> WHERE ARE YOU?

> CALL ME

> YOU ARE IN BIG TROUBLE

> YOU CAN'T RUN, CARRIE

I skimmed down the list of messages until another caught my eye.

> Where are you, babe? I'm so worried

I had pressed call before I could stop myself. Despite it being three in the morning, he answered immediately.

"Carrie?"

"It's me."

"Oh my God! Where are you?"

I swallowed hard as tears stung my eyes.

"I'm in Athens."

"You're *where*?"

"I had to leave Turkey," I said. "I had no choice."

Atakan listened in silence as I relayed the horrors of the past few weeks.

"You should write a book," he said when I had finished.

I gave a hollow laugh. "Bestseller."

"Where will you go?" he continued. "What are you going to do?"

They were the same questions I had been asking myself since we sailed out of Bodrum a few days earlier. I had no idea.

"I have a friend in Spain," I said. "From there, I don't know. We're taking the ferry to Italy in a few days, so we'll spend some time there. I promised Elif a holiday." I looked at the sleeping little girl. "She deserves it."

"You both do," replied Atakan. "And I want photos. I want to see you holding up the Leaning Tower of Pisa and eating Cornettos on a gondola in Venice."

I laughed despite myself. "I promise."

"Please don't tell anyone you've heard from me. You know how gossip is in Maralya."

"Never."

"I love you, babe."

"I love you more."

When our conversation was over, I returned to bed, listening to the night-time sounds of Athens that drifted in through the open window. Scattered conversations. Laughter. Music from a nearby bar. I lay awake until the sounds were replaced by the screech of opening café shutters, the distant wail of sirens, hurried footsteps on the pavement.

That was the first night I cried. Hot, silent tears that finally carried me into a deep and dreamless sleep.

Chapter Nine

Maralya, Turkey. February 2015

The estate agent, a short, squat woman with glasses, surveyed me from behind her clipboard as I wandered through the empty rooms. She kept looking at her watch and I assumed she had another appointment, but I didn't care. This was important, and I needed to take my time.

The apartment was over two floors, comprising the top floor and attic of a large, detached house in a leafy area of Maralya close to Caretta beach. It had its own separate entrance at the side of the house with a red front door in need of a coat of paint. Next to the door was a broken flowerpot, its inhabitants dry and unloved, and a fence beyond which stretched a large empty expanse of lawn.

If I stood on my tiptoes and looked through the window of the attic bedroom, the one I had already decided would be mine, I could see a small blue triangle of sea.

We took the curving staircase back downstairs, where the kids were arguing about who would have which room.

"I want this one!" declared Cem, folding his arms across his body and sticking out his bottom lip.

"But you said you wanted the other one," replied Elif with an exasperated sigh that belied her diminutive years. "You can't have both!"

The estate agent glanced at her watch again as I stepped out onto the spacious balcony and looked out across the street. On the other side of the road, there was a small park, a tennis court, and a discount supermarket. After the fields and farmland of Kirazlı, it felt good to be back in civilization.

I glanced down, looking for a tree stump, a wall, an overturned dustbin, but there was nothing. Nothing for Serkan to climb on and no way for him to get in. Like many homes in Turkey, there were iron security bars on the windows to protect against burglars. Someone had looped a shiny glass *Nazar* or "evil eye" through the security bars with a piece of frayed string. The nazar is ubiquitous in Turkey and can be found everywhere from buildings and shops to jewellery or simply pinned onto clothing to protect the bearer from harm.

"I'll take it."

The kids squealed with delight and jumped up and down, hugging each other, their argument forgotten. Of all the places we had seen, this was by far their favourite. The estate agent smiled a relieved smile.

A few days later, a removal van was parked in the driveway, shaded by the same trailing grape vines I had fallen in love with all those years ago.

The chickens had been re-homed with a friend to see out their days in peace, rather than end up in the pot, as I feared if I had let one of my neighbours have them.

Despite my hopes of slipping away unnoticed, the presence of a removal van had brought my neighbours out into the street. They gathered around me in a curious throng as I smiled and tried to answer their questions as vaguely as I could. I had no idea if any of them were in contact with Serkan, but I suspected that at least one of the men would be.

In Turkey, it is common for men to "keep an eye on" their friend's wives and girlfriends. A kind of "wives and girlfriends' police," or as I had nicknamed them, the "WGP." I had often returned home from shopping in Maralya or having lunch with a friend to find that Serkan already knew exactly where I had been and with whom. Although I found this vaguely sinister, with nothing to hide, it had never really bothered me. Until now.

I took a last walk through the empty rooms. Without its furniture, the villa felt huge and rather melancholy. I felt I had let it down somehow, failed to make it the family home it could have been. I remembered again my dream in London. Evenings on the balcony, children playing in the garden. But all I heard in my head as I walked from room to room were screaming arguments, slamming doors, tables being kicked over, and walls being punched.

From the bedroom window, I gazed out at the garden.

"When did you last clean the windows?" intruded Serkan's voice in my head.

I moved away, descending the marble staircase as a lone dog hair caught my eye.

"Get this bloody dog out!" An image flashed into my brain. Serkan opening the back door, shoving Alfie hard with his foot as the dog scrambled to get out of the way, his nails slipping on the tiled floor.

In the kitchen, I opened the empty cupboards one by one.

"When are you going to learn to cook like my mum?"

"You didn't put in enough salt."

"You should have cooked the tomatoes longer."

It's over. I told myself. He will never speak to you like that again.

From outside, I heard the removal van doors being slammed shut. Taking a deep breath, I turned and walked out of the villa, locking the heavy wooden door behind me for the last time.

On the driveway, one of the removal men, a short, wiry man with spiky black hair and stubble, was smoking a cigarette. He frowned and narrowed his eyes at me.

"Are we ready to go?" I asked in Turkish.

He nodded, still watching me curiously.

"I know you," he said eventually, taking a last drag of his cigarette. "You're Serkan's wife."

I felt my stomach lurch.

"Where's Serkan?" he continued.

"He's in London," I replied, not looking at him.

From the back seat of the car, the kids caught my eye and waved, Alfie happily sandwiched between them. I turned back to the removal man.

"Look, Serkan doesn't know about this," I told him in hushed tones. "We're not together."

He narrowed his eyes further.

"I'd appreciate it if you didn't tell anyone."

He nodded again. "Of course."

He threw the cigarette butt on the ground and crushed it with his foot.

"It's none of my business."

***

The purple couch was hard and uncomfortable. I had bought it cheap, second-hand, a few days earlier, leaving the large red corner couch at the villa. Apart from being too big for the new apartment, the old couch had never recovered from having its covers cut off with scissors, boil-washed and sewn back on by Gülşen a few years earlier.

A wave of relief washed over me. Never again would my mother-in-law descend uninvited to scrub, boil, and strip everything to within an inch of its life, frequently breaking things in the process. It was the constant threat of Gülşen, being brought over to "clean properly," that had kept me obsessively cleaning the villa like an unpaid maid.

When the villa was sold, I would buy a new couch to go in my new apartment. A place that was mine, that he could never again hold over my head like a guillotine's blade.

After a much-needed cup of tea on the uncomfortable purple couch, I headed, exhausted, upstairs to my attic bedroom. I paused at the children's bedroom door and gently pushed it ajar. The children had finally agreed to share a room and use the other bedroom as a playroom. They lay splayed out on their backs, their chests rising and falling as they breathed, Alfie stretched out, sentry-like on the floor between them.

He has no idea where I am.

The thought covered me like a thick blanket as I closed my eyes. Safe in the knowledge that for tonight at least there would be no jangling of his key in the lock. No roar of his motorbike in the driveway. No invasion into my room and my body at three in the morning.

No fear.

Chapter Ten

Maralya, Turkey. March 2015

We settled into the new apartment as if it had always been home. Every morning I rose at seven to walk Alfie around the park, hurrying him along as he stopped to examine an interesting blade of grass or lift his leg against the trunk of a tree.

After breakfast, we piled into the car and made the ten-minute drive back to Kirazlı, where I dropped the children at school before continuing to work.

The weather was already warming up, and I signed the children up for tennis lessons at the tennis club in the park, spending Saturday mornings on a bench with a book, listening to the thwack of balls across the net as Alfie dozed at my feet. Afterwards, we would go to the discount supermarket, where I would treat the children to an ice cream.

Almost a month had passed since we had moved out of the villa, and I still hadn't spoken to Serkan. I knew I was putting it off. Delaying the inevitable, but I didn't care. I wanted to enjoy the calm before the storm for a little longer.

"Beautiful day," said a voice behind me as I sat on the bench one Saturday. Alfie staggered to his feet, wagging his tail as he came nose to nose with a honey-coloured Labrador.

"I'm Jackie," said the middle-aged woman. She had dark, wavy hair, greying around her ears, and laughter lines around her eyes.

"Carrie." I smiled.

"We're neighbours," she continued. "My garden backs onto yours. I've seen you pegging your washing out."

I looked up at the sound of plimsolls on tarmac running towards us.

"Can we get ice cream now?" Cem crashed down on the bench beside me, panting heavily. Elif crouched down and stroked the yellow dog's ears.

"You like dogs?" smiled Jackie. "You should come over to mine. I've got four puppies at the mo."

Elif's face lit up! "Can we, mum!" she begged. "Please!"

Jackie was a volunteer for the local animal rescue charity, she explained. An insurmountable task given the number of strays that roamed the streets of Maralya.

Jackie's garden was as tidy and landscaped as the villa's had been wild and overgrown. Circles of light-brown, recently dug earth surrounded newly planted rose bushes. Delicate, star-shaped jasmine wove its way through a trellis up the side of the house, and large orange fish shimmered in a lily-padded pond.

We sat on pink cushioned chairs under a huge pink parasol, the table between us laden with plates of Battenburg, lemon drizzle, and homemade Victoria sponge. Jackie picked up the china teapot, white with pink roses, and poured hot amber liquid into matching china cups.

Around the manicured lawn, the dogs chased each other in wide circles, pink tongues lolling from their mouths.

"Well, if you ever need a dog sitter..." Jackie smiled as the dogs play-pounced before switching directions and continuing the chase. "They certainly seem to have hit it off!"

I took a sip of tea, enjoying the familiar taste and marvelling at this little slice of English village life tucked away in the middle of Maralaya. It was a few seconds before I realised Cem was holding my phone towards me. He'd been playing a game on it, with the volume turned down.

"Mum," he was saying. "It's Baba."

I froze as my stomach dropped to the floor. I stared at the phone for a few seconds before reaching out and taking it tentatively. Serkan's voice boomed from the device long before I placed it to my ear.

"Carrie?" he spat. "What the hell is going on?"

I imagined him at the villa, walking through the empty rooms. Shock and disbelief turning to burning rage with every step.

"I've left you, Serkan," I said.

There was a stunned silence, followed by a hollow laugh.

"Don't be so stupid. Get back here now."

"Please don't talk to me like that." My voice was surprisingly calm.

"I'll talk to you however the fuck I want..."

There was a rustling sound. Muffled voices. Kadir's voice came on the line.

"Carrie?"

"Hi, Kadir."

"Carrie, he's really upset. He wants to see the kids; can you bring them...?"

"I'll meet him on the seafront," I said. "Manzara café. In an hour."

***

The wind was strong at the beach, beating restaurant awnings, flapping tablecloths, and bending the spindly palm trees that lined the promenade. I pushed against it, ignoring the acrobatics in my stomach and the children arguing about whose turn it was to hold Alfie's lead. The hard lump of dread in my chest grew heavier with every step.

Manzara was one of the few cafes that stayed open in winter, scraping a living from the stubble-faced, backgammon-playing men who filled the wooden tables, smoking and making a glass of *çay* last two hours. A solitary waiter paced up and down between the tables like an animal in a zoo, a leather-bound menu wedged under his arm.

At a table in the corner, in the shade of a swaying palm, Serkan sat stony-faced. I was relieved to see Kadir sitting next to him.

"Baba!" Spotting his father, Cem ran towards Serkan, who gave him a dismissive hug, keeping his eyes fixed on me.

"What the hell do you think you're doing?" he hissed as I pulled out a chair and sat down.

"Please Serkan. Let's not do this in front of the children."

"Kids, go and play!" he barked.

So much for missing them.

As the children and Alfie ran off towards the beach, Serkan glared at me.

"Well done Carrie," he said, his voice dripping with sarcasm as he gave a slow clap.

Kadir took a sip of his *çay* and stared at the red and white checked tablecloth.

"Serkan, I can't do this anymore. I've tried, I really have, but…"

"Have you met someone?"

I stared at him. Did he seriously think that was the reason I left him?

"Of course not!"

"Why did you move out?"

"I thought it best. For everyone."

"Where are you living?"

"I can't tell you that, Serkan."

The waiter arrived to take our orders. The thought of eating or drinking anything made my stomach churn, but I ordered two glasses of *ayran* for the children.

Neither of us spoke. People strolled past enjoying the Saturday sunshine. Couples hand in hand, families with children, people walking dogs. Further along the seafront, someone had caught a fish, carefully removing the metal hook from its lip before leaving it flapping and gasping on the ground.

"You know I'll find you," he said.

"I know."

The waiter returned and placed two glasses of white, foaming *ayran* on the table in front of us.

"Elif! Cem!"

Grateful for the distraction, I stood up and called towards the beach, waving my arms until the children looked up from their game.

Though I didn't look at him, I could feel Serkan's eyes on me, as heavy and oppressive as the air before a storm.

The children arrived and clambered onto their chairs, out of breath from running. They reached for their glasses and sucked the salty yoghurt drink through their straws.

My head jerked up as Serkan's chair scraped the ground. He stood up, knocking the table so that some of Elif's *ayran* sloshed onto the red and white cloth. A flicker of fear passed across her face, but he hadn't noticed. His eyes remained fixed on me, and for a moment I wondered what he would do.

Usually, Serkan was careful to keep up the pretence of the jovial, good-natured husband when other people were around, saving his outbursts for me and the children. His rages witnessed only by Gülşen who could be relied upon to take his side.

I imagined him kicking the table. Broken glass, and spilled *ayran*. The waiters restraining him like a wild animal.

He can't do anything. I told myself. *Not here.*

Feeling the weight of his stare on me, I remained still on my wooden chair. My hands found each other in my lap, grasping each other for support.

Eventually, the stalemate was broken. "Let's go," Serkan muttered to Kadir, dropping his gaze and shoving the chair hard against the table so that Elif's ayran spilt again.

I held my breath, watching as he walked away, almost making it to the door before he stopped. When he turned, I had just enough time to register the fury in his eyes as he strode back towards me.

"You've made a big mistake," he hissed, leaning towards me across the table and jabbing his finger in my face.

"*Abi*!" called Kadir from the other side of the restaurant. "Let's go."

I recoiled as Serkan stayed where he was, his face inches from mine as he considered his next move.

"Big mistake, Carrie," he whispered, staring deep into my eyes. He smiled then, his lip curled into a sneer as he pulled back, shoving the table one more time for good measure, before turning and walking away.

Chapter Eleven

Maralya, Turkey. April 2015

"I want music on," complained Cem the following day as we made the ten-minute drive to school.

"Not today."

I gripped the steering wheel a little tighter as we headed into Kirazlı's main street. Past the overpriced mini market, piles of fruit and vegetables stacked up outside. The Barber's shop, clean white towels flapping in the breeze, and the café where an elderly man sat sipping *çay*.

"But whyyy?"

"Because I said not today."

In my rear-view mirror, Cem folded his arms across his chest and stuck out his bottom lip. Next to him, Elif stared back at me, silent and serious. A wave of guilt washed over me. Serkan had only been back a day and already everything was different.

My heart began to race as I turned left at the mosque. Past the field where a solitary cow swished her tail against the flies. I reached the crossroads and slowed to a stop.

In the school playground, children milled about in uniforms of red and grey. Trousers for the boys, the girls demure in knee-length culottes over thick white tights. Cem's teacher Tarik *Bey* stood in the open doorway, hands in his pockets, his smile exaggerated by his handlebar moustache as children streamed past him into the school building.

I scanned the playground for Serkan's face, but there was no sign of him. Letting out a sigh of relief, I pulled up in front of the school gates.

"Have a good day!" I said as the kids climbed out of the car. "And remember what I told you."

"Don't go with Baba," parroted Elif.

I smiled. "Not yet," I said. "You'll see Baba soon, but today just wait for me, OK?"

"OK," they chorused, clambering out of the car. I watched as they crossed the playground to the entrance. Tarik *bey* giving a friendly nod in my direction as they disappeared inside.

At the hospital, I parked the car as close to the entrance as I could, scanning the car park as I hurried inside.

The reception area was empty except for an elderly man sitting alone in the corner, falling asleep as he leaned forward on his cane.

There was no sign of Serkan. "*Günaydın* Carrie!" The girls waved in unison from behind the desk.

"*Günaydın,*" I smiled weakly, reaching into my bag for my phone as I continued down the corridor to the office.

"Carrie!" Atakan spun around in his swivel chair as I opened the door. "Guess who's here!"

I continued past him to my desk, my phone pressed to my ear.

"Babe, you look awful!" said Atakan. "Has something happened?"

"*Efendim?*" said Azra's voice in my ear.

"Serkan's back," I said.

"Shit," replied Atakan and Azra simultaneously.

"Have you spoken to the school?" said Azra.

"Yes, a while ago. They won't let the kids leave with anyone but me."

"OK, good," she continued. "He will have received the divorce papers by now. Give him a day or two to simmer down and I'll call him to arrange a meeting at my office."

"OK."

"Be vigilant," she said. "The most dangerous time for a woman is right after she leaves. If he calls you or shows up at your apartment or the hospital, tell him to talk to me. If he persists, call the police."

"OK."

"And remember what I told you, Carrie. NO contact!"

"OK," I said again.

I ended the call and looked at Atakan. We didn't say anything, but I could see the worry in his eyes.

"Who's here?" I asked him, changing the subject as I switched on my computer.

***

Margaret Crosby was waiting for me outside the orthopaedic surgeon's office. Her skin looked even greyer than usual; her wispy hair was greasy at the roots.

"Oh, there you are dear," she said as I approached. "It's my knees! Bloomin' arthritis."

I sat down next to her, leaning forward as a wave of nausea rose from my stomach. I hadn't eaten any breakfast.

"Are you alright, dear?" Margaret peered at me through wisps of grey hair. "You're looking a bit peaky."

I spent the day on tenterhooks, jumping every time the office door opened, glancing around for him as I escorted patients to doctors or answered calls to the emergency room.

When it was time to leave, I braced myself, expecting him to be waiting at the exit, or lurking next to my car, but there was nothing. He was not at the school when I picked up the children, nor outside the apartment when we arrived home.

After dinner I walked Alfie around the park, spinning around at every rustle in the trees or snapping of a twig underfoot. That night I lay awake in my attic room, straining my ears for the sound of a motorbike. A voice. Footsteps outside.

The silence was deafening.

The week slipped by agonisingly slowly as I waited for the other shoe to drop. For the bomb to detonate. For the punishment I knew was coming.

Would he vandalise my car? Appear from behind a tree as I walked Alfie late at night? Snatch the children from school?

It was almost two weeks after our meeting at Manzara that Serkan did something so surprising, so out of character and so unexpected, that it caught me completely off-guard.

This tyrant, this ogre, this bully who had held me in the grip of fear for so long, did the one thing I never thought he would do.

He fell apart.

Chapter Twelve

Kirazlı, Turkey. May 2015.

"I love zis song!" declared Cem from the back seat as Rhianna came on the radio. I reached forward and turned up the volume as he sang along.

It was my favourite time of the year. Before the heat and humidity got too much. The warm air was soft against my skin. My feet in flip-flops. Socks put away for the next six months. In Kirazlı, the stark winter branches were alive with baby leaves and the gardens were brazen with colour. Purple wisteria cascaded like silk scarves down the sides of houses. Pretty but deadly oleander trees lined the streets, their delicate pink and white flowers belying their lethal toxicity. Majestic palm trees reached for the sky.

I braked hard to avoid a mother hen as she crossed the road, chicks following in a line like tiny yellow balls of fluff on a school outing.

Cem swayed from side to side in his booster seat to the music as I turned left at the mosque, past the muddy field and the solitary cow.

I reached the crossroads and stopped.

Standing alone in front of the school, Serkan stared back at me, his face an unreadable mask.

I clicked the radio off. The happy atmosphere died instantly, leaving a sober silence. For a moment, we stared at each other. Every fibre of my being wanted to turn the car around and drive home. Instead, I took a deep breath, pulled out into the road and slowed to a stop in front of the school gates.

'It's Baba!' Cem pointed out of the window as Serkan began striding towards us.

"Go straight inside," I instructed. "I'll pick you up later."

The children grabbed their bags and made their way through the gates. Locking the car doors from the inside, I watched until they disappeared through the double doors. Almost immediately, Serkan's face loomed at my window.

His appearance shocked me. His face was puffy, his eyes red and bloodshot. He looked like he hadn't slept in days. We stared at each other, his expression desperate, pleading, his eyes filled with tears. He tapped on the glass and motioned for me to wind down the window.

I stared straight ahead and inched the car forward. "Please Carrie," he said, gripping onto the wing mirror as if he could single-handedly prevent me from driving away.

"We've got great kids, a beautiful home…"

I opened the window an inch. "Serkan, you need to talk to Azra."

"I don't want Azra. I want you."

A solitary tear ran down his bloated cheek. "I know I treated you badly. You didn't deserve it, Carrie. I love you. I've only ever loved you."

My mind drifted back to the beginning. How everyone had tried to talk me out of marrying someone from such a different culture and background. But I knew better. I believed that love was enough. I had clung to that belief for so long. Long after the love had died. Too long.

"Can we just talk?" Serkan pleaded. "We can meet tonight at Manzara. I'll buy you and the kids dinner."

Azra's words intruded into my brain. "NO contact. He can only communicate with you through me."

"Can't we at least be amicable?" I had replied.

"After the divorce," insisted Azra. "I've dealt with hundreds of divorces, Carrie. Trust me. This is the only way."

A small group of curious children had formed around the car. Serkan refused to relinquish his grip on the wing mirror as I stared straight ahead and moved the car forward another inch.

The stalemate was broken by a sharp rap on the passenger side window. Cem's teacher, Tarik *Bey* smiled in at me. He was wearing a slightly crumpled brown corduroy suit and a tie with blue diamonds on it that had blown over his shoulder in the breeze. His handlebar moustache tilted upwards slightly at the corners, the ends shiny with wax.

"*Iyi misin?*" he asked in Turkish. Are you Ok?

I shook my head silently.

"Everyone inside!" I heard him say, clapping his hands at the onlookers until they reluctantly dispersed. Making his way towards Serkan, he gently steered him onto the pavement and leaned towards him, speaking in a low voice. His expression hovered somewhere between seriousness and sympathy, his eyebrows set in a low frown, like a teacher talking to a disobedient child. Eventually, Serkan nodded and took a few steps away from the car. Pulling out into the road, I pressed my foot down on the accelerator.

In my rear-view mirror, Serkan stood in the middle of the road, staring after me as I drove away.

Chapter Thirteen

Puglia, Italy. May 2016.

"Why have we stopped?"

Elif failed to hide the worry in her voice as the police officer strode towards our car, his eyes fixed on our license plate, radio pressed to his lips.

Behind us, cars were disembarking from the ferry, trailing past us like ants in a line.

"I don't know."

It was the truth. But I had an idea. An idea too terrible to say out loud. An idea that had been wedged firmly at the back of my mind since we left Bodrum, fluttering to the surface as we arrived in Kos and again in Athens. Pushed to one side as ridiculous and farfetched as we arrived here at the port of Bari in the Puglia region of Italy.

Now the idea was staring me in the face as clearly as the man standing at my window.

The police officer was tall, with aviator shades and a distinct five o'clock shadow, despite it being ten in the morning. His expression was unreadable as he motioned for me to lower the window. A solitary bead of sweat trickled down his temple as he launched into a stream of Italian.

I shook my head. "Do you speak English?"

The man continued in rapid Italian before accepting, from my blank expression, that he was wasting his time.

"*Passaporto.*" He held out his hand.

I rummaged in my handbag for the smooth plastic of our passports and handed them over. The man glanced briefly at the burgundy covers before flicking disinterestedly through them. Elif and I sat in silence.

Handing the passports back, he circled the car with slow, elongated strides, stopping to examine our license plate again as he conversed on his radio.

I pictured myself in a darkened room. A faceless official behind the desk. Asking for a lawyer.

Eventually, the man stopped talking, clipped the radio onto his belt and reappeared at my open window.

"*Come,*" he said in English, motioning for me to get out of the car. I unfastened my seatbelt and stepped out onto the tarmac, following him around to the boot where he lifted his palms in an upward motion.

"*Open.*"

I unlocked the boot and lifted the hatch, watching as he peered inside at the two suitcases, the small portable barbeque, and the cylindrical blue tent. He gave a small nod of his head and stepped back.

"*Close,*" he said, palms motioning downwards. I closed the boot and looked at him, awaiting the next instruction.

"*Passare.*" He flicked his hand dismissively, unclipped his radio and held it to his mouth.

I stared at him.

"*Passare!*" he said again, motioning towards the exit with an outstretched arm. His radio crackled as he walked away.

"Are we going?" said Elif as I got back into the driver's seat.

"I think so."

I started the engine and headed slowly towards the exit, glancing in my rear-view mirror for signs that I had misunderstood. A raised arm. A wave. A shout of protest. But the police officer had turned his attention to a long-distance lorry that had been pulled over behind us. Two officials in high-visibility jackets emerged from the back, torches clutched in their hands. Like us, the lorry had Turkish plates. A wave of realisation washed over me as I remembered the Syrian refugees in Bodrum, hands outstretched as they huddled together in the shade of a tree. The customs official wasn't looking for us. He was looking for stowaways.

Leaving the bustling port of Bari behind, we headed up the Puglian coast, through a series of fairytale towns in shades of sand and terracotta. Houses slumbered behind wooden shutters in the late afternoon sun. Laundry flapped lazily across narrow cobbled streets. Sunlight danced across the bright cobalt blue of the Adriatic.

I saw myself in a hotel room in Bodrum, tracing my finger along the map as I said the names out loud.

Giovinazzo.

Molfetta.

Bisceglie.

"Where are we going?" said Elif as another hour passed by.

"I don't know."

All I knew was that the more I drove, the further away the events of the past year became.

We left the coastal towns behind and climbed higher along the winding mountain roads of the *Gargano* National Park, through mile after mile of dense forest with no towns in sight. We would need to stop soon and find a place for the night, I thought as a sign appeared ahead. A picture of a deckchair and two wavy lines depicting the sea.

Vieste

"The sea!" exclaimed Elif as we descended the steep mountain road towards two parallel strips of gold and blue. It was exactly what we needed.

We rented a bungalow in a holiday village opposite the long, sandy beach. The next seven days were filled with expedient nothingness. Our mornings, swimming in the warm, shallow sea or lazing under the Italian sun. I dug out the paperback I had found in Bodrum and lost myself in its dog-eared pages. In the afternoons we explored the cobbled streets and whitewashed buildings of the old town, browsing an open market where glistening olives and wheels of cheese lay shaded by hanging necklaces of garlic and red peppers. We filled our tiny kitchen with *mozzarella, prosciutto, focaccia,* and fresh *tagliatelle*.

Slowly, I felt the meat returning to my bones.

When I was a child, I used to have a snow globe. Tiny log cabins surrounded by miniature pine trees in a festive scene. I remember shaking it as hard as I could, making the "snow" swirl around furiously before watching it settle back down.

That's what we were doing in Vieste. Settling.

***

It was our last morning in Vieste. I sat alone on our little terrace, a large mug of black coffee on the table in front of me. Elif was off trying to photograph the lizards that ran like quicksilver across the pathways, disappearing as fast as they came.

The pain came from nowhere. Raw. Visceral. Punching me in the solar plexus so hard it made me catch my breath. I closed my eyes and leaned forward, clutching my chest as I waited for it to pass. I forced myself to breathe slowly in and out, clinging to the comfort of familiar sounds. Snatches of conversation from the other side of the fence in undulating Italian. The far-off cry of a seagull. The crashing of the distant tide.

After several minutes, the pain began to subside, reducing in intensity to the omnipresent ache that had lived in my chest since I left Turkey. I sat up and opened my eyes, anchoring myself to my surroundings. Identical white bungalows with dark green doors and shutters. A low stone wall. Neatly trimmed hedges. Freshly washed laundry flapping on the line.

It was time.

"He can't hurt you," reassured the voice in my head as I reached for my phone. I closed my eyes, listening to the ringing across the miles.

"Carrie?"

Serkan's voice was hesitant, heavy with disbelief.

"Yes."

"Where are you?"

"I need to speak to Cem," I said as calmly as I could muster.

"Where the hell are you?" Serkan's tone hardened. "Where is my daughter?"

"She's with me, she's fine."

"What do you want?" he snapped.

"I want to speak to my son."

A sarcastic laugh. "Oh, you have a son?" he jeered. "So now you remember?"

I gripped the phone tightly.

He can't hurt you.

"Please, let me talk to Cem."

Another sarcastic snort followed by a lengthy silence. I wondered for a moment if he had hung up.

"Hello?" Cem's voice.

Relief flooded my body. He sounded fine. Normal. Happy.

"Hi, sweetie, it's Mummy," I said, forcing down the hard lump that had lodged in the back of my throat.

I could hear him breathing. The way a child breathes. Too close to the receiver. Tears sprung to my eyes.

"Where are you?" he said, eventually.

I tried to keep my voice steady. "We had to go away for a while."

Elif, back from her lizard-hunting expedition, had joined me at the table and was listening intently.

"OK," said Cem, accepting my pitiful explanation.

I moved on to safer subjects. School. Friends. His favourite football team. He answered my questions, though it was clear from the tone of his voice that his father was listening to every word. By now Elif had worked out who I was talking to and was making pleading eyes as she reached for the phone. I passed it to her, listening as they talked. Laughing about a schoolteacher and a mutual friend until her voice became stiff and polite and her answers vague.

"Baba wants to talk to you," she said.

Reluctantly, I took the phone.

"Where are you Carrie?" he demanded, his voice hard. "You've really messed up this time."

An iridescent lizard darted from the flower bed and streaked across the path. Pausing for a fraction of a second, it cocked its head to one side as if it had forgotten something important before disappearing from sight.

"Well, you must be somewhere in Turkey," continued Serkan, a hint of smugness in his voice. "I blocked you from taking Elif out of the country."

A flurry of Italian filled the air as our neighbours emerged from the bungalow next door.

"*Bongiourno,*" said the man with a nod and a smile.

I smiled back.

"Of course," I said.

There was an uncomfortable pause.

"Are you with *him*?" Serkan said eventually.

A jolt hit me squarely in the chest.

"He never turned up," said Serkan. "In court."

I didn't say anything. There was nothing to say.

"The police are looking for you, Carrie," he continued. "They'll find you. It's only a matter of time."

A voice filled my mind. His voice. Intimate. Husky. Whispering across the days, weeks and kilometres that separated us as if he were standing right beside me.

Barbaros.

"*Her şey zaman,*" it said.

Everything in time.

Chapter Fourteen

Maralya, Turkey. May 2015.

Azra's office was located on the ground floor of an apartment block in a well-to-do area of Maralya, close to her six-bedroomed house.

I crossed the manicured lawn, past the swimming pool to the shiny black front door. A pale-yellow retriever with liquid black eyes gazed down silently from an upstairs balcony.

I had been there many times before, sharing breakfast over her polished mahogany desk on summer mornings as the kids splashed about in the pool, or drinking *çay* on rainy winter afternoons. For someone with an apparent abundance of money, Azra seemed to do remarkably little work.

As the intercom clicked a response, I pushed open the heavy black door and made my way along the corridor to her office.

The door was open. As I entered, Azra nodded, unsmiling, from behind her mahogany desk. She was dressed in a grey tailored suit, her black curls tamed into a neat bun, eyes framed by black-rimmed glasses. There was no trace of the party girl; glass of wine in one hand, cigarette in the other. In place of my friend sat a polished professional.

Serkan was already there, sitting in one of the plush overstuffed armchairs. He looked up, a nervous smile flickering across his face as I entered the office and perched in the other armchair.

Azra shuffled some papers and turned towards Serkan.

"Have you received the petition for divorce?"

He gave a defeated nod.

"Good, then I'll start."

Azra had told me to leave the negotiations to her. I examined my nails as she began.

"I have made a request to the court for the villa in Kirazlı, the car, custody of both children and the four apartments in Maralya."

She smiled at Serkan, who stared at her open-mouthed.

"That's everything!"

"Yes."

I tried to catch Azra's eye, but her unblinking gaze was fixed on Serkan. There must be some mistake. I hadn't agreed to this. I didn't want to take everything from him.

"You can't…" he spluttered eventually.

"But Carrie paid for them," said Azra.

"So where will I live?"

"You are a man, Serkan. Work. Take care of yourself."

I got the feeling she was enjoying this.

Serkan turned to me. "Is this what you want?" he whispered.

"Please do not address my client directly."

He turned back to Azra, a flicker of defiance in his eyes as he sat back in his chair. "I'll sell the villa," he said. "I can sell it tomorrow if I want to."

"You are welcome to try." Azra flicked nonchalantly through the papers on her desk. "But you will find there is a court order preventing you from doing so."

Serkan appeared to visibly deflate, sinking slowly into his chair like a punctured tyre. He opened his mouth to speak and closed it again.

There was an excruciating silence.

"Unless..." Azra tapped her pen on her desk and stared at Serkan. He lifted his head slowly to look at her.

She raised one eyebrow. "What do you want?"

"I want the flats."

Azra turned her gaze to me.

"What do you think, Carrie?"

I opened my mouth to speak, but she had already turned her attention back to Serkan.

"*Two* of the flats," she said. "On the condition that we sell the villa as soon as possible, deposit the money into Carrie's bank account and sign the divorce papers immediately."

Serkan glared at her, his gaze unwavering.

"*All* of the flats."

Azra leaned back in her swivel chair.

"Of course, we could always go to court..." she said airily. "Let them decide. But I must remind you, we can not only prove that Carrie paid for all the properties, but her bank statements show you have not paid a single household bill in the past five years."

"I left money..." protested Serkan weakly. "In the book."

I turned to face him, incredulous. At least he had the shame to look away, I thought, as he averted his eyes.

"Add to that Carrie's testimony of your violent behaviour..."

"Violent!" He snorted in disbelief, turning back to me.

"You read the petition?" Azra leafed through the papers until she found what she was looking for.

"Swearing...kicked over a table...punched the wall...his hands around my throat..." she let the words hang in the air. "I could go on."

"I've got a bit of an anger problem..." Serkan muttered, looking down at his lap.

Azra shook her head. "It doesn't look good for you, Serkan. The best scenario is to settle now and present the court with an agreement. Otherwise, this could drag on and on." She fixed him with a stare as cold as steel. "You could lose everything."

Serkan stared down at his lap. The air in the room was suddenly as thick and heavy as the plush, velvet curtains that hung from the floor-to-ceiling windows. The seconds counted down by the antique wall clock, its gold pendulum swinging back and forth. I stared at a square of wall, the paint a shade darker, unfaded by the sun as if a picture had once been there.

I had never noticed it before.

Eventually, Serkan lifted his head. "OK," he said with a defeated sigh. "Find a buyer for the villa and I'll sign."

Azra smiled. The cat that got the cream.

"I want to see my kids," he said as he stood up.

"Carrie has been awarded full temporary custody," said Azra. "You have visitation rights once a week until permanent custody is decided. If you fail to return the children at the agreed time, that is a breach of the custody order and a criminal offence."

Serkan nodded.

"Carrie, which day works for you?" said Azra, turning to me.

"Saturday?" I said. "I can drop them on Saturday evening, and pick them up on Sunday afternoon?"

Serkan nodded again. He didn't look at me.

"Good!" Azra smiled and rubbed her hands together as Serkan walked out of the office, slamming the door behind him. A few minutes later, the revs of his motorbike filled the room as he sped away.

Azra leaned back in her swivel chair and grinned at me. There was a glint in her eye, like a tiger about to pounce. I had never seen this side of her before.

"I kind of feel sorry for him," I said. "He looked so defeated."

Azra scoffed. "Worry about yourself, Carrie. He will be fine."

"I was hoping we could be friends," I continued. "We were married for a long time. We have children."

"When you get the money from the villa and the divorce papers are signed, you can do whatever you like," she replied. "But for now, absolutely no contact. Trust me, Carrie. I know what I'm doing."

Chapter Fifteen

Maralya, Turkey. May 2015.

Serkan was waiting on the broken wooden bench in the shade of the fig tree outside the flats where he was staying with Gülşen. A packet of sunflower seeds in his hand, he bit the middle out with his teeth before dropping the shells onto the growing pile on the ground. A group of local boys played football in the street, shouting back and forth to each other as they skidded in the dust.

"Baba!" Cem had unclipped his seatbelt and opened the door before the car had even come to a complete stop.

"My boy!" Serkan ruffled Cem's hair before turning his attention to his daughter.

"Hi, Elif."

She smiled at him as she climbed out of the car, book clutched tightly in her hand.

"What have you got there?" Serkan peered at the book as Cem ran up the stone steps towards Gülşen's flat on the third floor.

"Matilda." Elif turned the book around to face him. "I can read it to you if you like."

"I would love that," Serkan replied with a broad smile. I watched them, simultaneously pleased by his newfound interest in his daughter, and saddened that it had taken this to change his attitude towards her.

As Elif followed her brother up the stone steps, Serkan approached my window.

"How are you?" he said.

It had been two weeks since our meeting in Azra's office. Outwardly, all was normal. I went to work. The children went to school. Every Saturday afternoon, I dropped them at the flats where they spent the night with Serkan and Gülşen before I picked them up on Sunday.

Could it really be this easy? I thought to myself as I lay awake at night in my attic room. Had the threats and promises of recriminations been no more than hot air? Had my fears been unfounded? A tentative hope flickered inside me. When the villa was sold, I would buy an apartment of my own. The children and I could stay in Maralya. In time, maybe Serkan and I could even be friends.

A cheer erupted from the end of the street as someone scored a goal. Serkan was smiling at me, waiting for an answer.

"Fine," I replied. "You?"

"Why don't you come up?" he said, tilting his head towards the stone steps. "Have a coffee?"

"You know I can't, Serkan."

"Of course you can..."

"I can't," I repeated, turning the keys in the ignition.

A glimmer of anger flashed in his eyes. Barely visible before he composed himself, but a glimmer all the same.

"I'll pick the kids up tomorrow at the usual time," I said before driving away.

***

"Ready?"

From her end of the balcony, Azra nodded, and we simultaneously lowered the ends of the plastic sign over the railings before securing it with rope.

Below us, Alfie scoured the garden of his former home, nose to the ground, zigzagging left and right as he followed the trail of enticing fresh scents.

The garden was wilder and more overgrown than ever. The rampant weeds, with which I had fought a valiant battle, left unchecked and fortified by months of rain and sun, had grown to several meters in height. The tenacious grape vines that snaked around the veranda had infiltrated the fruit trees, tightening their grip, millimetre by millimetre, and choking everything in their path. The roof of the chicken-less coop had caved in under the weight of rainwater and fallen leaves. The hammock, frayed and rotten from exposure to the elements, hung forlornly between the lemon and plum trees.

Azra and I surveyed our handiwork from the car as we drove away.

Sahibiden Satılık Villa /Villa For Sale Direct From Owner proclaimed the sign in meter-high black letters above mine and Azra's telephone numbers.

"Lunch?" she grinned at me.

***

Along Caretta Beach, the cafes, bars, and restaurants were stirring into life, sleepy and unprepared, like animals emerging from hibernation. The dull drilling and hammering of last-minute repairs droned in the air as we selected a table in the sun.

The first tourists of the season, milk-white and conspicuous in shorts and T-shirts, fanned themselves in twenty-six-degree heat as Azra and I pulled our jackets closer around ourselves in the brisk sea breeze.

"He watches the apartment," I said.

Azra placed a cigarette between her lips.

"Are you sure?"

I nodded.

At first, it was just a feeling. A sound late at night. A shadow moving behind the trees as I looked out of the living room window through the metal bars. The familiar sound of his motorbike as it sped past. In the beginning, I put it down to my own paranoia. My brain playing tricks on me. But deep down, I knew. I could feel his eyes on me. Watching me.

There was a repeated clicking sound as Azra tried to light her cigarette against the salty breeze. She cupped her hand around it, finally taking a deep drag and breathing out smoke into the sea air. "We need to scare him," she said. "You have to go to the police."

***

Maralya police station was a soulless, rectangular building in government-issue beige with metal bars on the windows and a large yard out front where off-duty police cars snoozed in the afternoon sun.

At the gate, two officers sat on wooden stools outside a Portacabin, smoking cigarettes. Between them, on an upturned crate, sat an overflowing ashtray and two half-empty glasses of *çay*.

"*Buyrun,*" said one of the officers with a smile. He looked me up and down the way many Turkish men look at Western women. As if I were a cake in a window.

"I need to make a complaint," I said.

The officers glanced at each other.

"I think this man is stalking me." I handed over a photocopy I had found of Serkan's ID card.

"You think?" the officer squinted up at me in the sun, a small, amused smile on his face.

"I've seen him," I said. "Watching my apartment."

"This is Cetin's son," said the officer as he stared at the photocopy. He passed it to his companion, who nodded in agreement.

"Serkan," he nodded. "Cetin's boy."

"I remember him when he was so high," the first officer continued, indicating the distance from the ground with his hand. He chuckled. "Always up to mischief."

I wanted to point out that Serkan was no longer a cute nine-year-old, but a 120kg man with a violent temper.

"Don't worry, *Hanımefendi,*" he said with a smile and a wink. He handed the photocopy back to me. "We'll talk to him."

Chapter Sixteen

Maralya, Turkey, June 2015

The blinding cyclops of the headlight shone straight into my eyes. The engine revved, as menacing as the roar of a lion and twice as terrifying. Dread flooded my body. I needed to run, but my legs refused to move as if stuck in cement. Serkan lifted the visor of his helmet, his eyes staring straight into mine as he revved the engine again. I closed my eyes. Waiting for an impact that didn't come.

Heart pounding, skin clammy with sweat, I opened my eyes to the shapes and shadows of my attic room. Alfie lay crouched on the floor, ears pricked as he stared at the window. He gave a low growl. Whatever had awoken me, he had heard it, too.

The unmistakable roar of Serkan's motorbike filled the room, sending Alfie into a cacophony of frantic barking. I swung my legs out of bed, the tiles cold beneath my bare feet as I crossed to the window.

In the street below, Serkan sat astride his motorbike, visor raised, his eyes fixed on me as they had been in the dream. We stared at each other in a silent standoff.

With Alfie at my side, I made my way downstairs, unlocked the balcony door, and stepped outside into the cool night air.

"What are you doing, Serkan?" I said.

He did not respond.

"Mummy!" Elif called from her bedroom.

"It's nothing, honey, go back to sleep."

Serkan glared at me through the open visor of his helmet and revved the engine again.

"Serkan, you need to leave," I said. "I'll call the police."

The door opened and Cem, messy-haired and creased with sleep, joined me on the balcony. He fastened his arms around my waist and blinked in the brightness of the motorbike headlight. He was closely followed by Elif, barefoot and yawning in her My Little Pony pyjamas.

"What's baba doing?" she said, stifling another yawn.

"Let's go back inside, it's cold out here." I herded the children back inside, where they huddled together on the sofa. Elif clutched her younger brother's hand, their eyes wide and fearful.

A rage began to build inside me. I had thought that the days of broken sleep, arguments and violent outbursts were over for them. This was supposed to be a safe place. A happy home free from fear. Furious, I grabbed my phone and returned to the balcony.

"If you don't leave right now, I'm calling the police," I said.

Serkan removed his helmet and wedged it under his arm. "Call them." His eyes were defiant, his smile mocking. "They can't do anything to me."

"It's three in the morning," I said. "The children need to sleep. Please leave us alone."

He glared at me, his eyes burning with rage.

"I'm not going to leave you alone!" he spat. "You're my wife! You belong to me! I'm not going to sell the villa. I'm not going to sign the divorce papers. Until the day I die, I am not going to leave you alone!"

He watched as I dialled the number Azra had given me for the police station.

"I need assistance," I said in Turkish, as a female voice answered the phone. "My ex-husband is outside my apartment and refusing to leave."

"Ex-husband? Are you divorced?"

I failed to see the relevance of this, but answered anyway, "We're separated."

"Do you have a restraining order?" continued the operator.

"No."

"Lock your doors and stay inside," she said. "We'll be there as soon as we can."

As I ended the call, Serkan, helmet still under his arm, revved the engine loudly and sped off down the road.

"Has he gone?" said Cem when I got back inside.

I nodded. "Let's go back to bed," I said.

"We want to sleep wiz you," said Cem. History repeating itself.

"Of course." I took his small hand in mine as we climbed the staircase, closely followed by Elif and Alfie.

It wasn't long before the ceiling and walls were patterned with blue and red lights. The doorbell chimed.

"Stay here," I told the children. "I won't be long."

The two police officers were waiting on the doorstep. One was older, hair greying around his temples with a noticeable paunch, the other in his early twenties, skinny with a protruding Adam's apple.

"Caroline *Hanım*?" said the older officer.

I nodded. "Thanks for coming."

"Has he gone?"

I nodded again.

The younger officer took Serkan's name, address and *kimlik* number, writing them carefully in his notepad.

"I want a restraining order," I said.

"Of course, *Hanımefendi,*" said the older officer. "Come to the police station first thing in the morning and file a report. My colleagues will be happy to help you. If he comes back, please call us again."

In my attic bedroom, the children were still awake.

"What did Baba want?" asked Cem in the darkness.

"I don't know, sweetie," I replied.

"He scared me," said Elif.

"Baba is going through a difficult time right now," I tried to explain. "He would never hurt you, you know that."

"Would he hurt you?" asked Elif after a few minutes.

I was unable to answer this.

Chapter Seventeen

Maralya, Turkey. June 2015

The room was small and dark, with a scratched desk and a faded picture of Atatürk on the wall. His eyes were an unnatural shade of blue as if they had been painted on as an afterthought.

The police officer typed as I recounted the events of the previous night, stopping occasionally to ask me to repeat something or clarify a detail. When I had finished, he read my statement back to me and printed several sheets of paper, which he passed across the desk for me to sign.

"There is a temporary restraining order in place for now," he explained. "We'll ask the courts for a permanent one and let you know their decision next week."

"OK," I said.

"If he comes anywhere near you, to your home or place of work, call us immediately."

"OK," I said again. "Thank you."

Outside, the sun was blinding, the temperature having already hit 30 degrees. I glanced at the clock on the dashboard as I got into my car. 10:15. I had called work to say I would be late, but a wave of guilt washed over me as I turned the key in the ignition. My inbox of files awaiting medical reports had been overflowing on Friday afternoon. I hated to imagine what it looked like now.

I stifled a yawn and flicked the indicator, about to pull out onto the road, when my phone rang. Probably work, I thought, as I reached into my bag. My heart sank as Serkan's face stared from the screen.

"How are you?" he said jovially as I answered. It was a pattern I knew well. The angry outburst followed by acting as if nothing had happened. This would inevitably be followed by accusations that I was overreacting or "crazy," quickly followed by further threats and anger.

I sighed. "How do you think I am, Serkan?" I said. "Thanks to you, we all had about two hours' sleep last night. The children could barely get out of bed this morning."

"Carrie, listen...." he began.

"No Serkan, YOU listen. I'm at the police station. I have filed a complaint. I have a restraining order. You need to stay away from me, or you'll be arrested."

I braced myself for the usual tirade of verbal abuse, but instead, there was a strangled sob on the other end of the line.

"Carrie, I'm dying! Please, Carrie! I can't live without you! I'm sorry Carrie, I'm so sorry..."

I didn't say anything, too stunned for a moment to respond.

"I'm losing my mind," he continued. "I want to kill myself, Carrie!"

I switched off the ignition and sat back in my seat.

"You're not going to kill yourself," I said.

"Please, Carrie. I'll try harder, I promise." He was sobbing heavily now. I could hear traffic noise around him and wondered for a moment where he was. I pictured him standing on a busy street, people staring as the tears ran down his face.

"Serkan, I'm not the one to help you through this," I said quietly. "Maybe you should talk to someone."

"I don't have anyone," he sniffed. "You are my best friend."

I felt myself weakening, my resolve sliding off me like rainwater off leaves. Closing my eyes, I forced my mind back. Back to the pushing, the shoving, the relentless put-downs and criticisms, the mocking laughter, and constant threats.

I sighed. "Turning up in the middle of the night, scaring the children. It's not OK, Serkan."

"I know."

"And I know you've been watching the flat. I've seen you."

"I'm sorry, Carrie. It's not too late. Don't sell the villa. Stop the divorce. Let's go home."

"Serkan...," I sighed.

"We can be friends," he continued. "Let's meet for coffee."

"I can't," I said before he could finish. "Azra said..."

"Fuck Azra!" he barked, his tone changing immediately as fury dripped from his voice. "Fuck Azra and fuck you, Carrie! You think I'm going to sell the villa? You think I'm going to sign the divorce papers? You think I'm going to just go away quietly and let you live your life? You don't know me! You don't know what I'm capable of!"

Ending the call, I threw the phone back into my bag as if it were suddenly red hot. Heart pounding, I pulled out into the street.

***

"Sorry I'm late," I said, pushing open the office door. As usual, the translation office was a hub of activity. Beyza was arguing with an insurance company in German, telephone receiver wedged between her shoulder and her ear. Atakan was speaking English to a harassed-looking woman in a bikini top and denim shorts. Her wet hair was dripping into a small pool of water beneath her on the office floor. Both the office phones were ringing.

"Patient in Emergency." Atakan thrust a file towards me. "Came in overnight. Drunk."

I glanced at the name on the file. *Julie Stevens.* Summer season had arrived.

The door opened, and Margaret Crosby drifted into the room flanked by a sour-faced blonde woman and a tall, dark-haired man.

"Hello Carrie," she said weakly, as if even opening her mouth was too much of an effort.

"Hi Margaret," I smiled. "How are you?"

As soon as the words were out of my mouth, I regretted them as Margaret launched into her usual list of vague ailments and non-specific aches and pains.

The stack of files awaiting medical reports that had doubled over the weekend glared at me from my desk. It's going to be a long day, I thought as Margaret's voice was drowned out by the shrill ringing of the telephone. I lifted the receiver to my ear.

"Foreign Patients department."

"We need a translator in emergency," said a voice on the other end.

"On my way."

"Have a seat for a minute," I said to Margaret. "I'll be right back."

Margaret sank onto the white leather sofa, gently assisted by the dark-haired man.

"Thanks, dear," I heard her say.

The blonde sat down next to her and glanced around the office with a bored expression on her face. She was wearing a blue tracksuit and gold hoop earrings, her hair pulled back in a severe ponytail.

I crossed the crowded reception. In Turkey, when a family member is sick, the entire family descends on the hospital in solidarity. Elderly men in flat caps, young women carrying fractious toddlers and rotund women in headscarves milled about, their faces lined with worry. In my pocket, my phone rang.

"Good news," said Azra in my ear. "I've had an offer on the villa."

"How much?"

The figure was reasonable. Not as much as I was hoping for, but not bad. And there was room for negotiation.

"What do you want me to tell them?" she said.

"Negotiate a bit more," I replied. "See how much higher they will go, but don't push too hard. I want it sold as soon as possible."

Doctor Mustafa was waiting for me in the emergency department. He smelled of strong aftershave and cigarette smoke.

"I can't get much sense out of her," he said in Turkish, as we walked together towards the cubicle. "She's been drinking all night by the looks of it. We just need some details."

"I'll try my best."

He swished back the curtains to the cubicle, where a middle-aged blonde woman lay in a foetal position, her eyes tightly closed.

"Julie?" I said gently. "How are you feeling?"

The woman groaned and opened her eyes briefly before squeezing them shut again and clutching her head.

"How much have you had to drink, Julie?" I asked as she rolled onto her back, shielding her eyes from the fluorescent light with a low groan.

"Got back as soon as I could!" came a sing-song voice behind me as the curtains swished open.

I turned to see a woman with white-blonde hair, tottering towards me on perilously high heels. Her orange foundation was thick on her face Her eyebrows were drawn on a little too high giving her a surprised expression. "I'm Steph," she said, thrusting some papers towards me. "Julie's friend."

"Were you with her last night?" I said.

"Yeah, we went to a bar and then a club. I just went back to the hotel to get her insurance papers."

"Can you tell me what happened?"

Julie suddenly lurched forward and began groping around for something. I grabbed a cardboard kidney dish from the table and handed it to her in the nick of time as she vomited profusely.

"We was out, dancin'," Steph continued. "Then suddenly Jules said she had a headache. We were waiting for a taxi back to the hotel and she just blacked out."

"Did she hit her head when she fell?"

The woman shook her head. "I don't know, I don't think so."

"How much had she had to drink?" I asked, taking the brimming kidney dish from Julie as she groaned and collapsed back onto the pillows.

"A bit. It was our last night," explained Steph, looking sheepish. She tried unsuccessfully to pull her fluorescent microdress down over her hips, before turning to Mustafa.

"Is she going to be OK, doctor?"

"OK, OK," Mustafa smiled as he patted her reassuringly on the shoulder. He turned to me. "Just let her sleep it off," he said. "We'll give her some IV fluids."

I followed him out of the cubicle, clutching Julie's insurance paperwork.

"Do you think it's worth getting a CT scan?" I said suddenly. Something about Julie Stevens didn't feel right.

Mustafa stopped and looked at me. "She's drunk," he said. "She'll be fine in a few hours."

"I don't know. I have a feeling there might be something else."

He shook his head. "Carrie, I'm the doctor. Leave the decisions to me."

"*Merhaba* Carrie," Doctor Tekin, the head doctor, nodded as I headed back towards my office. "Is everything OK?"

"Yes, fine. I'm just a bit worried about a patient in Emergency."

Tekin listened carefully as I voiced my concerns.

"I'll request a CT scan," he said when I had finished.

"I don't want to make any trouble with Mustafa, he is the doctor..."

"Carrie, you are a highly experienced nurse," said Doctor Tekin, waving my concerns away. "Leave Mustafa to me."

The office was empty except for the dark-haired man sitting alone on the sofa. Atakan must have taken Eleanor to the doctor with the blonde woman, I thought as I photocopied Julie's documents, sat down at my desk, and reached for the first file. An email icon flashed in the corner of my screen. It was from my sister.

Found these gorgeous shoes in the sale. What do you think about them for Elif? They match her bridesmaid's dress perfectly!

Gorgeous! I typed in the reply box. *Not long now, the kids are so excited!*

It was a few minutes before I felt it. The weight of his eyes on me. I glanced up at the dark-haired man, our eyes meeting for a fraction of a second before I looked away. Willing myself not to look at him, I forced myself to focus on my computer screen as I began the first in my pile of medical reports.

On examination, the patient was found to have severe tenderness and guarding to the left lower quadrant.

His gaze continued to bore into me, demanding a response. My discomfort grew. Where was Atakan? Beyza? Unable to stand it any longer, I shot him another glance, assuming he would realise he'd been caught staring and look away. Instead, he held my gaze and smiled, confident in his good looks and charm. I did not smile back.

I knew the type well. Classically handsome in a swarthy Mediterranean way. Black hair, slick with gel. Olive skin. Deep-set eyes under well-groomed brows, and designer stubble. In a holiday town like Maralya, men like him were two a penny, preying on unsuspecting tourists in the summer months in the hope of easy sex, or even better, money or a passport.

The office door opened and Margaret, clutching the blonde woman's arm, shuffled into the office, with Atakan close behind.

"Prescription," said Margaret, waving a piece of paper. "I need to come back in a week for a check-up."

I smiled at her, grateful for the distraction.

"I hope you feel better soon," I said.

"Thanks love."

"Ready?" snapped the blonde with the ponytail at the dark-haired man. He gave a barely perceptible nod.

"Oh, this bloomin' arthritis! It makes me so tired..." trailed Margaret's voice as she disappeared down the corridor with the blonde woman.

The dark-haired man remained where he was.

The phone rang and Atakan pounced on it.

"They need a translator in CT," he said airily as he disappeared out of the door, leaving the man and I alone again.

I forced my eyes back to the words on the screen, but my mind was blank. Why didn't he leave? I thought as I re-read the same sentence for the fourth time. Eventually, he got to his feet, walked towards me and extended his hand.

"It was nice to meet you...?" he said. A space hung in the air where my name should be.

"Carrie," I heard myself say as my fingers touched his. His skin was soft, his hand warm.

"Carrie," he repeated, holding me with his gaze. His voice was husky and intimate, barely above a whisper.

He had been holding my hand for too long, but I couldn't move. Something I had considered long dead began to stir inside me. I was suddenly aware that I was holding my breath.

The door flew open, and Beyza blustered in, clutching a handful of paperwork. Two harassed-looking parents followed, the father clutching a crimson-faced toddler, sweaty-haired and crying.

"I'll just make some photocopies," she said, motioning for them to sit down. "Then we'll go straight to the doctor."

I looked back at the dark-haired man. He held my gaze for a few seconds more, an unreadable expression on his face. Half smiling. All-knowing.

I was unable to look away.

"Nice to meet you, Carrie." He smiled, his eyes crinkling up at the corners.

"I'm Barbaros."

Chapter Eighteen

Maralya, Turkey. July 2015

"Baba!"

I turned, splashing boiling water onto my hand as I poured the steaming liquid into my coffee cup. Cem had pulled back the net curtain and was waving at the street below.

"Baba!" he said again.

Swearing under my breath, I ran the tap, holding my hand under the cold water as my phone rang.

"Bad news," said Azra. "The buyer has pulled out of the sale."

My heart sank. Having accepted the offer, for the past three weeks, Serkan had repeatedly delayed the sale of the villa. His excuses ranged from he was too busy to sign the paperwork, to the price was too low. Without his signature, we could do nothing.

"I'm not surprised," I said, patting my hand dry with a tea towel. "He was never going to sign."

"We'll find another buyer," reassured Azra.

"And he will refuse to sign again," I said with a sigh. I looked out of the window. On the other side of the road, Serkan stared back at me.

"He's outside," I said.

"Call the police!" said Azra. "Don't talk to him, Carrie. Remember. No contact!"

The restraining order had done nothing to curb Serkan's uninvited visits to the apartment. I would frequently look outside to see him lurking on the opposite side of the road or sitting astride his motorbike, staring up at the window. He would appear in the next aisle at the supermarket as I was shopping, while I walked Alfie around the park, or at the beach when I took the children. He never said anything, just stared at me from a safe distance away, ready to zoom away on his motorbike if I called the police. In the end, I called the police so often that they stopped coming.

Every Saturday evening, he was waiting on the broken bench under the fig tree as I dropped the children at the flats. I didn't speak to him, stopping only long enough to see them disappear up the stone steps before driving away.

But today something was different. Something in his eyes. In the set of his shoulders and the tilt of his head. A brazenness.

He walked up to the house and looked up at the balcony.

"Carrie! Come out. I need to talk to you."

I opened the balcony door and stepped outside.

"Let's go for a walk," he said, gesturing towards the beach. "Have a *çay*. It's a beautiful day."

"The buyers have withdrawn their offer on the villa," I said. "They got sick of waiting."

He shrugged. "The price was too low."

"I was happy with the price."

"How's Rebecca?" he continued, changing the subject. "Not much time now until the wedding. The kids must be getting excited."

"She's fine." Distant alarm bells began to ring in the depths of my mind. Serkan never asked about my sister.

"You know..." he pushed his hands into his pockets and looked up at me. "You can't take the children out of the country without my permission. Especially with things as they are between us."

"But it's their aunt's wedding..."

He smiled, "Of course," he said. "The problem is Carrie, we are in the middle of a divorce. How do I know you'll bring them back?"

"Of course, I'll bring them back..." I stuttered. "This is their home."

Serkan looked up at me, a slow smile spreading across his face.

"How about that *çay?*" he said.

We walked towards the beach, Alfie almost choking himself as he strained at the leash. It chafed against the circular red welt on my hand where the hot water had scalded me.

"What happened to your hand?" said Serkan.

"I burnt it," I replied. "Coffee."

He reached for Alfie's leash. "Let me take him."

We stopped at Manzara, wordlessly choosing the same table, in the shade of the swaying palm, where we had sat in March. Though barely four months had passed, it felt like a lifetime ago.

The season was well underway, and the café was busy. Shiny-faced couples in oversized sunhats fanned themselves in the heat. Toddlers lay splayed out in strollers with a glazed look in their eyes. Flies buzzed and crawled over half-eaten plates of congealed pizza.

"Kids, go and play!" ordered Serkan, unclipping Alfie from his leash.

The kids and Alfie ran towards Carretta Beach. The sand was circled with raffia parasols beneath which tourists, ranging in colour from cerise to burnt umber, roasted like chickens on a barbeque. Brown-skinned vendors, weighed down with cold drinks and sunglasses, traipsed up and down the scalding sand. Overhead, a kite climbed and dipped in the cloudless blue sky. I watched it, envying its freedom.

A waiter appeared, the armpits of his otherwise pristine white shirt darkened with sweat, pen poised above his notepad.

"Wine?" smiled Serkan.

"*Çay* is fine," I replied.

I remembered the last time we were here. The spilt *Ayran* on the red and white tablecloth. The scraping of the chair as he stood up. His face inches from mine. *You've made a big mistake!*

It was the first time we had been alone since Serkan had returned from the UK. No Kadir or Azra to provide a buffer. An awkward silence beat down on us with the midday sun. On the next table, a sparrow hopped lightly on the red and white checked cloth, pecking at the crumbs of a leftover burger.

The drinks arrived. Glad of the distraction, I picked up my glass and took a sip of my too-hot *çay*, burning my tongue. The second time that day Serkan's presence had caused me to scald myself.

"I miss you."

I replaced the glass on its saucer and forced myself to swallow the boiling *çay*.

"Serkan, please don't..."

"I love you, Carrie," he said.

"You've punished me enough," he continued. "I'll change, I promise."

I stared at the tiny glass saucer, the two cubes of sugar, stained brown by the *çay* where it had spilled.

"This isn't about punishing you, Serkan." I forced myself to look at him.

"You don't love me anymore?" His eyes were pleading, imploring me to give him something, a tiny crumb of hope to hold on to.

The word NO filled my mind, rising in my throat where it lodged, refusing to come out.

I looked back at the sparrow as it flitted away.

"You changed," I said, my voice barely audible as I stared down at the red and white squares.

His fist crashed down on the table, making my glass rattle on its saucer. "I'll change back!" he said. "Just give me another chance!"

I stood up.

"Don't leave!" His hand shot out and grabbed my wrist, letting go immediately as I jerked my arm away.

"I'm sorry," he mumbled. "Please sit down."

Laughter drifted towards us. The children were walking back up the beach, lured by the promise of chocolate milk.

"They must be excited," said Serkan, taking a swig of his beer. "About the wedding. It would be such a shame if they couldn't go." He wiped his mouth on the back of his hand.

The children joined us at the table, reaching for their milkshakes and slurping the thick brown liquid up through their straws. Alfie collapsed in a heap at my feet, pink tongue lolling from his mouth.

I sat back down.

"I want the children to go to the wedding," said Serkan softly, reaching across the table and stroking my burnt hand. "But I need to trust you. I just want us to be friends Carrie, is that so much to ask?"

The knot of discomfort tightened in my gut. I wanted to get up, walk away and never come back.

Instead, I nodded my head. Obedient. Compliant. Submissive.

Serkan tightened his fingers around my hand. A gesture of victory, dominance and ownership disguised as one of tenderness and love.

Turning back towards the beach, I watched the kite flier running to catch his kite as it fell from the sky.

Chapter Nineteen

Somerset, England. July 2015.

"You may kiss the bride!"

Elif and Cem exchanged looks of amused disgust as Rebecca lifted her veil and leaned in to kiss her new husband. The champagne-infused congregation, perched on hay bales, applauded and raised their glasses. A mercifully sunny day in an otherwise cold and wet July, the ceremony was held in a garden vibrant with lavender, roses, and hollyhocks, and backed by the lazy hum of bumblebees. Beautiful in a way that only England in summer can be.

At the after-party, woozy from the champagne, I sat with my newly married sister, watching the children take centre stage on the dance floor. Elif in a white dress, its floaty material billowing out as she twirled. Cem, heartbreakingly handsome, and surprisingly clean, in a cream three-piece suit and tie. It was good to see them having fun. As much as I had tried to protect them, the separation and impending divorce had inevitably taken their toll.

"The kids are really enjoying themselves," said my sister, as if reading my mind.

I nodded. "They have been looking forward to this for months."

James, my new brother-in-law, joined the children in the centre of the circle, Elif's skirt fanning out as he twirled her around. I smiled as Cem spun around by himself, almost losing his balance.

"Are you sure you want to go back?" said Rebeca, her blue-grey eyes suddenly serious. My sister and I had barely spoken about my impending divorce, as if the mere mention of the D-word would put a curse on her own nuptials. We sidestepped and skirted around the issue as if it were a drunk relative at a party.

"It's our home," I replied simply. "I have friends. A good job. The children are settled in school. I've been there for nearly ten years."

"I know."

"Anyway," I said, feeling suddenly tired, though from the champagne or the conversation topic I did not know.

"Serkan and I are trying to be friends."

I wondered if my words sounded as unconvincing to her as they did to me.

***

The following morning, I forced my eyes open, trying to ignore the pounding in my head as I stared at the tiny gap of grey sky between the curtains of my sister's spare room. A steady patter of rain tapped lightly on the windowpane.

"My foot hurts."

The door opened and Elif hobbled in, bed-headed and sleepy-eyed.

"Too much dancing," I said, rolling over and closing my eyes as she climbed in beside me.

Two hours, a coffee, and a hot shower later, I realised Elif was still hobbling.

"Let me look at that." I crouched down and gently removed her sock as she winced in pain. The big toe on her left foot was bruised and swollen.

"Is it broken?" she said.

"I don't know," I replied. "We fly home in a few hours. I'll take you to the hospital for an X-ray, just in case."

I rummaged around in my sister's medicine cabinet, located some Elastoplast and carefully splinted Elif's damaged toe to its neighbour.

***

"Yes. Broken."

The orthopaedic surgeon slouched low on his swivel chair, clicked the mouse, and zoomed in on the X-ray on his computer screen, expertly locating the crack running down the outer edge of Elif's big toe.

He looked at Elif and smiled.

"You must rest," he told her. "No running, no jumping, and no swimming."

Her mouth fell open.

"For three weeks."

Elif looked at me. "No swimming!" she repeated in horror. As the temperature outside scraped forty-seven degrees, this was no overreaction.

After a trip to the emergency room where Elif's toes were strapped neatly together, she swung ahead of us on crutches as we stepped outside into the bright sunshine.

"Ice cream!" cried Cem, running towards the hospital cafeteria. A week of rain, grey skies and temperatures hovering in the mid-teens had taken their toll.

"Excuse me," said a voice behind me as I selected a table in the shade and sat down.

A middle-aged blonde woman sat at the next table; her head wrapped in a pristine white bandage.

"I'm Julie," she stood and extended her arm. "I remember you. You were here when I was brought in."

Julie. The name rang a bell.

"Subarachnoid bleed," she tapped the white bandage on her head. "If it hadn't been for you, I could have died."

Julie Stevens. I remembered her lying in Emergency, shielding her eyes from the light. Unrecognizable from the well-dressed woman in front of me.

"They thought I was drunk." She picked up her coffee, balancing it carefully on its saucer.

"Do you mind if I join you?" she said, pulling out a chair and sitting down opposite me without waiting for an answer.

"What's your name?"

"I'm Carrie," I smiled. "Did the operation go well?"

She nodded, the relief clear on her face. "Yes, everything was fine. They discharged me a week ago. Back today for a check-up before I fly home."

"That's good to hear."

"How did you know?" she asked me, squinting in the bright sunshine. "That I wasn't just another drunk tourist?"

I hesitated. "A hunch," I replied. "I was an intensive care nurse for years. You get a feeling about these things."

"I'm a nurse too!" exclaimed Julie, her eyes wide. "I work in cardiology. What a coincidence!"

The children returned with their ice creams, Elif carefully resting her crutches against the table before lowering herself into the chair next to me.

"What happened to you?" Julie smiled at Elif.

"I broke my toe," replied Elif, peeling away the wrapper of her yellow and green Twister. "In England. We went to Auntie Becky's wedding."

"I live in England," said Julie. "But I love Maralya. I come here every year on holiday."

Cem bit into the top of his magnum, wincing briefly at the cold.

"What happened to your head?" he said.

"I had an operation."

"Did it hurt?"

"It did a bit," Julie replied. "But thanks to your mum, I'm OK now."

"My mummy's a nurse," Elif informed her, taking a lick of her rapidly melting ice cream. "She makes people better."

"Babeee!" Atakan's voice floated through the air towards me. "You're back!"

He sashayed towards me, clutching an armful of patient files.

"I missed you!" he said as we kissed each other on both cheeks. Atakan rolled his eyes. "The office has been crazy."

"I'm back tomorrow," I said. "Elif broke her toe."

Atakan looked at Elif, pushing out his bottom lip in an exaggerated, sad face.

"*Canım benim!*" he said.

"I wanna see Baba." Cem, bored since making short work of his ice cream, squirmed in his chair.

"And where is Baba?" Julie asked him.

"Baba make fish," Cem replied.

Julie and I laughed.

"Serkan works in a fish restaurant on the seafront," I explained. "The Mermaid. You probably know it."

Julie looked at me as if a light bulb had just gone off in her brain.

"Wait!" she cried suddenly. "You're Serkan's wife!"

"We're separated," I explained. "How do you know Serkan?"

"I've been going to the Mermaid for years!" continued Julie. "It's one of my favourite restaurants. Serkan and I are friends on Facebook! I remember him telling me about you. My wife, Caroline, who works at the hospital. He seemed very proud of you," she added with a smile. "My wife this and my wife that."

I smiled back, wondering why it was that Serkan could say he was proud of me to everyone but me.

"We'd better go," I said to Julie. "The kids haven't seen their dad for a week, and they miss him."

Julie reached for her phone. "Give me your telephone number," she said. "I fly home tomorrow, but I'll be back at the end of the year, and I'd like to buy you dinner."

We swapped numbers, and I stood up to leave. Julie took my hands in hers. "Thanks again Carrie," she said. "I owe you."

I smiled at her. "Us nurses have to stick together."

***

The restaurant was quiet. Stray dogs slept under the tables, flies buzzing lazily around their faces, making their muzzles twitch. Two blonde tourists with sunburnt shoulders were deep in conversation over a plate of calamari and a bottle of white wine. Serkan sat alone in the corner reading the sports pages of a newspaper, a half-empty glass of beer on the table in front of him.

"Baba!" Cem ran towards him, arms outstretched.

Serkan looked up from his paper in surprise, his face lighting up at the sight of his son before grabbing him, lifting him up, and plastering his face with kisses.

"Elif broke her toe!" announced Cem, as Elif hobbled towards him on her crutches.

"She's fine," I said quickly. "It was an accident. She had an X-ray and there is a small fracture on her big toe. She just has to be careful for the next three weeks."

I pulled out a chair for Elif and helped her sit down.

"You came back," said Serkan as Cem settled onto his lap.

"I told you I would."

"Thank you."

"Thank you," I replied. "For trusting me. The wedding was amazing. The kids had a great time."

I ordered a coffee while the kids filled Serkan in on the events of the past few days, chattering excitedly over each other as they tried to fit in all the details.

"I'm not allowed to swim, Baba!" Elif told Serkan. "For three weeks!"

Serkan looked at me. "What are you going to do?" he asked. "About childcare?"

Since the schools had closed in mid-June, I had hired a childminder to care for the children while I was at work. Laura was a British woman with two kids of her own, and the children loved going to her, spending most days at the pool or beach. With Elif out of action for the next three weeks, this would no longer be an option.

"I can ask my mum to look after her," suggested Serkan.

"No!" Elif immediately interjected, turning to me.

"I'll take her to work with me," I said. "She can sit on the sofa in the office. They won't mind."

"I want to go to the hospital with mummy. Can I?" Elif looked imploringly at me. "Please?"

"Of course, you can," I said.

"What about Cem?" continued Serkan, kissing the top of his son's head.

"I guess he'll still go to Laura's."

Serkan looked at me across the table as if weighing something up in his mind.

"Let me look after him," he said eventually. "At least until Elif's toe is better."

Cem's face lit up.

"I want to stay wiz Baba!" he declared, tightening his arms around his father's neck.

I looked at Serkan dubiously.

"You can drop him at the flats on your way to work," he continued. "I can bring him here for the lunchtime shift. It's not usually busy. You can pick him up after work before I start the evening shift."

It made sense.

"I don't know," I said.

"Please Carrie," said Serkan, kissing Cem's head again.

"I missed them so much when they were away. And you. I know I lost you, Carrie. I understand that now. I'm just so happy that we're friends."

There were tears in his eyes.

"Let me help you," he continued. "Let me look after Cem. Be a proper dad again."

"Just until Elif's toe is better?" I said.

"For as long as you like," he smiled.

Chapter Twenty

Maralya, Turkey. August 2015.

On the broken bench in the shade of the fig tree, Cem stared down at the wasps buzzing drunkenly over the rotten fruit on the ground. Serkan, astride his motorbike, watched through the open visor of his helmet as I tried to reason with my son.

"Come on sweetie," I said. "You'll see Baba again tomorrow."

"I don't wanna stay wiz you." Cem refused to meet my gaze. "I wanna stay wiz Baba."

I turned to Serkan, silently demanding an answer.

"I haven't said anything!" he exclaimed, eyes widening in mock indignation. He inserted his key into the ignition and revved the engine.

"Come on, mate," he said half-heartedly to Cem. "Stay with your mum tonight and I'll pick you up tomorrow."

"Let's go," I smiled reaching for his hand.

"No!" cried Cem, pulling away from me, clinging to the trunk of the fig tree as he started to cry.

For the past three weeks, I had dropped Cem at Serkan's every morning, taken Elif to work with me, and picked him up again in the evening.

About two weeks previously, Serkan had suggested Cem stay overnight during the week to save me from dropping him off and collecting him every day. Since then I had picked Cem up on Friday evenings and dropped him and his sister back on Saturday afternoons.

This Friday, however, something was very wrong.

The heat beat down, merciless even at six in the evening. I looked up to see the silent shape of Gülşen at the windowpane, watching us.

"I have to go to work," said Serkan. "Leave him with my mum tonight. Let's talk tomorrow."

I turned to my son in a desperate, last-ditch attempt. "Cem honey, what's wrong? Come and stay with us tonight. We can make popcorn. Watch a movie."

He shook his head, darting a quick glance at me, before looking back down at the ground.

"OK, sweetheart." Tears pricked my eyes. "You can stay here tonight. I'll see you tomorrow, OK?"

I watched, helpless as Cem ran up the stone steps to join his Grandmother. When he had disappeared from sight, I turned to Serkan, just in time to see the flicker of quiet triumph in his eyes before he slammed his visor shut and sped away.

***

The next morning, I opened my eyes, blinking in the bright triangle of sunlight that sliced through my attic room. The thin sheet I had kicked off during the night rose and fell with the oscillating fan. Its low hum was joined periodically by another sound, high-pitched and barely audible. Rolling onto my back with a sigh, I turned my head towards the door. Alfie, head lowered in a half apologetic, half desperate stance lay crouched in the doorway imploring me with his eyes. I glanced at the digital clock on the bedside table. 10:32.

"Sorry, boy," I mumbled, swinging my legs out of bed, and wondering why I had slept so late. Then I remembered. Unlike Cem, invariably charging into my room at seven in the morning to explain the finer points of his latest action figure, Elif stayed downstairs, quietly making herself some cereal and switching on the TV.

After a hasty trip to the park where Alfie relieved himself against a lamppost, I stuffed a load of washing into the machine, trying to ignore the nagging sense of unease that was building in my gut.

Over the years, I had listened as Serkan, and Gülşen talked long into the night. The misfortunes of others appeared to be the only thing that provided relief from Gülşen's foul temper and aching back as she gleefully picked over the bones of friends, family, and neighbours for hours at a time.

Now, I was the subject matter, and my son was hearing every word.

I pushed the thought aside. Cem was confused. He was so young and had always idolised his father. It was natural that he would feel some anger towards me as the one who left. The past two weekends, with Elif out of action, had forced us to stay inside watching films and playing games with the air conditioning on. Maybe that was why he had refused to come yesterday, I thought. A simple explanation.

Today would be different. A day at the pool and his favourite chocolate milkshake would fix everything.

"What are we going to do today?" said Elif from the table, her schoolbooks spread open in front of her.

I smiled. Yesterday, after a final X-ray, Elif had been given the all-clear to swim.

"We could go to the pool!" I smiled.

Her face lit up. "I can swim?"

"Yes, you can!"

She hesitated. "Is Cem coming?"

I stared out of the window at the empty street below.

"I hope so."

At eleven-thirty, I called Serkan. There was no reply.

I vacuumed the floors and stripped the beds, Cem's pristine and unslept-in as if making a point. Elif sat alone at the table doing her homework, opposite the space where her brother should have been. She frowned in concentration as her handwriting looped between the lines.

Just after midday, I called Serkan again, listening to the ringing until a robotic voice came on the line. *The person you are calling is not available.*

I sent an optimistic text.

Let me know what time I can pick Cem up.

I kept busy, trying to ignore what I already knew.

With no word from Serkan and Elif itching to get back in the water, we made our way out onto the hot, flat streets and walked to a local hotel where we often used the pool.

"*Merhaba Yenge!*"

The barman greeted us warmly.

"Where have you been?" he teased Elif, pinching her cheek. "I miss you!"

"I went to England and broke my toe, so I couldn't swim," she explained.

The barman frowned and poured her a cherry juice. "Oh! Very bad!"

"But I'm OK now," said Elif with a huge smile, peeling off her shorts and T-shirt to reveal her blue swimming costume underneath.

"Be careful!" I shouted as she leapt into the shimmering blue water with a splash.

"And the boy?" said the barman, shrugging as he looked around. "Where is…?"

"He might come later," I said hopefully, though to myself or the barman, I wasn't sure.

The afternoon stretched on. Though she didn't say anything, I knew Elif was bored by herself and missed her brother. Finally, at seven o'clock, my phone rang.

"How are you?" Serkan was nonchalant. There was no mention of the missed calls or unanswered messages.

"I thought I was going to see Cem today," I said.

Serkan hesitated. "I took him to the beach."

I thought for a minute, unsure how best to respond.

"Serkan, what are you doing?"

"He wanted to stay with me," he said flatly.

"Well, can I see him now?"

"He's tired," said Serkan. "Let's meet tomorrow. We can have lunch. The four of us. Together."

I had no choice but to agree.

***

They were already waiting at Manzara when we arrived. Serkan was picking the label off an amber bottle of beer. Cem sucked a chocolate milkshake through a straw.

"Hi, Cem!" I said, looking at the huge plastic water gun on the table in front of him. "Is this new?"

He nodded silently, keeping his eyes down.

We sat divided. Elif and I on one side, Serkan and Cem on the other.

During our marriage, Serkan had made no secret of his preference for the favoured boy, leaving me to balance the deficit with our daughter. I stared across the table, wondering when we had become two different teams.

Slurping up the final dregs of his milkshake, Cem grabbed his water gun and ran off towards the beach with Elif in hot pursuit.

"Elif's toe is better," I said to Serkan. "She had an X-ray yesterday, and the fracture is completely healed."

Serkan took a swig of beer. "That's good."

"Cem can come home."

"No rush."

I stared at him. "I'm not rushing. We agreed..."

"So, the kids will go back to Laura's?" He looked at me for the first time since I had arrived.

I nodded.

"Can you afford it?"

We both knew the answer. My hopes of selling the villa quickly had failed to materialise. Since our first buyer had pulled out, there had been no further offers, leaving me to pay rent on an apartment I could barely afford. The cost of childcare on top was crippling, and Serkan knew it.

"I'll manage," I said.

"Carrie." Serkan leaned towards me across the table, a soft smile on his face. "What's wrong? You can tell me. I'm not your enemy."

The red and white tablecloth blurred behind my tears.

"My son doesn't want to see me."

Serkan laughed and shook his head. "Carrie, he's a child. He's confused, that's all. Give him time."

"And you promise you are not saying anything to him, or in front of him?"

"I promise."

"And your mother?"

He looked into my eyes, his gaze unwavering.

"I would never let her say anything bad about you to anyone. You are my children's mother."

Reaching for a serviette from the white plastic dispenser on the table, I dabbed my eyes.

"Why doesn't Cem stay with me until the end of the school holidays?" continued Serkan. "I don't want you to pay for childcare you can't afford. Let me help you."

The kids came running back from the beach, Elif squealing with delight as Cem sprayed her with water from the plastic gun.

"Let's order!" Serkan reached for the menu.

"Isn't this nice, kids?" he beamed at them as they sat down.

"All the family, back together!"

Chapter Twenty-One

Torre Mileto, Italy. June 2016.

The darkened road wound ahead with no end in sight. My robust optimism that we would find somewhere to stay before sundown was fading as fast as the rapidly diminishing light. The thought crossed my mind again. Should I park somewhere? Sleep in the car? The minivan would be spacious enough if I flattened down the back seats. I pushed the thought aside. What if we were attacked or robbed?

Another forty minutes dragged by.

"I'm hungry," said Elif from the back seat.

"Not long now," I replied, wishing I felt as confident as I sounded.

Hope flickered inside me as a light glowed ahead. A roadside motel? A Bed and Breakfast? At the very least, a café or a small supermarket?

It turned out to be a petrol station, though it was clear from the prefabricated cabin and solitary pump that this was no well-stocked Shell or BP garage with rows of shiny confectionary, fridges full of soft drinks and novelty air fresheners. It also appeared to be empty. Through the grimy window, I could just make out a desk cluttered with mounds of paper, cans of oil and assorted engine parts. I sighed, about to drive off when a flicker of movement caught my eye. A blurry figure had emerged from behind the stacks of paper and was walking towards the door with the slow, deliberate steps of someone who hadn't moved in a long time. I glanced at the petrol tank, still a third full since I had filled it up that morning, but a combination of guilt at disturbing the man and uncertainty when we would have the chance again found me reaching for my purse.

"*Diesel per favore*," I said, as he appeared at my window with a toothless smile. He nodded and made his way to the petrol cap, slowly unscrewing it with arthritic fingers as I watched him in my mirror.

"Hotel?" I said with a hopeful shrug as he returned to my window. I handed over a fifty euro note. He furrowed his brow, reaching into his back pocket and shaking his head as he leafed out change from a battered wallet. I remembered the cylindrical tent we had bought in Bodrum before we left.

"Camping?" I made a triangular "tent" with my fingers. He shook his head again, glancing at the back seat, where Elif was fighting sleep, her head lolling against the window.

"Camping, no," he replied sadly.

I started the engine. The car it was.

"*Grazie, Signore.*"

I made my way to the exit, preparing to pull back out onto the empty road when he appeared in my rear-view mirror, waving his arms wildly. I pulled the handbrake and watched as he returned to his cabin, moving as fast as his stiff joints would allow. Several minutes later, he returned with a scrap of paper, which he handed to me.

Written in spidery handwriting were two words: TORRE MILETO

"Camping?" I said.

"*Camping si!!*" replied the man, pointing at the scrap of paper with another toothless grin.

"*Grazie!*" I replied.

I continued along the empty road, lured by the image of a hot meal and a soft bed for the night. With any luck, the campsite would have internet, so I could figure out where we were and plan the next leg of our journey.

I kept driving.

I must have missed the turning, I thought as another hour went by. My eyelids were drooping, my back stiff as I shuffled in my seat. Time to call it a day.

I pulled over to the side of the road and turned to look at Elif. By now, she was fast asleep, her head resting against the window, her eyes closed. I wondered how I was going to break it to her that we were going to spend the night hungry, sleeping in the car. Deciding to let her sleep a little longer, I leaned back against the headrest as a white rectangle in the distance caught my eye. A road sign.

We had passed a multitude of signs. My hope of finding a place to spend the night diminishing with each one as they informed us of a steep incline, the speed limit, or the possibility of deer in the vicinity.

Sleep beat down on me in waves as I started the engine, pulled back out onto the road and headed towards the white rectangle. I stared at it in disbelief, all traces of tiredness evaporating as the words lit up under the headlights.

Torre Mileto

"Elif!"

"Hmm?" drifted back her reply.

"We're here!" I said. "This is the place the man was telling us about!"

My relief was short-lived. Far from being a lively holiday resort like Vieste, with a strip of campsites, hotels, and restaurants to choose from, Torre Mileto seemed to consist of a small, square tower and a car park beyond which a grey, angry sea crashed onto the beach. Maybe the old man had been mistaken, I thought as I passed a solitary bar, closed and in darkness. A flash of yellow caught my eye. A weather-beaten sign on a rusty gate, open and hanging from its hinges. In the centre, a small black triangle and a single word.

Camping

I drove through the gate into an empty field and parked under a tree before getting out of the car and gratefully stretching my aching back.

"*Buonasera!*"

A man emerged from a small prefabricated cabin. He was tall and looked to be in his mid-seventies. He was wearing a cowboy hat.

"Camping?" I said, making the triangular finger tent again.

"*Camping Sii!*"

I looked at Elif, fast asleep in the back seat. She must be starving.

"*Ristorante?*" I glanced around the empty field as if in the hope that one might appear.

The man thought for a minute and shook his head.

"*Supermercati!*" he said suddenly, pointing towards the road and tapping his watch in the universal sign for "hurry!"

Climbing back into the car, I turned the key in the ignition, yanking my seatbelt across my body as I pulled back out onto the road through the rusty gate. Elif lurched forward in her seat.

"Where are we going?" she said.

"Food," I replied as I sped off down the empty road.

A middle-aged woman looked up in faint surprise from her mop and bucket as we rushed in through the sliding doors. Grabbing a basket, I scoured the aisles, throwing in bread, cheese, a packet of crisps, a bottle of Fanta for Elif and a bottle of red wine for me.

It had been a red wine kind of day.

"What are we having for dinner?" said Elif, picking up a packet of burgers. "I'm starving."

I glanced at the bread, cheese, and crisps in the basket.

"Picnic?" I said hopefully.

"Can we have a barbeque?" she said, holding up the burgers and fixing me with a winning smile.

He was in my mind before I could stop it. Crouched next to the barbeque, fanning the flames as the smell of chicken wafted through the air. Eyes crinkling up at the corners as he smiled.

I had forgotten about the portable barbeque still in the boot of the car.

"Great idea!" I said, taking the burgers and adding a pack of chicken legs and a large bag of salad. We made our way to the checkout.

There was no sign of the campsite owner when we returned. The cabin was closed and in darkness. Only a dim light from the toilet and shower block on the far side of the field remained. I opened the car boot and rummaged around by the light of my phone for the shiny blue cylinder we had bought in Bodrum before we left. **Easy-Assemble Two-Person Tent** announced the label confidently.

"Let's see how easy to assemble it really is," I said, as Elif clapped her hands in delight.

"We're camping!" she exclaimed as I slid the tent from its shiny, blue casing. A quick pull of the cord on the top and the tent sprang to life. With a bed for the night, the next priority was food.

We placed the small portable barbeque in the glow of the car headlights and scattered firelighters and charcoal throughout the metal tray.

Elif and I watched as the flames danced and leapt high into the air, devouring the firelighters and spreading slowly through the base.

Elif was impressed. "What do we do now?" she said, sipping Fanta from a plastic cup and glancing hungrily at the packets of chicken and burgers.

"Now we wait!"

I pulled open the bag of salad and poured the contents into a bowl.

"Hello!"

From nowhere, a lone figure dwarfed by an enormous backpack sailed past us on a bicycle.

"Hi," I waved back.

The cyclist dismounted a few meters from us, and removed his backpack on which he sat, swigging water from a plastic bottle.

With no chairs, Elif and I perched inside the open boot, watching our new neighbour, silhouetted in the semidarkness, as he unpacked the contents of his backpack.

"He looks sad, mummy," decided Elif as the man placed a saucepan on top of a tiny gas camping stove. The faint blue flame flickered lamentably before dying out.

I opened the wine, poured some into a plastic cup, and took a sip.

"Why don't you ask him to join us?" I said.

As the flames on the barbeque began to die down and the charcoal started to turn white, I unwrapped the burgers and chicken and spaced them out across the grill.

"Mummy, this is Luca."

The man smiled. He was young, in his twenties, with glasses and thick curly hair.

"Carrie," I smiled back.

"We thought you looked sad," explained Elif. "Are you?"

Luca laughed. "Not really," he replied. "I was trying to cook pasta, and the gas ran out."

"You can have some of our food," decided Elif immediately.

Luca smiled sheepishly and glanced at me.

"Of course," I said, motioning towards the barbeque. "There's too much for us."

I poured Luca a plastic cup of wine and switched on the car radio, which was tuned into some obscure Italian pop station. With the party in full swing and the chicken and burgers cooked to perfection, I spread a blanket out on the grass, and we sat with our backs against the trees, swapping life stories over plates piled high with food.

"We came from Vieste," I said. "Ended up getting lost in the middle of nowhere. I thought we were going to spend the night in the car."

"Vieste is about an hour away," said Luca, with a frown. "I'm heading there next." He took out his phone. "Here," he said. "There's a straight road from Vieste. The SS80." I looked at the map on the screen. With no internet data and a non-existent sense of direction, I had taken multiple wrong turns and ended up lost in the depths of the Gargano National Park.

At around midnight, the remaining lights in the campsite went out, plunging us into total darkness.

"Wish I'd packed some candles," came Luca's voice in the dark.

"Wait!" I said, standing up.

Using my phone as a light, I made my way to the car and opened the glove compartment. My fingers closed around the cold metal cylinder. Still there from the day I left him.

I returned to Elif and Luca and placed the silver tea light on a tree trunk. The three of us watched in silence as the silver hearts turned in slow circles above the flame.

Our stomachs full, we lay back on the blanket under a sky embroidered with a million tiny stars.

"You see that?" said Luca to Elif, pointing skyward. "That yellow ball?"

"Yes."

"That's Venus," he said. "Another planet."

"Do people live there?" asked Elif.

"Not there," Luca replied. "But maybe somewhere else in the universe."

Tiredness and quiet contentment settled over me like a warm blanket as I listened to Luca pointing out the constellations of Big Bear and Little Bear, *Ursa major* and *Ursa minor*. Italian pop music from the car radio drifted overhead in the warm night air, melting away the stress of the day. I gazed up at the star-filled sky, wondering how what could so easily have been the worst experience of our travels so far had somehow turned into the most magical night of all.

Chapter Twenty-Two

Maralya, Turkey. September 2015.

The goat's mouth moved in a circular motion as it surveyed me from beneath the fig tree with yellow eyes.

"Iyi bayramlar!" One of the second-floor tenants smiled from her open front door, broom in hand as Elif and I climbed the stone steps to Gülşen's flat on the third floor.

"Iyi bayramlar!" I replied, wishing her a good festival. The dark-eyed child behind her looked up at me curiously, thumb in her mouth, a one-armed doll clutched in her hand.

On the third floor, I pressed the doorbell, unleashing a cacophony of robotic birdsong as Elif and I removed our shoes and added them to the neat row along the wall. The front door flew open and Gülşen, head wrapped in a bright orange scarf, glared at me, a bloody meat cleaver clutched in her raised hand.

"Iyi bayramlar!" I smiled.

With a dismissive grunt, my former mother-in-law took a step back, wiping her brow and smearing blood across her forehead. Across the living room floor, slabs of meat were spread out on plastic sheets around a large plastic bowl glistening with chunks of pink flesh. The smell of slow-cooked lamb mingled with the smell of death in the oppressive September air.

"Hi guys!" beamed Serkan from the pristine white sofa, reaching for the remote control and turning down the sound of the football match that blared from the TV. Next to him, Cem sat, absorbed in a video game.

Kurban Bayram, "The Feast of the Sacrifice," is a tradition across the Muslim world where an animal, usually a sheep or a goat, is slaughtered and the meat shared amongst the poor.

Lured by the promise of her grandmother's legendary lamb *kavurma*, Elif had agreed to spend the day with Serkan and Gülşen.

"Are you hungry?" smiled Serkan as Elif perched on the armchair opposite. She nodded.

He turned his attention to me, patting the sofa next to him. "Good to see you, Carrie," he smiled. "Why don't you stay for a bit? Have a drink?"

Since Rebecca's wedding, there had been a noticeable change in Serkan. There had been no more uninvited visits to the apartment in the middle of the night. No more threats or angry outbursts. With Cem still refusing to spend time with me alone, the four of us would spend Sundays together, having lunch, or at the beach or pool. My hopes of remaining amicable had begun to feel like a real possibility.

"Sure."

I pushed my feet into a pair of guest slippers by the door, stepped carefully around the slabs of meat and sat down next to him.

"*Çay?*" he said.

I shook my head. The smell of raw meat was making me queasy. "No, really, I'm fine…"

"*Anne, Çay yap!*" Serkan barked towards Gülşen, ordering his mother to make a pot of tea. Gülşen muttered under her breath as she threw another chunk of meat into the plastic bowl. She rose stiffly, wiping her hands on her bloodstained apron, and made her way to the kitchen.

"Back to school next week." I smiled at Cem as he looked up from his video game. "Are you excited? I've got your new uniform ready at home."

Cem glanced at his father, silenced by the briefest lift of his eyebrows before returning to his video game.

"How's work?" said Serkan, changing the subject.

"Quietening down," I said. "The season's nearly over."

The summer had dragged on. The villa remained unsold, and the divorce proceedings sat as stagnant as a mosquito-infested swamp.

Now, with the end of summer in sight, a restlessness had taken root inside me, growing with each passing day. It was time for Cem to come home. Time to sell the villa and buy a place of my own. Time to move on.

"Any news on the villa?" I said.

Serkan looked at me, holding my gaze for a second too long before turning back to the TV. He shook his head.

"I hope it sells soon," I continued. "I want to buy somewhere as soon as possible."

"No rush," replied Serkan, as Gülşen placed a silver tray of *Çay* on the table.

***

I had meant to go straight home, housework and laundry my only plans for the day. Instead, I found myself back on Kirazlı's familiar tree-lined streets. Driving towards the villa, I tried to avert my eyes from the carcasses that hung from trees, and the tethered sheep and goats that awaited their fate.

In the field next to the mosque, the solitary cow flicked her tail, pulling at grass bleached blonde by months of sun. I turned right at the crossroads, climbing the hill until my former home came into view.

I could see immediately that something was different. As I got closer, the feeling grew. The villa didn't feel like mine anymore.

I pulled up outside the gate and stared at the unfamiliar car parked beneath the trailing grapevines. A skinny sheep was tethered to the lemon tree. Someone else's laundry flapped on the line.

The "For Sale" sign Azra and I had tethered to the balcony in March was gone.

Still staring in disbelief, I reached for my phone.

"*Efendim?*" Serkan sounded distracted. In the background, I could hear a cartoon blaring from the TV.

"Serkan, what's going on?" I said. "I'm at the villa. Someone is living here."

A lengthy silence and a heavy sigh. "It's better if we talk in person," he said. "Come."

When I got back to the flats, an ominous circle had formed around the fig tree. The white goat strained pitifully at the end of its rope, its plaintive bleats echoing through the late afternoon air. I kept my eyes fixed on the floor as I climbed the stone steps to the third floor.

"Carrie…" Serkan stood at the open front door, "I know you're angry, but…"

I pushed past him into the apartment. Elif and Cem sat immersed in a cartoon on the TV, bowls of *Kavurma* on their laps.

"Sit down," said Serkan. "I'll explain everything."

"Who are they?" I said.

"Friends of mine. Tenants."

"How long have they been there?"

He shrugged. "A few months."

"A few *months*?" I stared at him, incredulous.

He glanced at the children and back at me. "Let's talk on the balcony," he said.

We made our way to the balcony and sat down on plastic chairs. Somewhere far away, a dog barked.

"So, you want everything your way?" said Serkan, gazing off into the distance.

"No…" I began. "We agreed. I get the money from the villa. You get two of the flats. We talked about this with Azra months ago…"

"No, *you* agreed!" Serkan hissed, leaning towards me. All traces of the past month's friendliness were gone. The old, familiar rage burned behind his eyes.

"The villa's in my name. I can do whatever I want with it. And I'm not selling."

I opened my mouth and closed it again like a dying fish gasping for air.

"Oh, and there's something else," he added, looking me straight in the eye. Before the words were out of his mouth, I knew what he was going to say.

"I want custody of Cem," he said. "He wants to live with me."

"But he has school…" I said feebly, thinking of the freshly washed and ironed uniform hanging on Cem's wardrobe door.

Serkan folded his arms across his chest. "I've registered him at a new school," he said.

The smell of roasting meat, heavy and sweet in the late afternoon air, wafted towards me, bringing with it a violent wave of nausea that grabbed and twisted my stomach. I ran to the bathroom and leaned over the toilet bowl, dry retching until the nausea finally passed. Easing myself into a sitting position on the cold tiles, I hugged my knees, remembering the last time I had sat like this. The bathroom floor of the villa. His fists pounding against the door. The night I ran to Azra's. The night Cem refused to come. A chilling glimpse of the future.

It was happening. Exactly as he said it would.

Serkan was sitting on the sofa in the living room. The look of quiet satisfaction in his eyes told me all I needed to know. He had planned this. And I had sleepwalked straight into the trap.

"I have to go," I said, my stomach clenching as another wave of *kavurma* wafted towards me. "I'll pick Elif up later."

The sun's glare was blinding as I stepped outside. I hurried down the stone steps to my car, glancing towards the fig tree as an excited babble of voices drifted towards me.

The image had seared itself onto my brain before I had a chance to look away.

A knife blade glinting in the sun. A headless carcass hanging from the tree. A pool of dark red, soaking slowly into the parched earth.

Chapter Twenty-Three

Maralya, Turkey. October 2015.

Shivering in the chill evening air, I squeezed Atakan's arm a little tighter, our conversation whipped away by the wind, drowned out by the black waves that crashed onto the beach. On the darkened promenade, "Angel's" shone like a beacon in a line of hotels, bars and restaurants that were closed for the winter.

A few tourists remained. Pasty, young couples with preschool children on cheap package deals. Elderly Germans travelling out of season in a bid to escape the summer heat. The occasional backpacker. Bored waiters paced up and down outside the few restaurants that remained open, leather-bound menus wedged under their arms.

The season had been poor. A combination of global terrorism, anti-Muslim flames fanned by a headline-hungry media and Prime Minister Erdoğan's apparent determination to turn Turkey into an Islamic state had taken its toll. Businesses had struggled to break even, and many waiters and bar staff had not been paid for working sixteen-hour days in the crippling heat. It would be a long, hard winter for many.

A faux English "pub," Angel's was bedecked by a range of UK memorabilia. Manchester United football scarves were strung behind the bar. Black and white posters of Queen and the Beatles vied with wall space among replica London street signs and Union Jack flags. Angel's was popular, both with Maralya ex-pats and tourists seeking roast dinners and steak and kidney pie in forty-degree heat. I normally avoided such places like the plague, but Melek, the owner, was a friend, the bar was warm and in winter our options were limited.

The door slammed shut behind us as Atakan and I blew in from the street, a wall of heat hitting us from the *soba* in the corner.

"*Hoş geldin!*" Beyza stood up and leaned in to kiss me on both cheeks before greeting Atakan in the same way.

"You alright?" smiled Mandy from across the table as I slipped off my coat and hung it on the back of my chair. Mandy had started at the hospital at the end of August. A fellow Brit, with a broad Leeds accent, and a wicked sense of humour. We had hit it off immediately.

"How's it going with you-know-who?" she asked, drawing a circle in the air next to her head and whistling in the universal sign for "crazy."

Since *Kurban Bayram,* there had been no more cosy family Sundays. I dropped Elif at the flats on Saturday afternoons and picked her up on Sundays. After Serkan's latest bombshell, I could no longer tolerate the forced "Family Time." My futile attempts to communicate with Cem were still met with robotic replies as he swivelled his gaze towards his father.

"Serkan still wants custody of Cem," I said. "And he's refusing to sell the villa."

"Bastard," muttered Mandy, shaking her head. "What are you going to do?"

"I guess we'll have to go to court," I sighed. "It could take years."

"I'm sure Cem will come around," said Beyza sympathetically. "He must miss you. You're his mum."

"Wait until the routine sets in," added Mandy. "Cold winter mornings. Getting up early for school. In a couple of months, Serkan will be begging you to take Cem back."

"I hope so," I sighed. "I just want this divorce over so I can move on with my life."

"Then you can marry me, Carrie!" squealed Atakan, clasping his hands together.

"Anytime, babe." I winked at him.

"Darling!"

Melek appeared, throwing her arms around my shoulders and planting a firm kiss on my cheek as she placed a glass of red wine on the table in front of me.

"How are you?" she said. "It's good to see you!"

"I'm good." I took a sip of my wine. "How are things with you?"

Melek grimaced. "Season very bad," she said. "No tourists. No money. I hope next year is better."

I nodded, looking around the almost empty bar. An elderly couple in the far corner sat in silence as they tucked into Shepherd's pie. At the bar, a dark-haired man in jeans and a leather jacket chatted to the barman in Turkish as he nursed a small beer.

"So?" Mandy leaned towards me, eyes bright with excitement, her unfeasibly long lashes spidery with mascara.

"What's the gossip, Carrie?"

"Have you met anyone?" said Beyza. "Now you're free and single?"

"No, because she is with me," Atakan retorted, taking my hand in his. He smiled sweetly. Butter wouldn't melt.

"But you are leaving me!" I protested with a smile.

It was a leaving-do of sorts. Next week Atakan was going to Istanbul to study English at university.

He squeezed my hand. "Never!" he said, his green eyes serious.

"Do you want to meet someone?" Beyza continued. "Another Turkish man?"

"Bloody Turkish men," muttered Atakan under his breath.

"They're not all bad," said Mandy, a dreamy look in her eyes as she thought of her fiancé, Hasan.

"How are the wedding plans?" asked Beyza.

"Bloody nightmare!" Mandy rolled her eyes. "My mum is taking over everything! But I have picked the dress!" She picked up her phone and turned the screen around to face us. The three of us leaned in to scrutinize the ivory dress's embroidered bodice and long lace sleeves.

"It's gorgeous!" I told her. "You must be so excited!"

"My Mehmet is perfect too," agreed Beyza, taking a sip of her beer.

"Has he asked you to marry him yet?" said Atakan pointedly. At thirty-two, Beyza was considered old by Turkish standards to be unmarried and childless. Nevertheless, she had skillfully hidden the fact that she had been living "in sin" with her boyfriend from her family for over a year.

She glared at Atakan. "No, but he will."

I took a sip of my wine and glanced around the room, my eyes locking for a second with the man at the bar. He looked vaguely familiar. A sinking feeling swept over me. Probably a friend of Serkan's.

Despite our separation and impending divorce, the Wives and Girlfriends police continued to keep fully Serkan informed of my movements. Every Saturday, he waited on the bench under the fig tree, a casual comment making it clear he knew exactly where I had been and with whom. No doubt tonight would be the topic of next Saturday's conversation.

"Do you know him?" said Mandy, nodding towards the man at the bar.

I shook my head. "Looks like a player," I said.

"He's been watching you all night," she continued. "I think you've pulled!"

"Who?" Atakan leaned towards us, ears pricked at the promise of gossip.

"The dude at the bar is checking out Carrie," Mandy filled him in. "I think he's gorgeous!"

Atakan subtly flickered his gaze towards the man and made an immediate professional judgement,

"He's hot, babe," he concluded. "You should go for it."

"Can you imagine what Serkan would do if he found out?" I took a gulp of wine as Atakan rolled his eyes. "Fuck Serkan, babe," he said. "You're not together."

"Atakan's right Carrie," Mandy agreed. "It's been nearly a year. He is going to have to get used to it. You are single. You deserve to have some fun."

I glanced at the man again. Dark hair shiny with gel. High cheekbones. Chiselled jaw sculpted with designer stubble.

He looked like bad news.

"I don't think I'm ready for another relationship," I protested weakly.

"Who said anything about a relationship?" retorted Atakan. "I'm talking about sex!"

Mandy howled with laughter. "Exactly!" she said, nodding enthusiastically. "You need to get laid, Carrie!"

Beyza's expression was serious. "Just be careful," she said. "You know how Turkish men can be."

"I'm going to the bathroom," I said, standing up and making my escape.

The floorboards creaked beneath my boots as I climbed the wooden steps to the ladies' room. Upstairs was closed and in darkness. It smelled of unopened windows and stale cigarette smoke. Chairs stacked on tables and a thin coating of dust were all that remained of summer. Drunken conversations and raucous laughter replaced by the whistling of the wind and the rattling of the windowpanes.

I reapplied my lip gloss, startled as a dark shape appeared behind me in the smeared mirror.

"Sorry, did I scare you?" said the dark-haired man from the bar.

"A bit." I turned around to face him.

The man was standing so close to me, I could smell his skin. A sweet, intoxicating mix of vanilla and something I couldn't put my finger on. In the semi-darkness, I could barely make out his expression. The silence vibrated in the air between us.

"Do you remember me?" he said after a few minutes had passed.

"Should I?"

"Carrie, right?" he held out his hand. "From the hospital?"

As our fingers touched, I felt a jolt of recognition. I had held that hand, looked into those eyes, before.

"Barbaros," I said as his name flashed into my mind. I felt suddenly swimmy with wine.

He smiled, his eyes crinkling up at the corners.

"You were with Margaret Crosby... and the blonde with the ponytail..."

He shook his head, keeping his eyes locked on mine. "Ancient history," he said.

His fingers brushed my arm, causing a jolt of electricity to run through me. He leaned towards me and for a moment I thought he was going to kiss me, surprised when instead he whispered in my ear.

"Give me your telephone number."

He pulled away, watching me with amusement, aware of the effect he was having.

I felt suddenly drunk despite having only had half a glass of wine. This felt dangerous. Intoxicating. Exciting. I couldn't remember the last time I'd felt like that.

Serkan's face flashed into my mind, bringing with it a surge of anger. Almost a year since I had left him, he was still in control. I continued to exist in a self-inflicted jail, fear dictating my every move. Mandy and Atakan were right. It had been nearly a year. It was time to have fun.

Barbaros took his phone from his back pocket. Emboldened by a mixture of anger and alcohol, I dictated my number as he tapped it into his phone.

"I'll call you," he said with a wink and a crinkly-eyed smile.

I could feel his eyes on me as I made my way back down the stairs, gripping the bannister for dear life.

"What took you so long?" asked Atakan as I sat down.

"I'll tell you later," I replied, gulping down the last of my wine and searching around for Melek to order another. I watched Barbaros descend the stairs and return to his seat at the bar. He didn't look at me, ordering another beer and lighting a cigarette as if nothing had happened. Now it was my turn to watch him, unable to stop myself from looking in his direction. He did not turn around again, chatting to the barman as he sipped his beer and smoking cigarette after cigarette, the stubs overflowing from the ashtray in front of him.

At around eleven-thirty, we decided to call it a night.

"Enjoy Istanbul!" Beyza embraced Atakan warmly. "We'll miss you!"

"Come and visit me!" he replied.

"Be good!" grinned Mandy. "And if you can't be good, be careful!"

Atakan and I walked back along the seafront arm-in-arm, listening to the waves as they crashed onto the beach. A sudden flash of lightning illuminated the night sky, followed a few seconds later by a ground-shaking clap of thunder.

"What happened in there?" Atakan asked eventually. "With the cute guy at the bar?"

Nothing got past him.

"He was watching you all night," he continued. "Then he followed you upstairs. When you came back, you couldn't tear your eyes away from him."

"Do you think the others noticed?"

"No babe. They were too busy talking about Mandy's wedding."

I stopped walking and let go of Atakan's arm. It was Saturday night, and the kids were at Serkan's. Suddenly, I didn't want to be on my own.

"Do you want to come back to mine?" I said.

"Sure, babe."

A light rain began to fall as I looked back towards Angel's. Standing alone, Barbaros stood silhouetted in the dark, the tip of his cigarette glowing orange in the blackness. For a few seconds, we stayed where we were, watching each other until he turned to leave.

Chapter Twenty-Four

Maralya, Turkey. November 2015.

Azra jerked the handbrake, narrowing her eyes as she sucked hard on her cigarette. The sombre playground, devoid of excited shrieks and laughter, was mirrored in her face. In place of children, a line of adults snaked through the open double doors beneath a drooping banner that hung from an upstairs window.

Seçim Sandığı (Polling station)

"If the AK party gets back in, this country is finished," she said, her normally cheerful expression lined with worry. "Erdoğan is a dictator. We will end up like Iran."

A confirmed atheist and fierce advocate of women's and LGBTQ rights, Azra was staunchly anti-Erdoğan. The man who once said that to put men and women on an equal footing was "against nature," and that women "should not laugh in public," did not inspire her vote. In contrast, Mustafa Kemal Ataturk, the founder of modern Turkey, was years ahead of his time. He considered men and women equal, modernized the new republic, and introduced secular rule, another cornerstone of Turkish democracy that was being slowly unravelled by Erdoğan's conservative AK party.

Azra hung back, phone pressed to her ear, as I joined the line behind a young couple. The woman was young, barely more than a teenager, strands of dark hair falling from her white headscarf. She wore a flowered skirt down to her ankles and a crocheted cardigan that hung from her slender frame. The man had a stern expression, accentuated by his bushy eyebrows that met in the middle and close-set eyes. The woman smiled at me as I approached, a glimmer of friendliness mixed with curiosity in her bright green eyes. I smiled back.

"*Haydi*!" said the man, prodding her sharply in the back. He shot a glance at me, immediately dismissing me as an irrelevant foreigner as he shoved her forward. The woman lowered her eyes, her face a passive mask as he continued his verbal lashing, unaware that I was listening to and understanding every word.

"Remember, you're voting for the AK party," he hissed at her as they moved through the double doors. "Don't think about doing anything stupid. You're my wife and you'll do as I say."

"Sorry."

I turned as Azra wobbled towards me on stiletto heels, her phone clutched in her hand. "Work."

The entrance hall smelled faintly of floor cleaner, old textbooks and freshly sharpened pencils. Pale blue walls smiled with rows of former students with identical uniforms and neatly brushed hair. A scratched wooden desk had been set up in front of the wide staircase. We passed our ID cards to the bespectacled official, who squinted as he ran his finger down the list and ticked off our names.

"*Ikinci odası,*" he smiled, passing us each a ticket and gesturing down the hall.

In the converted classroom, another official exchanged our tickets for ballot papers. As her husband disappeared behind one screen, and Azra the other, the young woman and I gazed in silence at the mishmash of projects that papered the walls. A map of Turkey painted pink. A bright green turtle on a tissue paper sea. Stick figures with too-big heads and spidery hands.

We both looked up as her husband strode out from behind the screen.

"Make sure you don't mess it up!" he barked at her.

Our eyes met fleetingly. Less than a second, but long enough for her to know that I knew. For me to see myself in her eyes. In the unhappiness. The fear. The shame.

At that moment, I hated him.

"Breakfast?" said Azra as she emerged from her booth, her sunny demeanour restored.

We found a table on the seafront in a hazy patch of sunlight. The storms of a week ago had given way to blue skies and spring-like temperatures and the few restaurants still open were peopled with a colourful mix of tangerine-skinned expats and locals enjoying *khavalti* in the sun. Stray dogs, skinny, matted, and weather-beaten from the first harsh weeks of winter, lay sprawled along the promenade, enjoying the warmth of the sun's rays.

"I have someone interested in the villa," said Azra, rummaging in her bag for a cigarette. "An investor. He knows about the tenants, and he doesn't care. But he wants a quick sale."

"But Serkan..." I began.

Azra stopped, cigarette packet in one hand, lighter in the other. There was a weariness in her eyes.

"Carrie, we need to sell," she said. "If we go to court, this could drag on for another two years."

She put the cigarette between her teeth and flicked the lighter

I sighed heavily. This month I had struggled to pay the rent and bills. I couldn't do this for another two years.

My phone buzzed a message.

> Good morning, beautiful!

Barbaros. Since our meeting at Angel's, he had messaged me every day. I remembered his face in the dark. The smell of his skin. His eyes crinkling up at the corners when he smiled. I stared at the message for a few seconds before pressing delete.

Azra tilted her head towards the phone in my hand.

"Call Serkan," she said. "Tell him if he doesn't agree to this sale, you'll sell the flats."

I opened my mouth to protest, silenced, as Azra reached across the table and placed her hand on mine. On her face, the same look of pity I had given the woman with the green eyes.

"Trust me," she said softly. "He can't do anything to you."

I wondered then when it had happened. When had my personality become so eroded, like a pencil sketch rubbed out so many times, that it left only the faintest lines? My needs, wants and desires pushed aside to make room for his until I didn't even know who I was anymore. To want was bad. To feel, even worse. In the year since I had found the courage to leave, nothing had changed. I remained in prison, too afraid to move on with my life.

Barbaros's face flashed into my mind, and I felt it again. The stirrings of something. Coming back.

"Are you ready to order?" A waiter appeared, pen poised above his notepad.

"Five minutes," said Azra, keeping her eyes fixed on mine.

My stomach was performing backflips, my finger hovering above the call button as Azra nodded in encouragement. I listened until he answered, closing my eyes, and trying to swallow the hard lump of dread that had lodged at the back of my throat.

"*Efendim?*" he barked, the impatience clear in his voice.

"I need to talk to you," I said, bracing the subject as delicately as a cat picking at fish bones.

"About what?"

"I have a buyer for the villa."

A lengthy silence, followed by a yawn, echoed down the line. I imagined him, sprawled on the white sofa, where he would spend the next six months, pocketing the rent from the flats and the villa. Last week I had walked around the discount supermarket, filling my basket with packet soup and pasta as I tried to stretch my last five lira until payday.

"I'm going to accept the offer," I said.

He snorted a laugh. "That's not up to you, Carrie."

"Then I'll sell the flats," I said.

"You can't!" he growled. "You wouldn't dare!"

"That's not up to you, Serkan," I said, concentrating on keeping my voice steady.

"I'll burn them to the ground!" he roared in my ear. "And the villa! I'll burn everything..."

I ended the call and dropped the phone on the table as if it were white hot.

Azra and I stared at it.

"What happened to you?" she said, her eyes wide.

"I think I'm coming back," I smiled.

***

That evening, with Elif at Serkan's, I sat alone on my uncomfortable purple sofa, an old film from the eighties playing out its predictable storyline on the TV.

On the coffee table, my phone buzzed.

> Please

Barbaros.

I stared at his photo. Deep-set eyes turned down slightly at the corners, a half-smile on his face. He was looking into the camera as if we shared a secret. I remembered the smell of him, the heat of his breath as he whispered in my ear, the softness of his fingers on my skin.

> Hi

I stared at the message, my heart starting to gallop in my chest before pressing send.

A flurry of messages, one after the other.

> Can we meet?

> Angel's?

> I need to see you

The thought of meeting Barbaros in public in full view of the Wives and Girlfriends police was as ludicrous as it was terrifying.

> I can't

> Husband?

> Ex-husband

> *I understand*

After that, there was nothing. On the TV, the end credits rolled across the screen. That's it, I thought to myself. There would be no more texts from Barbaros. Whatever it had been was over before it began. Surprised by my own disappointment, I got up from the sofa and made my way to the kitchen, where I flicked the switch on the kettle and dropped a tea bag into a mug.

Bleep.

A single word stared out from the screen.

> *Come*

***

The road was in gridlock. The streets teemed with people, and the traffic was at a standstill. Rousing music competed with loudspeakers and blaring horns as men leaned out of car windows waving banners and Turkish flags. I flinched as someone fired a gun into the air. The traffic crawled on, inching its way past the flashing lights of police cars as officers tried to regain order.

The address Barbaros had given me was in an area I knew well, close to where Atakan's mum and stepdad lived. I parked the car in a side street, away from the prying eyes of the Wives and Girlfriend's Police. Following the directions Barbaros had given me, I passed identical white apartment blocks and gated complexes, until I found myself standing in front of a complex of holiday apartments. The complex was in darkness, the paint peeling from the smiling dolphin sign that arched over the wrought-iron gate.

Yunus Holiday Apartments

Pushing open the gate, I made my way through the neglected gardens. Last spring's kittens, now skinny adolescents, lurked wide-eyed in the flowerbeds, awaiting the return of the tourists that fed them. A solitary lamp flickered next to the swimming pool in which dried leaves and a few feet of stagnant water festered uninvitingly. I found the door number he had given me, took a deep breath, and rang the bell.

It opened immediately.

Barbaros was even better looking than I remembered.

"*Hoş geldin*," he smiled, stepping back to let me pass.

The apartment was small, in complete darkness except for a small television set that flickered in the corner of the living room, the volume turned down low.

"Wine?" asked Barbaros as my eyes adjusted to the dark. Apart from the TV, there seemed to be no personal effects at all. No photographs or books. No pictures on the walls. Nothing to tell me who this stranger, in whose home I found myself, was.

I nodded and perched on the edge of the couch.

As reality seeped in, the recklessness that had driven me here began to evaporate. What was I doing? In this apartment? On this couch? How far had I come from the married mother of two? Respectable housewife? Party hostess? Downtrodden wife? I would have a glass of wine, make my excuses and leave.

Barbaros returned with two glasses of red wine and placed them on the low coffee table. He sat down next to me.

On the TV, a young woman in a leather miniskirt was silently belting out a song at the top of her lungs.

"I thought you changed your mind," he said. I reached for my wine and took a nervous gulp. A heady recklessness hit me with such force it made my head spin.

"Traffic," I replied, uncomfortable under the scrutiny of his intense eyes. "It's crazy out there."

Barbaros took my wine glass from me and placed it on the table. He reached for my hands, intertwining his fingers with mine.

"Look at me," he said.

It was then that I felt it. Fear. Raw, primal fear that seized and twisted my gut, making me want to run from this place and never come back.

Not fear of Serkan, or of the stranger in front of me, but fear of what was to come. The certainty that if I went down this road, I may never find my way back. The knowledge that this would not end well, and the realisation that I was powerless to stop it.

A shudder of something passed between us, as powerful as a lightning bolt and as gentle as the breeze. A breath. A flicker. A heartbeat. His eyes looked into mine as if he could see straight into my soul.

My fear dissolved into nothingness, swept away by a surge of desire. Keeping my eyes locked on his, I pulled him towards me.

Chapter Twenty-Five

Rome, Italy. June 2016.

I gripped the steering wheel in both hands, straining my eyes as I inched towards the faint blur of red brake lights ahead. The music from the car stereo was drowned out by the drumming of hailstones and the rhythmic mechanical whir of the wipers as they tried and failed to clear the deluge of water that bucketed from the slate grey sky.

In my rear-view mirror, worry flickered in Elif's eyes as she looked up from her sketchpad in the backseat.

Half an hour earlier we had been singing along to the car stereo as we crossed the narrow breadth of Italy, clear blue skies and sunshine turning to ominous black clouds and heavy traffic as we joined the multi-lane intersection crawling into Rome.

"It's fine, sweetie," I reassured her as a zigzag of lightning forked in the leaden sky, followed immediately by a deafening clap of thunder. Fear tingled in my fingers, my chest tightened, and for a second, I was back there. In this car, with Barbaros as the world closed like a thick black curtain across my mind.

But things were different now. I was different.

I glanced at Elif again in my rear-view mirror.

"It's OK," I smiled, fixing my eyes on the brake lights ahead. "It's just a shower. It'll be over soon."

Over the past two years, I had learned a few things about fear. One, that like this storm, everything passed if you held on long enough. The other, that the only way to the other side, was straight through the middle.

Eventually, the rain slowed, the hammering died down to a patter, and the sky opened up like a skylight of pale blue. Through the windscreen, cars, motorbikes, buses, and trams competed for space as umbrella-wielding pedestrians dashed across the road.

And there in front of us, bathed in a bright shaft of sunlight, as if it had somehow planned such a dramatic entrance, was the Colosseum.

"Mum look!" cried Elif. "I know this place! I've seen it in pictures! Can we go, mum? Please!"

I took a deep breath and exhaled slowly. The windscreen wipers screeched against the glass as they swished away the last remnants of water.

"Of course we can," I said.

***

The sun had disappeared behind the clouds by the time we made our way back to the Colosseum later that afternoon. Audio guide pressed to her ear, Elif soaked up her lesson on ancient Rome, stopping to relay any interesting facts to me as we explored the ruins. "The Romans were horrible!" she concluded as we stood on the balcony, gazing down at the amphitheatre below. "I'm glad people aren't like that anymore."

I stared down at the rows of empty seats, imagining the air ringing with jeers and laughter as the audience bayed for blood. My own character assassination played out in the modern-day amphitheatre of social media, sprang to my mind. My reputation torn to pieces as savagely as the animals and slaves of ancient Rome. Judged and found guilty by people who did not know or care for the truth. In 2000 years, I wondered, had we really changed at all?

This was my second trip to Rome. Over a decade earlier, Serkan and I had saved for months for a weekend break, as excited as schoolchildren to be on our first holiday together.

Now, as I wandered the same streets with Elif, memories confronted me at every turn. The old Serkan, the one I had fallen in love with, was everywhere. I felt his presence as Elif and I sat on wooden pews, heads tilted in quiet awe towards the ceiling of the Sistine Chapel. His face lined with laughter instead of rage, as Elif and I photographed each other on the Spanish steps. His eyes filled with love, not contempt as we wandered through the cool, echoing silence of St Peter's Basilica. The early years of our marriage was a place I hadn't visited for so long it was as if it had never existed. Before screaming arguments and icy silences. Before he put his hands on me in anger instead of love. Before we went so far down that path that we couldn't find our way back.

It was on a family holiday to Maralya as a teenager that I first met Serkan. Intrigued by his winning smile and Michael Jackson dance moves, I smiled at the shy boy and attempted a conversation in broken English. Over the next week, I ran into him everywhere; on the bus to the beach, at his friend's Turkish delight shop, and finally outside my hotel, where we had our first kiss under the olive groves. After I returned to the UK, we kept in touch with love letters and sporadic phone calls until I returned to Maralya with a friend around three years later. Our romance began and after two years long-distance, we married and returned to the UK.

I remembered the first night Serkan and I stepped out of our hotel onto the streets of Rome all those years ago. The stillness and warmth compared to the blustery cold of London. The exotic smells that wafted from restaurants. The sing-song Italian that streamed from bars as we strolled hand in hand through the winding streets. We had stopped in our tracks, gazing in wonder at the Trevi fountain haloed in white marble against the night sky.

Now, fifteen years later, I walked the same streets with our daughter as if barely a day had passed.

"Where are we going?" said Elif.

"It's a surprise," I smiled as we turned the same corner. There it was. Exactly as I remembered.

An image filled my mind. Serkan and I, young and in love, standing side by side in front of the Trevi fountain. My hand in his, we smiled as we threw our coins backwards over our shoulders to ensure our return to Rome. And return I had, in circumstances I could never have imagined. With only one of my children. Running from the man I thought was my best friend.

In front of the fountain, throngs of people jostled to take pictures, arms outstretched, heads pressed together, selfie sticks in the air.

"Let's throw a coin!" said Elif as she took my hand and pulled me through the crowd. A myriad of languages filled the air, elbows jabbed into my ribs. I stumbled slightly as someone stepped on my foot.

Elif continued to push forward until we reached the front. We jostled for space in front of the fountain as I dug around in my purse for coins.

"One. Two. Three!" Elif shouted.

Closing my eyes, I took a deep breath and threw my coin backwards into the cascading water.

Chapter Twenty-Six

Maralya, Turkey. November 2015.

I devoured him with a hunger I didn't know I felt. Wave upon wave of pleasure, each more intense than the last. Simultaneously desperate to reach the summit and never wanting it to end. Finally, a force so powerful that it started in his body and ricocheted through mine. A glimpse of perfect bliss before floating back down to earth like feathers on a warm breeze.

Afterwards, we lay there in the dark. For a long time, we didn't speak.

"What was that?" I said eventually.

He smiled, his eyes crinkling up at the corners.

"That, baby," he said. "Was good."

We were on his rickety double bed, which was actually two single beds pushed together. The low murmur of the TV filtered in from the living room as the barking news anchor-man declared the AK party's election victory.

Barbaros reached for a cigarette from an open packet on the bedside table. He flicked the lighter, the tip of his cigarette glowing orange in the dark. I ran my fingers across his flat stomach, tracing the smooth contours of his chest. The intoxicating smell of him made me want to breathe him in forever. He smiled at me in the semi-darkness.

"I could fall in love with those eyes."

His words jolted me back to reality. This wasn't what I came here for. I pulled away and sat up.

"What time is it?"

He picked up his phone from the bedside table. "Almost three."

"What! It can't be!" I clambered across him, trying to locate my clothes from where they were scattered all over the floor.

"I have to go."

"Will I see you again?"

I hesitated. There was no way I could take such a risk again.

"Maybe," I lied.

He sighed and took a drag of his cigarette, watching me as I self-consciously pulled on my knickers, fiddled with the clasp of my bra, pulled my sweater over my head, and pushed my legs into my jeans. In the cracked mirror on the bedroom wall, a stranger stared back at me, mascara smudged beneath her eyes.

Stubbing out his cigarette in the ashtray on the nightstand, Barbaros picked a pair of neatly folded shorts from a drawer. and pulled them on. We walked in silence to the front door, cold air and reality rushing in as he held it open for me. I had no idea of the appropriate thing to say.

"Thanks!" I grinned, turning to leave.

"Carrie..."

When I turned back, his eyes were different. The self-assured confidence was gone, replaced by something sad and broken. A melancholy so strong it caught me off guard. Another wave of fear swept over me. The urge to leave before it was too late.

"Goodbye Barbaros," I said, pecking him hastily on the cheek.

The heels of my boots echoed around the empty complex as I passed the flickering lamp by the swimming pool and through the metal gate with its peeling dolphin sign. As I stepped out onto the street, I glanced around for signs of Serkan, unable to shake the feeling that he *knew*. I could feel his eyes on me, watching me, as I found the side street where I had parked and headed towards my car.

The celebrations were over, and the streets were eerily quiet. I stopped at a red light, my body tensing as a motorbike roared into view and stopped beside me. The teenager revved the engine as he waited impatiently for the lights to change before speeding away, his helmet wedged under his arm.

I don't know what I was expecting, but the apartment was exactly as I'd left it. Remote control on the coffee table. Tea bag still in the mug next to the kettle. Clean plates stacked next to the sink. After a quick circuit around the park with Alfie, I peeled off my clothes and stood under the shower, letting the hot water wash away the smell of him, and with it, all traces of guilt.

In my attic bedroom, I stared at the ceiling, unable to sleep. I had done the unthinkable. I had had sex with another man.

Snapping on the bedside lamp, I reached for my phone. Despite the lateness of the hour, I needed to talk to him right now.

"I had sex with Barbaros."

"OMG! Tell me everything!" Atakan sounded wide awake. In the background, I could hear the pumping music of a club.

"It was amazing."

"Babe, I'm so happy for you!"

"He lives near your mum," I continued. "Yunus holiday apartments. Do you know it?"

"Why does he live in a holiday apartment?" laughed Atakan. "Carrie, who is this man?"

"It doesn't matter," I replied. "It's not happening again."

"We'll see."

"Goodnight aşkim."

"Goodnight, my love."

Chapter Twenty-Seven

Maralya, Turkey. November 2015.

Tiny dust particles danced in the beam of light that streamed in through the window, spotlighting the paper in front of me like an actor on a stage. The paper I had been waiting for for so long. The day I had almost given up hope of ever seeing had finally arrived. Earlier in the week, the villa had been sold, and the money deposited into my bank. The flats had been transferred into Serkan's name. The divorce was about to be final.

But there was no celebration in my heart, only a dull, leaden ache.

"Carrie?" ventured Azra from behind her mahogany desk. "Are you OK?"

I had been staring at the document for a long time. A signature away from freedom. The marriage that had kept me shackled to my tormentor, severed with the stroke of a pen.

A breath away from giving up custody of my son.

"It really is for the best, Carrie. Cem is settled with Sekan. He's at a new school. Things will carry on as they are now. Elif will stay with you, Cem with his dad," continued Azra. "Plus, if we go to court…"

"It will take years and I'll probably lose." I finished her sentence for her. I'd heard it countless times.

Cem's face flashed into my mind. *I wanna live wiz baba.* Tears blurred the words on the page.

Discomfort twisted in my gut as I reached for the pen and scrawled my name, passing it to Serkan, who did the same. I did not look at him, refusing to let him see me cry.

"That's it?" I said, standing up. I didn't want to be here.

Azra nodded. "That's it."

"Carrie..."

I had reached the door, my hand already on the handle, when his voice stopped me in my tracks. Of course, it was too much to expect that he would let this moment pass without a jibe or a barbed comment. I turned slowly, preparing myself for the characteristic smirk, the sadistic glimmer of triumph in his eyes, but there was nothing.

"I'm sorry," he said.

I let the words hang in the air, waiting for the inevitable twist of the knife.

I'm sorry I ever met you. I'm sorry I had kids with you. I'm sorry I didn't leave you first...

But there was nothing.

"I'm going to fix things with you and Cem," he said. "You're his mum. He loves you. I'll talk to him, I promise."

I nodded. "Thank you."

"I want us to be friends, Carrie," he continued.

"I mean it this time. I know it's over. I lost you, but I want you in my life. No more games. No more arguments. I don't want the children to see us fight anymore. Will you give me another chance?"

Serkan looked at me, his eyes a mixture of sincerity and longing like a child asking to stay up past bedtime. He seemed smaller somehow, stripped of the layers of bravado, threats and pride until only sadness remained. Despite everything, at that moment, I felt sorry for him. It was over. I couldn't fight anymore.

I felt suddenly exhausted. I wanted to crawl into bed and sleep for a week.

"Sure," I said.

Chapter Twenty-Eight

Maralya, Turkey. December 2015.

Mandy and I exchanged amused glances as the waiter placed plates of roast turkey, roast potatoes, salad, and rice on the table in front of us. The obligatory fresh bread and bowl of natural yoghurt were already there. Azra and Beyza viewed their meals with a mixture of curiosity and suspicion. At the opposite end of the table, my dad caught my eye and smiled.

Christmas day in Turkey is a surreal affair. For the largely Muslim population, it is a day like any other, though in Maralya, local restaurants gamely put on a "Christmas menu" for the ex-pat community, complete with an old CD of festive carols, a hastily decorated artificial tree, and something vaguely resembling Christmas dinner.

"Can we do quackers now?" said Cem, unable to tear his eyes away from the shiny, gold cylinder next to his plate.

"Yes!" I smiled at him, unable to hide my delight that he had agreed to join us.

Everyone took a cracker, and we linked arms around the table.

"One. Two. Fwee!" shouted Cem as the crackers snapped apart, sending their contents flying.

"I won! I won!" he cheered, retrieving his tiny plastic prize from the floor. Elif foraged in her remaining half, carefully unfolding her purple hat, and placing it on her head.

With the divorce sealed in ink and the villa sold, there seemed to have been a mental shift in Serkan. A resigned acceptance. True to his word, he appeared to be encouraging Cem and I's improving relationship.

Two weeks earlier, he had been waiting on the bench under the fig tree as I picked Elif up from the flats.

"Can we decorate the tree today?" she said as she climbed into the back seat.

"That's a great idea!" I said.

"Twee?" repeated Cem, glancing at his father and then back at me. "Cwismas twee?"

"Do you want to help decorate the tree?" I said, turning to Serkan. "Can he? I'll have him back by seven."

"Of course!" Serkan grinned and opened the back door as Elif scooted across to make room for her brother.

Last night, lured by the presence of his grandpa and the promise of a stocking full of gifts, Cem had agreed to spend the night with us for the first time since the summer. Even the children's ungodly awakening at five thirty had failed to wipe the smiles from my dad's and my faces as we watched them open their presents. When it was over, the living room a wreck of torn wrapping paper and discarded packaging, my dad reached under the tree for a small box I hadn't noticed before.

"Just a small thing I found in Copenhagen," he said, passing it to me.

He must have slipped it under the tree when I wasn't looking.

The children stopped playing and watched as I carefully removed the pink ribbon and expensive gold and silver paper. Inside was a plain white box from which I extracted two bubble-wrapped parcels. Inside the first was a small tumbler, its glass façade covered with intertwined silver hearts. I unwrapped the second smaller package to find a silver ring, above which extended a silver parasol and four delicate hearts hanging like raindrops suspended in time. A tea light candle holder.

"It's beautiful," I said, leaning in to give my dad a kiss. "Thank you."

We lit a tea light candle and placed it inside the cylinder, watching as the silver parasol began to turn in slow circles, driven by the heat of the flame.

The silver tea light turned circles now in the centre of our unconventional Christmas table, where roast potatoes and turkey competed with rice and salad. The Christmas tree, like the only one in fancy dress at a party, stood conspicuously next to swaying palms, and Bing Crosby's "White Christmas" floated through the air, at odds with blue skies and sunshine.

Azra sat opposite me, her yellow paper hat at a jaunty angle on her head.

"I've always wanted to try a real English Christmas dinner!" she grinned, taking a forkful of rice.

I didn't have the heart to tell her.

"How are things with Serkan?" she said. "Since the divorce?"

I thought for a minute.

"Strange."

Despite the outwardly friendly façade, I couldn't shake my suspicion that Serkan was still spying on me. We ran into each other more often than could be attributed to mere coincidence, even in a small town like Maralya. He would appear from nowhere as I browsed the supermarket aisles or had coffee with a friend, a look of unconvincing surprise on his face.

"What did you do last night?" I had said to Elif as we ate dinner one Sunday a couple of weeks earlier.

"We went to the park," she said, nodding her head towards the window.

I stared at her. "Which park?"

"That park." She pointed across the road.

The familiar feeling of dread began to build inside me.

"Why didn't you go to the park near Baba's house?"

"He said he likes this park," she shrugged.

My plan never to see Barbaros again had backfired spectacularly. Like the gravitational pull of the moon to the tides, I made my way to his apartment every Saturday night and every Saturday night I told myself it was the last time. When I wasn't with him, I was thinking about him. Memories of us lingered like shadows waiting to hijack my unguarded mind, pulling me back to the sex and the smoke and the darkness. We never went out, instead spending Saturday nights lying together on his threadbare couch, my head on his chest, as we listened to music or watched a film on the TV. Barbaros had a penchant for cheesy rom-coms and uplifting "lifetime" movies. Nothing with any violence.

"I've had enough violence in my life," he explained sadly.

Sometimes we talked, though mostly he talked, and I listened. He was born in a rough area of Istanbul. Beaten every day by an alcoholic father, he went off the rails as a teen and fell in with a bad crowd. He was good with numbers, the kind of person who could do complex sums in his head and had trained as an accountant. He was born with a heart condition, he told me. An arrhythmia.

"Do you take medication?" I said. "It could be dangerous."

Taking a sip of his *çay*, he flicked ash from his cigarette into a saucer. "These are all the medications I need."

"Cigarettes and *çay?*"

"Painkillers," he replied, his eyes clouding over, lost in some faraway place. Then, just as quickly, he was back in the present, his mask restored. He stubbed his cigarette out and pulled me towards him.

"I just want a quiet life, Carrie," he whispered into my hair. "A normal, quiet, peaceful life."

I never asked him anything about his life or why he was living in a holiday apartment out of season with barely any belongings. I didn't ask how he spent his days or what he did for a living. Our relationship existed in a bubble, a realm that had nothing to do with our real lives. I would end it soon, I told myself, but right now, Barbaros was exactly what I needed.

"You were miles away," said Azra from across the table. I reached for the wine and refilled our glasses, raising mine towards her.

"Thank you," I said. "For everything. I couldn't have done this without you."

"To freedom," she said.

"To freedom!" We clinked our glasses together.

"So, what are your plans now, free woman?" she asked with a grin.

"I'll start looking at apartments in the new year," I said. "Something small and easy to look after. Maybe with a pool."

Azra nodded.

"And I might get a new car," I mused, thinking how good it was to be in control of my own finances again. "Mine struggles up hills."

"Yes! A sexy little run-around!" Azra clapped her hands together.

"Oh, and a really comfortable sofa!" I added. "That purple one is horrible!"

"You deserve it," she said, reaching across the table to give my hand a squeeze. "You've been through a lot. I'm proud of you Carrie."

Azra lit a cigarette. She looked so funny in her lopsided party hat, glass of wine in one hand, cigarette in the other, that I reached for my phone.

"Smile!" I said as I captured the moment.

I sat back and gazed around the table. Mandy and Hasan, paper-hatted and smiling as they posed for a selfie. Beyza, reapplying her lipstick in the reflection in her boyfriend's sunglasses. Cem and Elif balanced on my dad's lap, explaining the finer points of their plastic cracker toys. In the centre of the table, the silver parasol turned in slow circles above the flame.

A new year filled with promise and possibility stood open-armed on the horizon. It was over. I would buy an apartment. Rebuild my relationship with Cem. Live the life I had been waiting for.

I closed my eyes, listening to the strains of Andy Williams drifting overhead.

It's the most wonderful time of the year...

And it really was.

Chapter Twenty-Nine

Maralya, Turkey. New Year's Eve, 2015.

I still don't know what woke me.

Barbaros shifting beneath me as he reached for his phone?

The white light that penetrated the dark?

The cigarette smoke that fogged the air?

A slow awareness began to filter into my consciousness as my eyes adjusted to the light. Something was very wrong.

"What is it?" I said.

Barbaros's eyes remained fixed on his telephone screen. He took a long drag on his cigarette.

"Your ex-husband just messaged me."

Suddenly, I was wide awake.

"That's impossible!"

He turned his phone around to face me. Serkan's Facebook picture stared out from the screen, intruding uninvited into the space that was ours.

> Call me urgently

Pushing back the heavy blanket, I climbed out of bed and began frantically gathering my clothes. I needed to leave. If Serkan knew about Barbaros, it was only a matter of time before he found out where he lived. Perhaps he already did.

Barbaros sighed.

"This is what I was afraid of," he said quietly.

"I'll talk to him." I pressed a kiss to his lips. "It'll be OK."

I slipped out of the front door, hurrying through the maze of darkened apartments. Past the empty swimming pool, the flickering lamp, and the dried-out flowerbeds. Through the arched gateway with its smiling dolphin sign.

My mind raced, tripping over itself as questions flooded my brain. How much did Serkan know? Had he followed me? Was he waiting by my car? I slowed my steps as I reached the side street where I had parked. A looming row of houses, faceless and silent. The grey shape of my car. I reached into my bag, my fingers curling around the cold metal of my keys, wincing at the too-loud click and flash of the central locking. I slid into the driver's seat and locked the doors. My frozen breath hung in the air like smoke.

Think, said the voice in my head. *Calm down and think.*

I forced my mind back to the beginning. To yesterday morning. The past twenty-four hours ran through my mind like a slideshow as I searched for the missing piece of the puzzle.

***

I was wiping down the kitchen surfaces after breakfast, as winter sun streamed in through the window. The silence interrupted as my telephone buzzed on the gleaming worktop. For once, there was no sinking feeling in the pit of my stomach as Serkan's face appeared on the screen.

"How are you?" he said jovially.

"Fine, you?"

"What time are you dropping the kids?"

Having spent Christmas with me, the children were to spend the New Year with Serkan and Gülşen, leaving me free to see in the New Year with Barbaros. In my attic room, my favourite little black dress, freshly dry cleaned, was already hanging on the wardrobe door.

"Six o'clock?" I said, running the cloth around the sink.

"My mum is making roast chicken," Serkan informed me.

"Great."

He hesitated.

"Why don't you join us for dinner?" he said as if the thought had just occurred to him.

"I can't. I have plans."

"Who with?"

I sighed. "Serkan…"

"OK, I know, I'm sorry. I was just asking. We're friends, right?"

I stared out of the window through the metal bars. The shiny blue Nazar glinted in the sunlight. In the park opposite, a toddler, snowsuited against the cold, tripped and fell as he ran towards his mother's outstretched arms.

"Please come," persisted Serkan. "Just for an hour."

Every instinct in my body screamed that this was a bad idea. Dinner with ex-husband followed by sex with new lover. A novel way to celebrate the new year.

"Please Carrie," he said. "You and Cem have been getting on so well."

It was a thinly veiled threat, and we both knew it.

"OK," I heard myself say. "But only for an hour."

I parked under the fig tree, the smell of wood smoke from the neighbourhood *sobas* assaulting my nostrils as I climbed the stone steps to the third floor. Serkan looked me up and down as I slid out of my coat, running his eyes over my black dress and high heels.

"Going somewhere nice?" he said.

"Just out with the girls," I replied, avoiding his gaze. I looked over at the children, cross-legged in front of the TV where the New Year celebrations were already in full swing.

"Azra?"

His tone was hard. A challenge flickered in his eyes. This was a bad idea.

"Maybe I should go."

I turned towards the door as his hand shot out and grabbed my wrist. He pulled me towards him, the fruity waft of wine on his breath hitting me squarely in the face.

"It was a joke, Carrie," he grinned. "What happened to your sense of humour?"

I pulled my hand away, rubbing my wrist.

"Look, I'm sorry," he smiled. "I'm just used to it, that's all. You are my wife."

I let the words hang in the air, wondering if he would correct himself.

"I'm not your wife, Serkan."

"Ex-wife," he said quickly. "I meant ex-wife."

We sat down opposite each other. The table between us was crammed with enough food to feed ten people. Roast chicken, sauteed vegetables, a mountain of rice, homemade chips and the ubiquitous bread and salad. Serkan reached for the half-empty bottle of wine in the middle of the table and poured us both a glass.

"Who's hungry?" he said, picking up a wooden-handled carving knife as the children joined us at the table. The discomfort in my gut turned to nausea as he sank the knife into the chicken. Glistening rivulets of oil oozed from its flesh and trickled onto the plate below.

I lifted my hand as he piled several pieces onto my plate.

"That's enough," I smiled. "Thank you."

"Me! Me!" Cem, thrust his plate towards Serkan as Elif waited patiently.

On the television, a woman in a silver sequined minidress and drag-queen-like makeup clutched a diamante microphone, her voice vibrating up and down the octaves. A dancing, clapping throng surrounded her, faces shiny with smiles.

In the kitchen, Gülşen stirred a pot of *Sütlaç*, Turkish rice pudding, on the stove. She didn't look up.

"Happy New Year," Serkan smiled and raised his glass. I did the same, and we clinked them together.

"Thanks for coming."

"Thanks for inviting me."

We ate in silence. I kept my eyes fixed on my plate, listening to the children's animated chatter. The clatter of Gülşen in the kitchen. The music from the TV.

Serkan drained his wineglass and poured himself another.

"Have you booked?" he said.

"What?"

"New year gets pretty busy," he continued. "You should have booked."

"It's fine," I said with a mouthful of chicken. I forced it down. Serkan had stopped eating and was staring at me.

"You might as well tell me where you're going, Carrie," he said. "You know I'll find out, anyway."

I reached for my wine. On the TV, the glittering woman had been joined by a shiny suited man, his face fixed in a grin as he clicked his fingers.

"Unless, of course, you're hiding something?"

We all jumped as his knife and fork clattered onto his plate. The kids stopped mid-sentence. Gülşen looked up, her wooden spoon frozen in her hand. On the TV, the clapping and singing continued, as if mocking us with its lively celebrations. Serkan glared at me.

"Are you seeing someone?"

I placed my knife and fork down and stood up.

"I should go."

"*Elinize sağlık,*" I nodded to Gülşen as I made my way towards the door. I reached for my coat and forced my arms through the sleeves.

"Happy New Year!" I said to the children with a too-bright smile. "Elif, I'll pick you up tomorrow."

She did not respond, careful to keep her expression neutral as she stared at her plate.

"Carrie, wait! Sit down please," said Serkan, standing up. I hurriedly pushed my feet into my high heels, closing my fingers around the door handle.

"Don't go." Cem's voice.

I stopped.

"You didn't finish your chicken," continued Cem, pointing across the table at my half-eaten meal.

"Of course," I smiled, stepping out of my shoes. "Silly me."

***

Shivering in the cold of the car, I switched on the engine and turned the heaters up full blast. I reached into my bag for my phone, staring in horror at the screen.

54 missed calls.

He answered on the first ring.

"WHERE ARE YOU?" blasted his voice in my ear.

"Serkan, what's going on?"

"WHERE THE FUCK ARE YOU?"

"I told you," I blurted. "I went out with friends."

"STOP LYING!"

"Serkan, stop! We are divorced..."

"I checked all your friends," he interrupted. "None of them know where you are."

"You WHAT?"

Terror curled around my heart as I pictured him driving around Maralya, checking my friends' houses one by one. Looking for me. This was more sinister than I had ever thought possible.

"Admit it, you're with him," he sneered.

"Who?"

"Barbaros!" He spat the word out as if it were poison.

"I know, Carrie. I know everything. I know his telephone number and I know where he works. Soon I will find out where he lives and then...you are both going to pay."

Ending the call, I threw my phone into my bag, turned the key in the ignition and pulled out onto the deserted road.

In the harsh fluorescent light of the police station, I felt cheap and conspicuous in my black dress. A row of orange plastic chairs lined the wall beneath an information poster on domestic violence. A woman, her left eye purple and swollen. Tape crisscrossed over her mouth. The telephone number at the bottom, torn and unreadable.

A flicker of distaste passed over the features of the overweight police officer as he looked up from his newspaper.

"*Buyrun?*"

"I need to make a complaint," I said in Turkish.

"*Otur,*" he indicated the row of plastic chairs before returning to his newspaper. I sat—wave after wave of tiredness beat down on me as the adrenaline began to subside. My eyes were closing and my head nodding forward when a male voice jerked me back to reality.

"Caroline, *hanım?*"

The officer was young. He had a clipboard in one hand and a pen in the other. Dark circles shadowed his eyes.

"This way, please," he said wearily.

I followed him down the brightly lit corridor. His shiny shoes on the tiled floor tapped in judgement of my messy hair, the mascara smudged beneath my eyes. The overweight officer's eyes bore into my back as I completed my walk of shame.

The interview room was small, with sickly, yellow lighting and no windows. The obligatory picture of Ataturk stared down from the wall, like a benevolent uncle. His stern expression softened by the kindness in his eyes. Pulling my skirt down a few inches, I perched on the plastic chair and handed over my *kimlik*.

"How can I help you?" he said.

"My ex-husband threatened me."

"Threatened you?"

"He thinks I have a boyfriend."

"And do you?"

"Do I what?"

"Have a boyfriend?"

I stared at him.

"We are divorced," I said.

The officer nodded and flashed a tight smile.

"And what exactly did he say?"

"That he would find me and make me pay."

In my mouth, Serkan's words seemed to lose their power, sounding silly and childish.

"I think he's been following me," I added. "Watching my apartment."

The officer stopped typing and frowned at his computer screen.

"I see you made a complaint before. In June?"

"Yes."

"And you had a restraining order?"

"Yes."

"But since June, nothing."

I sighed. "We've been getting along. He's been better..."

"Until you got a boyfriend?" interrupted the officer.

"We are divorced," I said again.

The officer didn't say anything, frowning at the screen as he typed. Finally, the printer behind his desk whirred into life, and spewed out several sheets of paper which he stapled together and handed to me.

He tapped the bottom of the paper and passed me a pen.

"*Imza.*"

I scribbled my name.

"There's a temporary restraining order in place for now," he said. "It will go to court next week, and they will give you their decision."

He reached into a drawer and passed me another sheet of paper with an address and telephone number on it.

"This is the Women's Protection Bureau. Someone from there will contact you in the next few days. If your ex-husband comes to your house or place of work, call us immediately."

I folded the paper up and shoved it into my bag. All I wanted was to go home, take a shower and crawl into bed.

"Thank you," I said, standing up and heading towards the door.

I drove the two blocks to my apartment and parked under the pale glow of a street lamp. For a few minutes, I sat there, staring out into the deserted street as condensation trickled down the windscreen. I scanned the street for any sign of him, any flicker of movement in the shadows, but there was nothing. Finally, exhaustion, coupled with the promise of a hot shower and a warm bed, forced me out of the car. I hurried up the narrow path to the front door, fumbling with the key in the darkness before turning it with a reassuring click.

It happened all at once. A hand clamped over my mouth. A weight behind me shoving me forward. The heat of his breath on my neck.

"Walk!" hissed Serkan in my ear.

Chapter Thirty

Maralya, Turkey. New Year's Eve, 2015.

I blinked in the harsh light of the hall as the door slammed shut behind us, stumbling on my heels as he forced me up the stairs. His fingers dug into the flesh of my upper arm.

"Open it!" he hissed as we reached the door to my apartment.

The key was still in my hand. I fumbled with it in the lock until the door swung open. The dark shape of Alfie body wagged at my feet before skulking away with his head down.

Serkan kicked the front door shut and spun me around to face him, tightening his grip on my arm. I flinched at the aniseed stench of *Rakı* on his breath as a glint of silver caught my eye.

"Sit down," he growled.

I stood, frozen to the spot, unable to look away from the wooden-handled knife in his hand. My mind flashed back to the previous evening. Rivulets of glistening oil as the same knife sank into the chicken's flesh.

"I said SIT DOWN!"

He lunged towards me, shoving me backwards onto the purple couch, glaring at me as anger oozed from his eyes. I managed to pull myself into a semi-sitting position and shuffle towards the far end.

"Serkan please," I whimpered. "We have children."

He sat down next to me. I recoiled at the smell of alcohol on his breath.

"Forget your children!" he hissed. "You are a whore, Carrie. A dirty whore. They don't need a mother like you."

"Can we talk?" I said, trying to keep my voice steady. Trying not to look at the knife in his hand.

"Talk?" he spat. "This isn't England, Carrie. This is Turkey. You fucked another man. And now you have to pay."

His face loomed over me in the dark, his eyes burning with hate. Somewhere in the background, Alfie began to whine.

"Shut up!" snapped Serkan in the direction of the dog. He sat back, running his eyes over my black dress and heels.

"You wore this for him?"

A look of pure disgust spread across his face.

"You even look like a whore!" he spat as Alfie's whining intensified.

"SHUT UP!!"

Roughly pulling off one of my shoes, Serkan threw it across the room. There was a high-pitched yelp and a clatter as it collided with Alfie's head. He pulled off the other shoe and threw it in the same direction.

Silence descended on us like a cloak. After what seemed like an age, Serkan turned away from me. He leaned forward, elbows on his knees, head down as he stared at the floor. The knife hung limply in his hand.

"How long?" he said, eventually.

"A couple of months."

He winced as the words hit him like a slap.

"Do you love him?"

I shook my head. "No."

"How many times?"

"What?"

He turned to me.

"How many times did you fuck him?"

I searched my brain for an answer.

"I don't know..."

"You KNOW!" he lunged back towards me, pressing the blade against my throat. His eyes burned with hatred in the dark.

"I used to go on Saturday nights when the kids were with you," I gabbled as he pressed the cold metal harder against my skin. "It wasn't serious. It didn't mean anything. It was just... it was stupid. I was stupid...."

The anger in his eyes melted away. He smiled briefly before his lips curled into a sneer.

"And now you have to pay."

"Serkan please..." I begged. "I'll go. I'll leave Turkey. You'll never see me again."

He smiled again as he ran the knife blade gently down my cheek, pleasure playing in his eyes as he stroked it across my throat.

Images filled my mind. Nameless faces almost nightly on the news. Women murdered by the men they once loved.

I wondered how long it would take to bleed to death.

"Serkan please!" I was begging now. "Please. Let's talk. About everything. I won't see him again. Think of the children. They need their mother. They need us. You'll go to jail, Serkan. They won't have anyone."

Serkan kept the knife where it was, seemingly considering his options. Finally, with a sigh, he moved the knife away. Slowly, I exhaled.

"I knew there was someone else," he whispered as he stared into space. "I knew it."

"We weren't together," I said softly. "We were divorced, Serkan. I met someone else. You could meet someone else."

"I don't want someone else!" he yelled, anger flashing in his eyes. "You are my WIFE!"

He lunged back towards me, his hand trembling in fury as he pressed the knife back to my throat. I froze.

"You are mine, Carrie! I own you! Divorce doesn't change anything. You are mine until the day I die!"

He pressed the blade harder into my neck until I felt it nick the skin. "I keep thinking about you," he hissed. Touching him. Him touching you...I should kill you right now, you dirty whore!"

"Serkan, please!" I managed to croak as I searched his face for a glimmer of recognition. A connection to the man I married. The father of my children, but there was nothing. The eyes of a stranger stared back at me.

As the insults and vitriol rained down, I escaped in the only way I knew how. I floated up and away. Out of my body. Out of that room. Above the rooftops and deserted streets of Maralya. Over the long, sandy outline of Carreta beach, accompanied only by the rushing of the tide. Higher still, above the clouds. Higher still. Until all I could see was blackness and all I could feel was nothing.

Chapter Thirty-One

Tuscany, Italy. June 2016.

I awoke, as I did every morning, wrapped in Barbaros's arms. Despite the miles between us, the physical addiction lingered, and at night he would creep into my unguarded mind, wrapping his limbs around me with the stealth of a serpent. If I kept my eyes closed, I could breathe him in, feel the warmth of his skin against mine, prolong the moment for a few seconds more until he inevitably slipped away.

That's the problem with love. Even when the brain knows it's over, the body and soul need time to catch up.

I opened my eyes. Grey light filtered in through the papery blind, casting a shadowy haze over the hotel room. The space next to me in the double bed was empty, and the arms wrapped around me were my own. I rolled onto my back and stared at the flat, white ceiling above.

Nobody in the world knows where I am.

The thought made me feel as comforted as it did alone. This hour of the morning, before Elif awoke and gave me a reason to fight as hard as I could against the blackness that sat so heavily on my shoulders, was the hardest time of day. During the day, buffered by the distraction and cheerful chatter of my daughter, I could pretend. But in the silence and stillness of the early morning, there was nowhere to hide. I closed my eyes. A slideshow of happy memories played behind my eyelids as I forced myself back from the abyss. Sunlit roads. Camping under the stars. A horse-drawn carriage through the cobbled streets of Florence. The Uffizi.

***

Elif tilted her head to one side as she surveyed the woman in front of her with a critical eye.

"I don't think so," she said in conclusion.

"You don't think so what?"

"I don't think she is the most beautiful woman in the world."

Botticelli's Venus stood atop her clamshell, her modesty preserved by her long, golden hair, breasts half hidden behind a coyly placed hand as she gazed at some unknown point in the distance.

"The goddess of love," I mused out loud.

"There's going to be a huge love between us Carrie," Barbaros's voice intruded into my mind. *"I can feel it."*

Venus refused to meet my gaze.

You have a lot to answer for, I told her silently.

We had been travelling for just over three weeks. Five days in Athens. A week in Vieste. Three days in Rome. We stopped when we felt like it and left when we grew bored. Sometimes we stayed in hotels, but when we could, we camped in the little blue tent I bought in a discount supermarket in Bodrum right before we left. These were the most magical nights. Grilling chicken on the portable barbeque and talking under the stars.

We got lost on purpose, driving down narrow lanes, past vineyards, and farmhouses just to see where they led. Mile upon mile of rolling landscapes in green, gold, and brown. Tuscan villages untouched by time. Winding roads flanked by sentry-like Italian cypress trees, upright and serious. Elif, in the back seat, sketched the scenery in one of her old school notebooks.

I kept my promise to Atakan, visiting Pisa where we photographed each other "holding up" the Leaning Tower.

Other than that, we ate. My appetite, missing and presumed dead in my final months in Turkey, had returned with a vengeance, and if there is ever a place to get your appetite back, it's Italy. I could feel the meat returning to my bones, padding out my jutting hips and filling the spaces between my ribs.

We continued through the cool rooms and high ceilings of the Uffizi. Elif stopped in front of another Botticelli masterpiece. The Primavera.

"You like this one?" An American woman smiled at Elif. "You have good taste."

The woman had perfect teeth the way most Americans do, and kind eyes.

"We're on a road trip through Europe!" Elif told her with a grin. She counted on her fingers, "We went to Greece first, now Italy, and then France."

"How wonderful!" replied the woman, smiling in my direction. "You must have an amazing mother!"

The pain was as raw and immediate as if she had driven a knife straight through my heart, catching me off guard with such force that I took a step back. The woman's smile faded; her eyebrows creased in a frown.

"Are you OK?"

I forced a smile. "Thank you," I said. "I'm fine."

I didn't allow myself to think of him often. Not yet. Though he was always there. In the guilt every time I bought Elif an ice cream. The space next to her when I kissed her goodnight. The empty chair at breakfast. Sometimes I would see a little boy in the crowd, around the same age with the same colour hair. Though I would know it wasn't him, I would stare, unable to tear my eyes away as I waited for him to turn around.

Before, when my life was normal, I had heard stories about mothers who left their children. I had sat in judgment, never fathoming why a mother would or could do such a thing. Now I was one of them. I had committed the last taboo. Fathers leave. Mothers do not. I wondered, now, about those women I had heard about. What was the full story? Did they question their decision every day as I did? Carry their loss around with them? An unfillable void. An unquenchable longing. An unatonable guilt.

***

The light was stronger now, haloing the blinds as it tried to penetrate the hotel room, signifying the beginning of another day. With the shape of Elif in her single bed showing no signs of awakening, I pulled back the duvet and padded across the carpeted floor to the bathroom. Under the harsh lights, I came face to face with myself in the mirror over the gleaming white sink. My reflection stared back at me, unable to hide the pain in her eyes.

I was aware that the full impact had yet to hit me, that my mind had mechanisms in place, shielding and protecting me from feelings I was not yet able to feel. It occurred to me that I had been numb, to a greater or lesser extent since that night, and I wondered if I would ever feel anything again, or indeed, if I wanted to. Like a burn victim, the bandages were wrapped thick over wounds that were layers deep. In the coming months and years, they would undoubtedly unravel to reveal the full extent of the damage. Would it hit me slowly, like coming round from an anaesthetic? Would the pain be sudden, searing like ripping off a band-aid? Would I scream? Cry? Fall apart? Find solace at the bottom of a wine bottle?

I turned on the tap, running my toothbrush under the cold water.

Today I had no choice but to keep going.

Elif needed me. I was all she had left.

Chapter Thirty-Two

Maralya, Turkey. New Year's Day, 2016

The purple couch was hard and unyielding beneath me. My neck screamed in pain as I moved my head. There was a high-pitched whine as I forced my eyes open, coming face to face with Alfie, his brown eyes full of concern. Another noise. Shrill. Intrusive. Periodically starting and stopping. Through the small gap in the curtains, I could see that it was light outside, but the living room remained cloaked in darkness. I lay completely still, barely daring to breathe as I listened for any sounds that may indicate his presence, but I could already feel that the flat was empty. Slowly, I moved my aching limbs and pulled myself up into a sitting position. My body stiff with pain and cold, I waited for the dizziness to pass as Alfie wagged his tail encouragingly.

The noise again. A low buzzing that bore into my brain. The slow realisation that it was my telephone.

My bag lay splayed on the floor next to the front door, where I must have dropped it last night. I took stiff, painful steps towards it and lowered myself gently to the ground.

Azra, in her yellow party hat, grinned at me from the screen.

"Hello."

"Carrie, where are you?" She sounded frantic.

"Home," I croaked. My mouth was dry.

"You need to get out of the house," she said. "Serkan knows."

"I know."

"He's lost it, Carrie. I'm afraid for your safety."

I made my way to the sink, where I filled a glass with water and gulped it straight down before filling it again.

"Carrie?"

Sunlight shone in through the bars on the window. The shiny, blue *Nazar* glinted in the light as it dangled from its frayed string. How naïve I had been to think they would protect me. That he wouldn't find a way in.

"Carrie?" said Azra again.

"I'm here."

"Come over to mine," she said. "As soon as you can."

Gripping the bannister, I headed upstairs. Alfie close behind.

Sun streamed into my attic room through the open blind. The bed unslept in. The empty coat hanger still hanging on the wardrobe door. In the bathroom, I peeled off my dress, dropped it in a black puddle on the floor and stepped under the hot water, closing my eyes as cell by cell, my stiff muscles gradually returned to life.

The buzzing again. Azra's face on the screen. I was wrapped in a towel, shivering in my attic room. I wondered how long I had been there. From the doorway, Alfie whined softly and wagged his tail.

I pulled on clothes and ran a comb through my wet hair.

We circled the park. Alfie, nose to the ground as he trotted along ahead. I wondered if he was watching.

A buzzing from the kitchen worktop greeted me as I pushed open the front door. I remembered Azra laughing as I held my phone up to take her picture. Andy Williams in the background.

"Carrie, where are you?"

"I'm on my way."

In the driver's seat, I turned the key in the ignition, pushed the car into gear, and pressed my foot down on the accelerator.

The car felt as if it was stuck in cement.

I tried again. Nothing. As I got out of the car to check the damage, I already knew what I would find.

All four tyres had been slashed.

It seemed Serkan had found a use for his knife after all.

***

I watched from the living room window as the two police officers circled my car. One of them took photographs from various angles, while the other chatted to Azra as he jotted down notes on a pad. Azra caught my eye and smiled as I stared blankly through the glass. I felt as if I were watching a film and it would be over soon. I would wake up, warm and safe in Barbaros's arms. I would tell him about the nightmare I had.

When the police had finished, Azra motioned for me to come downstairs.

"You'll catch a cold," she said, glancing at my still-wet hair as we sat side by side in the back of the police car. The radio crackled from the front seat.

I stared out of the window. A round-faced woman, pegs between her teeth, was pinning out washing on a line. Three scruffy boys, in too-small clothes rode too-big bicycles, weaving precariously along the side of the road.

I needed to get Elif back.

It dawned on me slowly that Azra was talking.

"He started calling about midnight, asking where you were. I said I didn't know. When I stopped answering the phone, he turned up at my house. I refused to let him in, and he stood in the garden, shouting at me to tell him where you were. He said he knew about Barbaros. That he's going to kill you. Both of you."

I turned my head and looked at Azra. There was a fear in her eyes that I had never seen before.

"I have dealt with hundreds of divorces, Carrie. Hundreds of men. Most of them want to kill their wives." She hesitated. "But Serkan is different. He's serious."

It was a different officer from the one last night, but the room was the same. No window. A desk. A computer. A plastic chair.

"You made a statement last night?" The officer flicked through some papers on his desk. He looked to be in his late forties, hair thinning around a bald spot on the top of his head.

I nodded.

"Apart from the threats last night, the harassment of your friend and the damage to your car, do you want to add anything else to your statement?"

Serkan's face flashed into my mind, inches from mine. His lip curled in contempt. The stench of Rakı. The blade pressed against my throat. I shook my head. "No."

The police officer reached for the telephone on his desk.

"I'll see if there's a space at the women's refuge."

"I don't want to go to the refuge," I said. "I need to get my daughter back."

The officer stared at me; the telephone receiver clutched in his hand.

"According to your lawyer and your statement last night, your ex-husband has made some very serious threats against you."

"I need to get Elif back," I said again.

There was a soft tap at the door. Azra peered around it, grinning at the officer.

"*Azra hanım!*" he stood up and they greeted each other warmly before turning their attention to me.

"I have advised her to go to the refuge," explained the officer as if discussing a naughty child. "But she refused."

"I need to get Elif back," I said, looking at Azra.

Azra's grin disappeared. Discomfort flickered in her eyes.

"Carrie, the custody agreement states that Serkan has Elif until tomorrow night," she explained softly.

I stared at her. Why was nobody listening to me?

"If he doesn't return her by tomorrow at five, we can open a court case for breach of the custody order."

She smiled as if this made everything OK.

"Open a court case?" I said, dumbfounded. "I need to get my daughter back."

"Carrie, the priority right now is your safety. Are you sure you won't consider the women's refuge? At least for a few nights?"

I knew the women's refuge. A large house at the end of a tree-lined street. Children playing behind the high-walled garden. Security cameras on the walls. An armed guard at the door. I used to drop off bags of clothes and toys that the kids had grown out of. It always seemed wrong to me that the women and children should be the ones behind bars while their attackers walked free.

Azra glanced at her watch. I was suddenly aware that I was taking up too much of her time.

I stood up and turned towards the door.

"You're going home?" she said.

I nodded. "Where else am I going to go?"

I waited for her to invite me to stay with her. To throw me a lifeline. To do her job, not as my lawyer, but as my friend.

Instead, she nodded.

"We have arranged a restraining order," she said. "If Serkan comes anywhere near you at home or work, call the police immediately."

***

The boy couldn't have been more than seventeen. Baggy jeans hung from his hips. A black Metallica T-shirt revealed his skinny arms despite the cold weather. His hands and forearms were streaked with black, and he smelled like engine oil. He circled my car and whistled, shaking his head.

"What happened, *Yenge*?"

"Ex-husband," I explained.

He shook his head again. "*Geçmiş olsun*," he said. May it pass.

After the boy had replaced my tyres, I watched him zoom away on his scooter before driving the car several blocks away and parking in a quiet side street. I walked back to my apartment, feeling the weight of

Serkan's eyes on me with every step. I made a mug of tea and sat stiffly on my uncomfortable sofa, staring through the gap in the curtains as it got cold. I watched as the sky faded from eggshell blue to sombre grey and eventually night. I sat in the dark, too afraid to turn on the light, sure that he was watching. Looking for signs that I was home.

My head was nodding, my eyelids closing as the shrill ringing of my telephone penetrated the dark.

"Carrie?" said Barbaros.

In the turbulence of the past twenty-four hours, I had barely thought about him.

"Are you OK?"

Hot tears sprang to my eyes. I bit my lip hard.

"Fine, you?"

He sighed. "Carrie, he's been sending me threatening messages all day. He knows where I work. It's only a matter of time before he finds out where I live. I'm an outsider, Carrie. I don't have anyone here. I need to leave Maralya."

"Can't you go to the police?" I said.

He sighed. "It's not that simple."

"Where will you go?"

"To Istanbul. To my brother's house," he hesitated. "What are you going to do?"

I stared straight ahead. A slither of moonlight shone through the gap in the curtains, capturing the silver tea light in a ghostly glow.

"I don't know," I said.

We didn't speak for so long, I wondered if he was still there.

"Pack your bag," he said eventually. "You're coming with me."

"I can't..."

"Pack your bag." There was a hard edge to his voice.

"But..." My mind was racing. "I can't just leave Maralya. What about the kids? Alfie? My job?"

Barbaros didn't let me finish.

"Carrie, listen to me. It's not safe here. Do you have any idea what men like Serkan do to women like you?"

Serkan's face flashed into my mind. The glint of the knife in the dark. The hate that burned in his eyes.

"Pack a bag," said Barbaros. "We leave in an hour."

I sat in the dark for a long time, staring at the moon through the gap in the curtains as if it alone held the answer. I don't know if it was the swivel of Alfie's head towards the window, the low growl, or the male voices from the street below, but suddenly I was on my feet.

I ran upstairs and pulled my suitcase down from the top of the wardrobe, emptying drawers and shelves as fast as I could. Zipping the case closed, I heaved it downstairs.

Alfie sat in the hall. He wagged his tail and whined softly. Crouching down, I buried my face in his thick fur, breathing in the smell of him. I kissed the top of his head and massaged his silky ears.

"I'll be back, I promise," I whispered into his fur.

I took a last look at the living room. In the corner, the Christmas tree, decorated by Elif and Cem, stood lopsided and with far too much tinsel. Unable to agree on a star or an angel, they had settled on both, sitting together at an awkward angle at the top. Framed photographs stared down from the walls. Cem, smiling shyly at the camera in his oversized sunhat, his long eyelashes casting shadows on his skin. Elif, bronzed and gap-toothed in her blue swimming costume, tiny beads of water glistening on her nose.

As I turned towards the door, a glint of silver caught my eye. The tea light, bathed in its shaft of moonlight, glimmered at me from the centre of the table.

I walked towards it and picked it up, turning it slowly around in my hand as memories flooded my mind.

Christmas day. The silver parasol turning in slow circles above the flame. Laughter and blue skies. Elif and Cem, paper-hatted on my dad's lap as they discussed their cracker toys. The day I thought everything was going to be OK.

The silver tea light clutched tightly in my hand, I pulled my suitcase towards the front door and walked out of my apartment for the last time.

Chapter Thirty-Three

Maralya, Turkey. January 2016.

He did not let go of my hand, his fingers intertwined with mine as he switched his other hand between the steering wheel and the gearstick. In my other hand, I clutched the silver tea light.

We didn't speak. I stared out of the window, lost in thought as the miles rushed by. Soon the apartment blocks, shops, bars, and restaurants of Maralya gave way to stretches of empty night-time motorway. The hard knot of fear in the centre of my chest loosened with every mile that passed.

Leaving Maralya was a decision I would question many times over the coming months, and to this day I don't know if it was the right one. All I know is that at that moment, on that freezing January night, I needed to get as far away from Maralya as possible.

Serkan needed time and space to calm down, I told myself. He would see sense. His rages, though terrifying to behold, invariably burnt themselves out. Though I had never seen him as angry as he was that night, the temper outbursts, threats, and violence were nothing new. In a few days, I would call him. Explain. Make him see that the children needed their mother. In time, his burned ego would heal, and Barbaros and I would return home.

I had to believe this was true.

Barbaros flicked the indicator and pulled into a motorway service station. The kind used by long-distance lorry drivers and hungry night-time travellers. Stale coffee in polystyrene cups. A hot-plated buffet congealing behind chrome and glass.

"Are you hungry?" he said.

I shook my head.

"Coffee?"

"OK."

The restaurant was almost empty. The fluorescent lighting and red and white plastic tables too bright after the darkness of the car. I chose a table in the corner. My reflection stared back at me in the black windowpane. Pasty-skinned and puffy-eyed.

At the next table, a stubble-chinned man flicked through a newspaper and stirred sugar into his *çay*. A young couple sat bleary-eyed, the remains of a pizza and a half-empty bottle of Coca-Cola on the table between them. A boy of about six ran and slid on the polished floor. On his mother's lap, his younger sister slept, her limbs splayed like a starfish, oblivious to the light and noise.

"Hey."

I looked up as Barbaros placed a white plastic tray on the table in front of me.

"Thanks." I took the coffee gratefully.

We sat opposite each other, self-conscious and awkward in the harsh glare of reality. It felt strange to be out in public. Our relationship so far had existed behind closed doors, in the dark confines of Barbaros's apartment. A twilight world of sex, wine, and cigarette smoke. Serkan, with the tenacity of a terrier, had flushed us out like rabbits.

As we drove on, exhaustion finally hit me, and I closed my eyes, resting my head against the window where I drifted in and out of sleep. When I awoke, we were parked in a layby, the ground outside covered in a thick blanket of snow. Next to me, Barbaros slept, his head wedged at an awkward angle against the window. I reached into the back seat for our coats, arranging them over us and turning on the car heater as he murmured a drowsy thank you. Huddled together, we slept as more snow fell against the windscreen.

Early the next morning, we boarded the car ferry to cross the Bosphorus to the European side of the city. Seagulls soared and dipped against the white sky; their cries joined by the low chug of the engine as we moved through the grey water. I pulled my coat closer around myself on the freezing deck as Barbaros smoked a cigarette. He was watching me intently.

"*Nasılsın aşkım?*" he said. How are you, my love?

"Fine." I smiled. "You were right. I feel better being out of Maralya."

"A fresh start," he replied, his gaze intensifying as if trying to gauge my response.

I stared at him.

"I can only stay a week, maybe two," I said hurriedly. "Just until this all blows over. I have to go back to Maralya. I have children. A job."

He inhaled deeply on his cigarette.

"I know."

The freezing wind whipped around our faces. Barbaros threw his cigarette butt overboard, where it floated on the foam. He pulled me towards him, enveloping me in his thick jacket.

"There's going to be a huge love between us, Carrie," he whispered in my ear. "I can feel it."

That feeling again. The same feeling I had the night we met. As if I were on a speeding train headed for disaster or being pulled out to sea by an invisible tide. Barbaros pulled back and gazed down at me, cupping my face in his hands. He stroked my cheeks with his thumbs.

"You're freezing," he said, moving a strand of hair away from my face. "Let's go inside."

At the bar, we warmed our hands around cups of overpriced coffee until the tannoy announced our imminent arrival and instructed us to return to our cars.

On the lower car deck, I climbed into the passenger seat and clicked on my seatbelt as Barbaros slid into the driver's seat beside me. He smiled. His chiselled features were shadowy in the dark.

"*Artık benimlesin,*" he said. "From now on, you're with me."

The bow doors opened, flooding the car deck with light. Barbaros looked different now. Eyes crinkling up at the corners, he smiled as turned the key in the ignition and reached for my hand.

Chapter Thirty-Four

Istanbul, Turkey. January 2016

> *Dirty whore*
>
> *You will never see your kids again*
>
> *We are happy without you*
>
> *Your kids hate you*
>
> *Stay away from Maralya, you're not welcome here*

  The texts went on and on. Day and night they came, vitriol spilling from him like pus from an infected wound. I read them repeatedly, like picking at a scab, unable to leave them alone.
  I was suddenly aware that the room was silent. Barbaros, his brother Ali and his wife Ticen were looking expectantly at me as if waiting for an answer.

"Carrie," said Barbaros softly, inclining his head towards the plate in front of me.

"You need to eat something."

The table in front of me was laden with food. Salad, fresh bread, rice, stuffed vine leaves. Opposite me, five-year-old Damla and her two-year-old brother Yusuf stared at me with serious eyes. Damla's hair was neatly parted in the centre, her immaculate braids flat against her scalp. I felt a wave of guilt that I had never been able to get Elif's hair like that, sending her to school with an off-centre parting, crooked bunches sprouting fountain-like from the top of her head. Ticen caught my eye, the empathy in her eyes unbearable as I smiled weakly and dutifully nibbled at a piece of cucumber. Next to me, Barbaros smiled encouragingly.

For the first two days, I slept. Drifting in and out of consciousness like someone with a fever. Sometimes, when I opened my eyes, Barbaros was sitting on the edge of the bed, holding a glass of water from which I took a grateful sip before descending back into oblivion. At other times I was alone, re-reading Serkan's messages, or calling his phone again and again in the hope of speaking to my children. Listening to the endless ringing across the lines until Barbaros took my phone away.

At night I was awoken by my own sobs, from dreams I couldn't remember, Barbaros holding me tightly until my body became still and my tears silent.

The apartment was tiny. Ali and Ticen had selflessly moved the children into their bedroom to make space for us. At night, Barbaros and I lay pressed together in Damla's narrow single bed with its pink Disney princess sheets as cartoon rabbits and elephants stared down from the walls.

After the first two days, I opened my eyes, looking around the dimly lit bedroom as if seeing it for the first time. A shelf of cuddly toys. A night light in the shape of a star. Colourful posters with the letters of the alphabet, and the numbers one to ten.

The events of New Year came back to me one by one.

Serkan found out

He threatened me with a knife

I left Maralya with Barbaros

I felt strangely removed as I examined each piece of information, like a forensics officer at a crime scene, before moving on to the next. When I had finished, I pushed back the covers and sat on the edge of the bed as I waited for the light-headedness to pass. I forced myself to stand, my muscles stiff, my legs weak as I took slow, deliberate steps towards the door.

In the living room, Barbaros sat alone on the plush yellow sofa, a glass of *çay* on the glass coffee table in front of him. He jumped to his feet as I appeared at the doorway, taking my arm and guiding me to the sofa as if I were a car crash survivor. I remembered the first time we met. My office. The blonde with the ponytail. Margaret Crosby clinging to his arm as she lowered herself onto the couch. *"Thanks, dear."*

On the television, a good-looking young man was arguing with a pretty, dark-haired girl, his face streaked with tears as he declared his undying love. The girl was backed into a corner, her hands over her face. I flinched as I noticed the gun in his hand.

"I need my phone," I said.

"Carrie..." began Barbaros.

"Azra," I whispered as another wave of light-headedness threatened to engulf me. I closed my eyes.

"I need to talk to Azra."

There were no more messages from Serkan unless Barbaros had deleted them. Only Jackie, asking what had happened and what she could do. I had messaged her, asking her to take care of Alfie, leaving her a key under the broken flowerpot by the front door. There were a few messages from work and friends, all asking the same thing. Where was I? What happened? Was everything OK?

It made my head hurt to even think about the answers.

I found Azra's number and pressed call, listening as it rang and rang. I pictured her staring at her phone, deciding whether or not to answer. When she finally did, her voice was strange and distant.

"*Merhaba, canım.*"

"Azra?"

"Where are you?"

Barbaros caught my eye and shook his head.

"Are you still in Maralya?" she continued.

"No."

"Good," she replied. "You did the right thing by leaving. He's still looking for you, Carrie."

"I need to get Elif back," I said.

"Have you heard from Serkan?" said Azra, ignoring me.

"He's been sending me messages," I said. "Insults. Threats."

"Keep them," she said. "We can use them in court."

"I need to get Elif back," I repeated.

"Carrie, I have to go," Azra said with a sigh. "I'm due in court. I'll call you when there's a hearing date."

"Hearing date?"

"Against Serkan for breaching the custody order."

"How long will that take?" I said.

She hesitated. "I don't know. These things take time. A few weeks…"

"A few *weeks*?"

Suddenly, I had a pounding headache. "I need to get Elif back," I said again, my voice now pleading and desperate.

"I have to go," said Azra. "I'm due in court in ten minutes. I'll call you when I have an update."

I could tell from her voice that she was lying.

I stared at the television. The boy's face shone with sweat and tears as he pressed the gun to the trembling girl's temple. Unrequited love as justification for murder. A bruised ego soothed forever. I flinched as the police burst in through the front door. The boy stepped back and dropped his weapon, his hands in the air. The end credits began to roll.

The police. I saw them, sitting in the sun, smiling amused smiles as they examined Serkan's *kimlik*. "*We'll talk to him.*"

Barbaros reached for my hand.

"*Düşünme,*" he said softly. Don't think.

The tears were in my eyes before I could stop them, stinging my eyes and blurring the picture on the TV. I picked up my bag from the floor, rooting around for a tissue as my fingers closed around a crumpled piece of paper.

"Women's Protection Bureau," it said above an address and telephone number. I remembered the young police officer handing me the paper. The bags under his eyes.

"*This is the Women's Protection Bureau. Someone from there will contact you in the next few days.*"

Nobody had.

The phone was answered on the first ring.

"*Efendim,*" said a male voice.

"I need your help," I said in Turkish. "I need to get my daughter back."

A tentative hope glimmered inside me as he listened to my story, occasionally stopping me to ask for more details or confirm names and dates.

"And you have legal custody of your daughter?" he said when I had finished.

"Yes."

"Can you hold for a moment," said the man as tinny music came on the line.

A plan had already begun to form in my mind. Half-baked and falling apart around the edges, but a plan all the same. The Women's Protection Bureau would help me get Elif back. I would take her straight to the airport. Go to the UK. Get legal advice about Cem.

The man was back.

"Madam, as you have custody, you have the right to go and get your daughter. If your ex-husband refuses, you can open a court case against him for breaching the custody order."

I felt suddenly weak. Had he not been listening to anything I said?

"My ex-husband can be violent," I said, closing my eyes as the pounding in my head continued. "I need someone to come with me. I am afraid for my safety if I go alone."

"I'm sorry madam, we are unable to intervene in domestic affairs," the man continued. "But if your ex-husband becomes violent when you go to collect your daughter, call the police immediately."

"Thank you," I said quietly, ending the call as my last slither of hope disappeared like water down a drain.

***

After dinner, I helped Ticen clear the table, running the tap and rinsing the plates until she waved me away. I would have been glad of the distraction. Instead, I returned to the living room for another evening of staring blankly at the TV.

Barbaros and Ali were still at the table, a half-empty bowl of salad and a bottle of lemon cologne between them on the pristine white tablecloth. They stopped talking as soon as I entered.

"Let's go out!" said Barbaros, standing up.

"Where?"

"For a walk," he smiled. "I can show you the neighbourhood."

We walked hand in hand through the freezing streets. After days inside, Istanbul was a riot of noise, smells and colour. Cold air and traffic fumes assaulted my nostrils. Babbling conversations and angry car horns sliced through my brain. The warm, sweet smell of roast chestnuts from street vendors hung heavy in the air. Barbaros pushed open the door to a small café, the heat making my cheeks sting as we sat down at a small table in the corner.

"How are you, *aşkım*?" he said, reaching for my hands across the table and rubbing them vigorously against the cold.

The tears were never far away, ready to well up and slide down my face at any moment.

"I miss my kids," I said wretchedly.

"You have to be strong." Barbaros looked into my eyes. "It's going to be OK."

The other customers slid curious glances at me as the tears rolled down my face, forming little rivulets by the sides of my nose. I reached for a napkin from the dispenser on the table.

"*Her şey zaman,*" said Barbaros, massaging my hands in his. "Everything in time."

I nodded, dabbing my eyes with the napkin.

"Carrie..." he began, hesitating as he looked into my eyes. "Ticen and Ali love you." He looked down at the tablecloth. "But you know, it's hard, with the kids. And the flat is so small."

I felt a rush of shame as his words sank in. So consumed had I been with the events in my own life, I had failed to think of the effect our stay was having on our hosts. We had been staying for almost a week. It was time to leave.

I nodded. "I'll go back to Maralya," I said. "Maybe if I speak to Azra in person or go to the police..."

Barbaros stared at me. "You can't go back to Maralya," he said. "It's not safe."

"I have to..."

"No!" Barbaros gripped my hands tightly. "You've read his messages. He wants to hurt you, Carrie. He wants revenge. Trust me. I know how Turkish men think."

"Maybe Azra can..." I began.

"Azra!" spat Barbaros. "Azra doesn't care about you! Can't you see? She barely even talks to you. As for the police, they're his friends, Carrie. Who do you think they're going to protect? Him or you?"

I stared at him as it dawned on me that he was right. I was alone. A wave of panic hit me at the thought of being without Barbaros. I couldn't do this on my own.

"We'll find somewhere," said Barbaros softly, stroking my hands. "We can rent a place near Maralya while we wait for the court date."

"We?"

"Of course," he smiled. "I'm here, Carrie. I'm not going anywhere."

Relief flooded through me. "Where will we go?" I said.

"I don't know," he shrugged. "But I don't want to stay in Istanbul. It's not good for me here."

"OK." I gave a fragile smile. "Thank you, Barbaros."

***

The following day, we stood on the doorstep to say our goodbyes. I embraced Ticen and kissed her on both cheeks. Though we barely knew each other, I felt an immense debt of gratitude to this woman who had taken me, a stranger, into her home and made me feel so welcome. I had bought flowers and *lokum,* for her and Ali, toys, and sweets for the children. Ruffling his niece's and nephew's hair, Barbaros reached for my hand again as we stepped outside into the biting January air.

Chapter Thirty-Five

Kuşadası, Turkey. January 2016

The apartment would have been beautiful if the circumstances were different. Five minutes from the beach. Quaintly decorated in nautical blue and white. On the sun-filled balcony, a two-seater swing chair swayed gently in the breeze.

The landlady seemed anxious that we be happy there, showing us the appliances one by one, where the extra towels and blankets were kept, fluffing up the cushions and straightening the seashell pictures on the walls. Barbaros paid a month in cash, peeling notes from his wallet as she stood open-handed. In April, the price would skyrocket as tourists descended in their droves, but it didn't matter. It would be over by then.

We chose Kuşadası for no other reason than that it was a few hours' drive from Maralya. That, and the fact that nobody knew us there.

The messages from Serkan continued, burrowing beneath my skin like worms where they festered, eating away at me from the inside. Sometimes I called him, bracing myself for an onslaught of threats and verbal abuse, but there was no reply. I sent plaintive messages, extending the olive branch as I had done so many times before.

> *How are you?*
>
> *Can we talk?*
>
> *How are the children?*

But my messages went as unanswered as my calls.

Barbaros took control of everything from signing the rental contract to preparing the meals I pushed around my plate. I was happy to let him, relieved to hand over the reins and take a grateful backseat in my own life.

The long, empty days stretched into weeks as I waited for news. A tantalizing hope that never materialised. I stared at my phone for hours. Waiting for the call that never came. "*Düşünme*," Barbaros would say to me as I stared into space. Don't think.

Sometimes in the afternoons, we walked along the beach. Stray dogs, scabby and listless, our only companions as we strolled along the promenade, or sipped *çay* in the wintery sun.

In the evenings, we lay as we had in Maralya, my head on his chest, his erratic heartbeat in my ear as a romantic comedy played out its predictable storyline on the TV. I went to bed early, succumbing to the constant exhaustion that weighed down on me despite the endless, nothing-filled days. Barbaros stayed up late, climbing in beside me in the small hours, pulling me towards him as our bodies found each other in the dark.

It was a chilly morning in late January. I awoke early as I did every morning, carefully disentangling myself from Barbaros's arms as he rolled onto his back with a sigh. Taking my phone from the nightstand,

I opened the bedroom door and closed it silently behind me. A fresh cup of coffee in my hand, I slid open the glass doors to the balcony and settled onto the swing chair to check my messages. The familiar weight of disappointment settled over me as I skimmed through the usual threats and insults from Serkan. Far from a change of heart, his fury seemed to have gained momentum since I left Maralya.

> I warned you
>
> You lost your kids
>
> They don't have a mother anymore

I stopped scrolling as I spotted two new messages from an unfamiliar number. The profile picture was of a middle-aged blonde woman smiling into the camera from behind a large glass of red wine. Her lips were painted a bright orangy red.

> Hi Carrie, it's Julie. You looked after me when I was in hospital last summer. I know this isn't any of my business and I don't know what's happened between you and Serkan, but I think you should see this.

Julie Stevens. I remembered her cowering on a hospital trolley, her hands covering her face. Drinking coffee in the sun, a pristine white bandage wrapped around her head.

"You're Serkan's wife!"

The second message was a screenshot of Serkan's Facebook page. I clicked to enlarge it, staring in horror at the image that filled the screen.

Elif and Cem were holding hands as they stared straight into the camera with serious eyes. Below the photo, Serkan's words screamed in angry capitals.

WHAT KIND OF MOTHER LEAVES HER KIDS TO RUN AWAY WITH HER BOYFRIEND AND DOESN'T EVEN CALL?

I stared at the screen in disbelief as a wave of nausea churned my stomach. Elif and Cem stared back at me from the screen as my fingers reached out to touch their faces. *What must they be thinking?* I put my phone face-down on the swing chair and looked around as if seeing the apartment for the first time. The blue and white decor and pictures of seashells on the walls were suddenly as preposterous as the walks on the beach, the romantic comedies, the endless glasses of *çay*. The pseudo-marital bliss.

What was I doing?

I stood up, stopping in my tracks as I came face to face with Barbaros. He stared at me through the glass, his expression unreadable.

"How long have you...?" I stuttered as I slid open the glass door.

"It doesn't matter," he said. His voice was calm.

He glanced at the phone in my hand.

"Who have you been talking to?"

"No one."

"Azra?" he continued. "Mandy? Atakan?"

"No one," I said again. "I was checking to see if there was any news from Azra..."

He sighed. A heavy sigh of disappointment, like someone dealing with a petulant child.

"I'm just trying to protect you, Carrie," he said softly. "You're not in your right mind. You could say something by mistake, tell someone where we are, and the next thing your ex-husband is banging on the door!"

"I have to go to Maralya," I said suddenly, pushing past him. "I need to talk to Serkan."

I froze as he reached out and grabbed my arm, gripping it tightly. We stared at each other.

"Barbaros, let go of me, please," I said, trying to keep my voice calm. For a second I thought I saw a glimmer of anger in his eyes before his features softened into a smile.

"Carrie, it's me. I'm not going to hurt you." He let go of my arm, rubbing it gently before taking a step back.

"What happened?"

I showed him the messages from Julie.

"*Şerefsiz!*" swore Barbaros under his breath.

"I need to go back to Maralya," I said. "This has gone on long enough. I need to see my kids." I walked past him towards the bedroom.

"Carrie, he's still out there!" called Barbaros after me. "His friends are still out there! Maralya is his territory, not mine. I can't protect you there!"

"I'll be fine."

This whole thing is crazy, I told myself, grabbing my suitcase and throwing it onto the bed. Running away with a man I barely knew. Leaving my kids, my job, my entire life behind. I flung open the wardrobe doors, pulling clothes from hangers, emptying drawers, and grabbing handfuls of toiletries from the bathroom. A memory flashed into my mind. Maralya. New Year's Day. Throwing these same things into the same suitcase as I prepared to escape.

What had I been thinking?

When I had finished, I zipped my suitcase closed and pulled it to the front door.

On the couch, Barbaros was leaning forward, his elbows resting on his knees.

"Carrie, please sit down." His voice was calm.

"I'll go to the police," I said. "I'll make them do something. They have to DO something!" I glared at him. "You might be afraid of Serkan, but I'm not."

Barbaros opened his mouth as if about to say something before changing his mind. I felt a pang of guilt. He had been so good to me. He didn't deserve this.

"I'm sorry," I said softly, "I'm really sorry, Barbaros." I turned, reaching for my car keys from the hook on the wall.

They were not there.

"Sit down," he said.

Panic started to spread through my body as I rattled the door handle. It was locked. I spun around to face him.

"You can't stop me from leaving!"

Barbaros reached for a cigarette, placed it between his lips, and flicked the lighter several times until the tip glowed orange. He sat back on the couch and took a deep drag, surveying me through a cloud of smoke.

He patted the sofa next to him. "Sit."

"I told you!" I protested. "I told you I couldn't stay, it was only until..."

"Until *what*?" he snapped.

He glared at me, his eyes were black, glinting like gunmetal.

"Nothing has changed, Carrie. He is still out there! He still wants to hurt you! I am trying to protect you! Why won't you trust me?"

We stared at each other. The pain and desperation in his eyes mirrored in my own. Two virtual strangers trapped in a living nightmare. The world was suddenly too raw, too real, as the warm blanket of numbness was ripped away. Reality hit me like a tornado, knocking me off my feet and sucking the breath out of me. I ran to the bedroom and threw myself face down on the bed, pushing my face into the pillow as the sobs consumed me. It was a pain like nothing I had ever felt, as physical as it was emotional. A pain so strong that I thought I would die.

A long time later, when there were no more tears, I rolled onto my back and stared up at the white swirls of the ceiling as my children's faces filled my mind. There was a soft click as the door opened. Light flooded in from the living room, silhouetting Barbaros in the doorway.

"What do you want from me?" I whispered.

"Nothing."

He sat down on the bed, pressing his thumbs under my swollen eyes, pushing away my tears.

"I just want you."

"I need to see my kids," I said.

"I know."

He leaned forward and kissed my eyelids, his lips were cool against my skin.

"We'll get them back," he said. "Both of them. But we need to do it properly. We have to be patient." He smiled at me. His eyes were different now, a soft chestnut brown. "I'm not Serkan, Carrie. You have to trust me."

He lay down next to me, encircling me with his arms. I pressed into his neck, inhaling the scent of him.

"*Her şey zaman,*" he whispered, stroking my hair.

Everything in time.

Chapter Thirty-Six

Kuşadası, Turkey. February 2016

Something strange was happening to me.

Like the proverbial frog in the cooking pot or the first sting of sunburn on a summer's day, by the time I realised, it was already too late.

As always, I awoke early. Our limbs intertwined under the thick duvet patterned with blue and white swirls.

Maybe it was the chill in the air, the prospect of another nothing-filled day, or the warmth of his body against mine, but that morning, something was different. The urge to pull away, to remove myself from his embrace and while away an hour or two on the swing chair was gone. For the first time, I stayed exactly where I was.

Sunlight filtered in through the blinds, the wooden slats casting stripes of light and dark across his skin. I moved my eyes across the flatness of his stomach, the curve of his chest rising and falling as he breathed. I took in the lines and shadows of his face. The crease between his eyebrows. The trace of a scar above his lip. The flicker of his lashes as he dreamed.

Almost involuntarily, I reached out and touched his face with my fingertips. The spell was broken. Barbaros stirred, murmuring something indecipherable as he pulled me towards him. I closed my eyes and inhaled his scent.

I wanted to lie like that forever.

***

"Carrie?" Barbaros was watching me across the breakfast table, a half-smile playing on his lips.

I was miles away. I looked down at my plate as I felt the heat rise in my cheeks.

"Shall I make some more *çay?*"

"Sure." I smiled shyly as, for a fraction of a second, our eyes met. I immediately looked away, but it was too late. He knew. The world had tilted ever so slightly on its axis. And everything was different now.

Barbaros stood up and began to collect the plates, taking them into the kitchen where I heard him scraping the uneaten food from mine into the bin. I picked up my phone from the table. Since the argument, it had sat between us like a referee. I tried not to look at it so much, and Barbaros tried to ignore it when I did.

There was another message from Julie. Another picture of the children. More accusations in block capitals screamed from the page.

I didn't notice Barbaros, having returned from the kitchen, looking over my shoulder.

"Düşünme," he said. "Why are you still reading this stuff, Carrie?"

"But other people are reading it and believing it."

He sat down opposite me, frowning as he poured us each another glass of *çay.*

"Can you guess his password?" he said suddenly.

The word lit up my brain like a lightbulb.

"I know his password!" I said. "I created the account for him!"

It was so brilliant and so obvious, I cursed myself for not having thought of it before.

Holding my breath, I logged into Facebook and typed in Serkan's email address and password. Immediately, his homepage filled the screen.

As I scrolled through Serkan's posts, the horrible truth was revealed. More pictures of the children. Lengthy rants in capital letters with no punctuation. An incoherent mixture of English and Turkish, much of it making no sense as Serkan vented his spleen for all the world to see. I turned my attention to the comments. Some were from people I knew, others from those who'd never met me. All were equally condemning in their judgement.

So sorry for you mate. You are a great father. At least they have you

Wow, I can't believe she would do that! I guess you never really know someone!

Sending hugs to you and the children. She doesn't deserve to be a mother. Selfish bitch.

I blinked back tears. A part of me wanted to respond. To tell my side of the story. To let them know what had really happened, but the last thing I needed was to get into a slanging match on social media. To turn my life into a circus for the entertainment of others. Instead, I swallowed the hard lump that had lodged itself in the back of my throat and deleted the posts one by one.

I meant to leave it there, like a ghost in the night. Log out and leave my ex-husband wondering where his posts had gone. Instead, I found myself turning to his private messages. Serkan, it appeared, never deleted anything, and some of the messages went back years.

The profile picture of a young blonde woman I didn't recognise caught my eye.

I clicked on the message.

> Can't wait to see you

> Not long now

> I miss you so much

> Me too, baby

I glanced at the date of the messages. Mid-November. Four years earlier. Apparently, Serkan's winter trips to the UK had been more pleasure than business. As I continued to read, it soon became clear that as well as a series of lovers to keep him warm through the cold British winters, Serkan had a steady supply of female visitors throughout the summer months. Some of the messages dated back to our first summer in Maralya. A time when I thought we were happy.

I thought back to all the nights that he had not come home. Sitting alone after the children had gone to bed. Staring at the TV. Missing him.

"What is it, *aşkım?*" said Barbaros, seeing the sadness in my eyes. I passed him my phone.

He cursed under his breath as he scrolled through the messages. "He didn't deserve you, *canım,*" he said, reaching for my hand across the table and giving it a reassuring squeeze. Suddenly, he stopped and frowned at the screen.

"Carrie, have you seen this?"

He turned my phone around to face me.

The message was in Turkish. There was a photo of me, my *kimlik* number and the registration number of my car. In the message, Serkan was asking someone to look for me. And they had agreed.

"Serkan has friends in the police," I said as my stomach sank through the floor. "He's asking them to look for me."

Barbaros nodded. His expression was serious.

"You need to sell your car," he said. "Today."

***

The red-faced salesman followed as we paced the shiny rows of waxed and polished cars. Far enough to give us space, but close enough to voice his approval if I stopped to run my hands over the smooth paintwork of a Renault Clio or open the doors of a Toyota Yaris to peer inside.

I reached the last car in the last row. It was more of a minivan than a car. White, with tinted black windows that gleamed in the sun. The smell of vinyl and beeswax invaded my nostrils as I climbed up into the driver's seat.

"We could have adventures in a car like this!" said Barbaros, climbing into the passenger seat beside me. He grinned and stretched out his arm. "Fethiye. Antalya. Kaş. Kalkan..." he winked. "Bodrum!"

His childlike enthusiasm was infectious, and I found myself smiling for what felt like the first time in months.

A quick trip to the bank and a few signatures later, and the car was mine.

"Congratulations!" said Barbaros, holding the keys towards me. "Let's go for a drive to celebrate!"

I stared at the keys. "I can't," I said immediately.

Since we left Maralya, Barbaros always drove. It wasn't something we discussed or decided. It was just what happened.

"Of course you can," Barbaros smiled. "It's your car, Carrie. Take it for a ride!"

The keys glinted in the sunlight, hanging between us like a dare.

I took them tentatively and climbed back into the driver's seat, pulling the seatbelt across my body and clicking it into place as Barbaros climbed in beside me. I closed my eyes and took a deep breath.

"Carrie," said Barbaros. "Are you ok?"

I nodded as I inserted the key in the ignition. My heart began to race as the engine purred into life.

This is ridiculous, I told myself. You can drive. You've been driving for years.

The gearstick slipped under my sweaty palm as I tried to arrange my feet over the pedals. I couldn't remember which was which. The car juddered and stalled. Suddenly, the world turned black. My throat began to close as I gasped for air. My chest was being squeezed from the inside. I unclipped the seatbelt, opened the door, and ran.

The world blurred like a kaleidoscope as distorted sounds drifted in and out. The whizz of passing traffic. The wail of a distant minaret. The indignant blare of a car horn. I kept running, twisting my ankle as I stumbled and tripped. I got back up, brushing the gravel from my knees as behind me, a lorry thundered past. I tried to scream as someone grabbed me from behind.

"It's OK," he whispered. "I'm here."

Barbaros.

He wrapped me in his arms as I sank into him, into the strength of him as he held me up.

***

We drove in silence. Barbaros's fingers entwined with mine as I stared out of the window and wondered what was happening to me.

"Where are we going?" I said after an hour had passed.

"You'll see," he replied with a smile.

I must have fallen asleep because when I awoke, we were on a winding road sloping down towards a glimmering blue sea.

Barbaros turned to me. "Welcome to Bodrum, baby!" He said, "My favourite place in the whole world."

We spent the morning exploring the fifteenth-century castle, holding hands as we gazed out across the turquoise Aegean. We had lunch in the harbour, where wooden *gülets,* tethered by frayed ropes, rocked gently back and forth in the blue-green sea. We wandered through narrow cobbled streets; white sugar-cube houses draped in cascading bougainvillaea, their wooden doors and window frames painted bright cobalt blue.

For a moment, I was able to forget. To feel like any normal couple enjoying a day out. To stop thinking.

The sun was low in the sky as we headed back along the coast road, curving around the Bodrum peninsula through towns and villages nestled into hillsides that sloped down towards the sea. A flicker of something like happiness fluttered in my chest. Fragile green shoots pushing towards the sun through a frozen earth.

My eyes were closing, my head resting against the windowpane, when Barbaros pulled off the road and parked in front of the faded red awnings of a roadside mini-market. A painfully thin dog lay sprawled next to the doorway, deflated nipples drooping from her concave belly. I wondered where her puppies were.

Barbaros disappeared inside the market, returning a few minutes later with a plastic bag which he placed on the floor next to my feet. We continued past fields bathed in a dusky pink light. Rows of olive trees. Whitewashed houses and trailing grapevines. He parked in front of a row of spindly palms, silhouetted black against a burnt orange sky.

"*Gel, aşkım*," he smiled.

The beach was deserted. A few empty cafes, closed for the winter. A discarded rubber ring. A skinny cat emerged from a dumpster before darting away.

Barbaros took my hand and led me towards the shore. The tide rushed up to greet us before pulling playfully back.

"Where are we?" I said, staring out across the sea at the silhouetted shape of an island straight ahead.

"Gümüşlük," said Barbaros. "My favourite beach."

We sat down on the sand. From the plastic bag, Barbaros produced a bottle of red wine, a corkscrew, and two plastic cups. He twisted the corkscrew, extracting the cork with a satisfying plop before pouring out the burgundy liquid.

"This is Rabbit Island," he said, following my gaze towards the craggy shape on the horizon. "We can walk there in the summer."

"Walk there?"

"Yes, on the city walls," he continued. "Myndos," he explained pointing downwards. "The ancient city beneath the sea." He turned to me and smiled, a light I hadn't seen before danced in his eyes. "This place is magical, Carrie. I used to come here for holidays as a child. To stay with my *Babanne*. It was the only time I got a break from my father's beatings."

His expression darkened as the familiar sadness returned. "It's over," I said, reaching for his hand. "He can't hurt you anymore." For a moment, I wasn't sure if I was talking about him or me.

We sat in silence as we drank our wine, lost in thought as we gazed at the pink-streaked sky. A thousand flamingos in flight. At that moment, I forgot about everything. The panic attack. The court date. The constant ache that lived in my heart. All that mattered was that moment. And at that moment, I was exactly where I wanted to be.

"Carrie, we need to move," said Barbaros eventually. "The lease is almost up on the flat. The new car is registered to that address. Serkan's police friend will find us in days."

I nodded.

"We can find somewhere else," I said. "Until it's safe to go back to Maralya."

Barbaros turned to face me. A mixture of sympathy and trepidation in his eyes, like a doctor looking at a cancer patient before giving them the bad news.

"Carrie, we can't go back to Maralya."

I looked down at the ground. An ant struggling with a leaf three times its size pushed heroically through the sand.

"Serkan will never accept you with another man," he continued. "If it hadn't been me, it would have been someone else. He will be watching your every move. Not just him. His friends and family. The whole of Maralya. He is destroying your reputation. Posting lies about you on social media. How are you going to go back there with people gossiping about you behind your back?"

It was then that I realised what I had known all along. The reason I had been so afraid to leave Serkan. The reason I had lain awake at night, trying to think of another way. The reason I had stayed for so long.

I remembered the Halloween party. A different version of myself. Naïve. Trusting. Clinging to Azra's words like a life vest in a stormy sea.

"Don't worry. You have a great lawyer."

Azra was right. There were laws in place. But there were other laws too. Unwritten laws. And I had broken every one of them.

"Stay here," whispered Barbaros. "With me."

His eyes were fixed on mine, searching for an answer.

Despite my best intentions, I was losing the fight.

"Bodrum!" cried Barbaros suddenly, raising his plastic cup towards the orange sea, like molten lava under the dying rays of the sun. "I've always dreamed of living here."

"So, let's live here," I said.

"What?" he spun around to face me.

I smiled at him.

"Let's move to Bodrum."

"Together?"

"Together."

He laughed out loud, throwing his arms around me, and pulling me towards him.

"You're crazy!" he laughed. "I love you!"

"I love you too," I whispered, realising as I said the words that they were true.

He pulled back. The smile was gone, his expression so serious that I had to look away.

For a long time, we didn't say anything. We watched in silence as the sun slipped below the horizon, stripes of yellow, pink, and deep purple mourning in its wake. A chill breeze fluttered over my shoulders. I hugged my knees closer to my chest and took another sip of wine.

"I love you, Carrie," he said.

I turned towards him, opening my mouth to speak.

"Shhh," he whispered. "Don't say anything."

Barbaros leaned towards me, pressing his lips to mine. He tasted of vanilla and salt and wine.

I felt suddenly anchorless, as if the ground had disappeared beneath me or I was falling through the sky. A place without walls or floors. Without beginning or end.

Falling.

Like Alice in Wonderland. Down the rabbit hole.

Chapter Thirty-Seven

Bodrum, Turkey. February 2016.

The car swung around a sharp bend in the mountain road, jutting out over a vast expanse of sea.

"Kos!" cried Barbaros, thrusting his arm towards the island that rose majestically from the water. The Greek island was so close I could make out the white buildings around its base and even the occasional car. I imagined the people that lived there. An unfamiliar language babbling in the air. A different country. A different continent.

The pretty village of Akyarlar sits at the southernmost tip of the Bodrum peninsula, directly opposite the Greek island of Kos. It was this tantalising proximity of European soil that lured Syrian refugees in their droves. They lined the sides of the road in makeshift camps, their children, grubby-faced and barefoot, their worldly possessions in plastic bags. I felt a pang of pity for them as we passed, wondering what lives they had left behind.

"Here it is." Barbaros pulled up in front of a small mini market where an overweight, red-faced man sat squeezed into a white plastic chair. The man took a swig from a bottle of Coca-Cola, watching as we parked the car before carefully extracting himself and extending his hand towards Barbaros.

"Süleyman," he barked, grasping Barbaros's hand in both of his and ignoring me completely.

Süleyman *Bey* informed us self-importantly that he owned the mini market and the six apartments above it as well as a seven-bedroom villa in the upmarket nearby village of Yalıkavak. He continued to brag about his empire to Barbaros as he wheezed up the four flights of concrete steps. Not once did he acknowledge my presence, though whether this was due to my gender or my nationality, I wasn't sure.

We reached a flat on the top floor and Süleyman *Bey* produced a large bunch of keys from his pocket, studying them slowly in turn as he searched for the right one.

"*Merhabalar!*" came a high-pitched voice behind us. A woman in a flowered headscarf stood in the doorway to the apartment across the landing, smiling broadly.

"*Merhaba.*" I smiled back.

The woman walked towards us, extending her hand. "*Fatma, ben,*" she beamed, as she squeezed each of our hands warmly.

Süleyman *Bey* opened the door to the apartment as Fatma launched into a stream of questions. Were we moving in? Where were we from? Were we married? Any children?

Barbaros sidestepped the questions as neatly as he could as Süleyman *Bey* tapped his foot impatiently.

"Well, I mustn't keep you," gabbled Fatma in Turkish, her bright smile never leaving her face. "It's just me and mother now. She's very old, but we do our best."

As if on cue, a softly creased face like an un-ironed pillow peered around the door.

"*Kim var, Fatma?*" croaked the elderly woman. "Who's there?"

"*Kimse yok, anneciğim!*" said Fatma, taking her mother's arm and gently steering her back inside.

"*Memnun oldum!*" she said, flashing us another smile. "Nice to meet you."

The flat was tiny, much smaller than it had seemed in the photos. Süleyman *Bey* collapsed on the sofa, gasping for breath as Barbaros and I showed ourselves around.

The flat consisted of an open-plan living room/ kitchen, two small bedrooms and a tiny bathroom. I stopped at the doorway of the second bedroom, devoid of furniture except for a single bed pushed against a pale pink wall. I imagined shelves crammed with books and toys. Brightly coloured posters on the walls. A My Little Pony duvet on the bed.

Elif's room.

Leaving Barbaros to negotiate with Süleyman *Bey*, I slid open the glass doors and stepped outside onto the surprisingly spacious balcony. Pressed against the wall was a battered leather sofa, weather-beaten by years of sun and rain. In the corner, a small glass-topped table and two chairs. I looked out past the long, narrow garden. A white mosque sat at the top of a hill, its blue minaret pointing skywards. At the foot of the hill, a shepherd leaned forward on his cane as he rested on a tree stump. A scruffy white dog sat by his side. Around him, his sheep grazed peacefully, the bells around their necks tinkling as they walked, their collars adorned with shiny blue *Nazar* that glinted in the late afternoon sun.

Barbaros's hands snaked around my waist as he planted a kiss on my cheek. There was a cough of disapproval behind us.

"What do you think?" he whispered into my ear. "It's small, but it's enough for us. And there's a room for Elif."

Süleyman *Bey* was waiting. The rental contract was spread out in front of him on the table, the pen in his hand tapping impatiently against the wood.

"It's fine." I smiled.

After signing the contract and handing over a month's rent, Barbaros took the keys and shook our new landlord warmly by the hand. With Süleyman *bey* gone, he closed the door and turned to me.

"Welcome home, baby," he smiled.

***

We had been in Bodrum for about a week. A cold morning with a bright winter sun that failed to produce any heat. Barbaros and I sat on the balcony, plates of cucumber, tomatoes, cheese and olives between us on the table. In the distance, the sheep's bells tinkled as they grazed on the hill. My breakfast stared back at me, the hard-boiled eggs as unappetising as rubber, the bread might as well have been made of cardboard. I could feel Barbaros's eyes on me as I cut the food up into smaller and smaller pieces and moved it around my plate.

"Not hungry?" he smiled.

I shook my head. Tears stung my eyes as I gave up and put my knife and fork down.

"Maybe later," he said, reaching across the table for my hand. "Shall I make you another coffee?"

The morning's tranquillity was shattered as my phone buzzed into life. I felt Barbaros's hand tighten around mine as we both stared at the face on the screen.

"Carrie..."

I snatched my phone from the table and pressed it to my ear.

"Serkan?"

There was a lengthy silence. Then Elif's voice.

"Mummy?"

She sounded so young.

"Elif?" I stuttered. "Sweetie? Is that you?"

Another excruciating silence.

"Elif?" I said again. "It's Mummy. How are you?"

A frantic whispering began on the other end of the line. Serkan's voice.

"Tell her," he urged. "Like I told you. Talk to your mother."

When she finally spoke, there was no trace of the little girl I had left behind. Only the forced, robotic mantra of something that had been practised many times.

"I'm fine," she said. "You don't need to come back. I live with Baba now."

My stomach dropped to the floor.

"Elif?"

The line went dead.

I sat in stunned silence as the terrible truth sank in.

The weeks in limbo. The endless waiting had all been for nothing. Serkan had already won.

It was a long time before I could speak. I stared out at the sheep on the hill grazing peacefully beneath the cold, white sky.

"Elif..." I said eventually, her name catching in my throat. "She doesn't.... she doesn't want me."

"You're her mother," said Barbaros softly. "Of course she wants you. It's him. He's telling her to say those things."

"He's poisoning her against me," I said, staring into space as the reality sank in. "Just like he did with..."

I grabbed my phone and scrolled down, searching for Azra's number. Since Istanbul, I had called her multiple times. At first, she would answer, her voice distracted and vague, always on her way to court or late for a meeting. "Don't worry, *canım*," she would say. "I'll call you as soon as there is any news." Lately, her phone had been going straight to voicemail.

I listened to the ringing across the miles until the familiar automated voice came on the line. *"The person you are calling is not available."*

"Forget about her, Carrie," said Barbaros, frowning as he typed a number and lifted his phone to his ear.

"Who are you calling?" I said.

"Who I should have called a long time ago," he replied. "Maralya family court."

I stared at my now cold coffee, listening to the tinny elevator music playing in the background as Barbaros was transferred between various departments. After what seemed like an age, he spoke, saying my name and *kimlik* number once before spelling them out a second time.

"*Teşekür ederim,*" he said eventually, ending the call with a heavy sigh. I looked up slowly, afraid to meet his gaze. The look in his eyes told me all I needed to know.

"The court has no record of you," he said. "Azra never opened a case."

Her face filled my mind. Wild black curls. Mischievous grin. I remembered breakfasts in her office, dinners on the seafront, beach days with the children. Summer nights sitting by her swimming pool, talking long into the night.

"There must be some mistake," I said.

Barbaros sighed again.

"*Canım*, there's no mistake. They checked twice."

I stood up, looking around for my bag.

"We'll get another lawyer," said Barbaros. "We should have done it ages ago. We should never have trusted her."

I wasn't listening. Elif's robotic mantra played on repeat in my head. *"I live with Baba now."*

"I need to see Azra," I said, making my way to the front door, where I pulled on my boots, and grabbed my coat. "I need to find out what the hell's going on." My hands were shaking as I reached for my car keys.

"Carrie," said Barbaros behind me. His fingers closed around my arm.

Anger surged through me as I spun around to face him. I glared at him; my car keys clutched tightly in my hand.

"No!" I said. "You can't stop me, Barbaros. Not this time!"

Neither of us moved. Our eyes locked as he contemplated his next move. Was he going to stop me from leaving like he had in Kuşadası? Lock the door and take away my keys? Hold me prisoner?

"But how will you get there?" he said softly.

"I'll drive."

"And if you have another panic attack?"

"I'll be fine," I said, reaching for the door handle.

Barbaros's grip tightened on my arm. I tried to pull away as he spun me around to face him.

"Let go of me!" I shouted. "You can't stop me from leaving, Barbaros!"

"I'm not going to stop you, Carrie," he smiled.

"I'm coming with you."

Chapter Thirty-Eight

Maralya, Turkey. February 2016.

It was the kind of cold that seeps into your bones; the sky, a thick blanket of white. Through the windowpane, our New Year's Day escape from Maralya played out in reverse as we made our way back along the coast road.

The journey was painfully slow, yet the winding road, sea views and silence turned to gridlock and blaring car horns before I was ready.

It was market day. The chaos of Maralya amplified ten-fold, as traffic, shoppers, and stallholders competed for space. Motorists and pedestrians weaved perilously between stalls piled high with aubergines and potatoes. A woman pushed a stroller into the road, stepping back in the nick of time as a motorbike sped past, a family of four piled onto the back. A shared taxi or *dolmuş* edged through the crowd, its horn blaring. A blue Nazar swung above the driver's head. The words *Allah Korusun* blazed in white across the windscreen. May God protect you.

The swimming pool was empty now, except for a few inches of stagnant water and a sludge of dead leaves. From the upstairs balcony, the pale retriever watched sooty-eyed as we crossed the manicured lawn to the shiny front door.

My finger hovered over the buzzer to Azra's office, her name in printed italics next to it.

Azra Yildiz

Avukat/Attorney at Law

HUKUK BÜROSU

Barbaros placed his palm over the intercom and shook his head. "If she sees it's us, she won't open the door," he said as he pressed the buzzer of one of the upstairs apartments.

"*Alo?*" echoed a male voice.

"*Posta.*" Barbaros winked at me as the door clicked open.

Outside Azra's office, I took a deep breath and pressed the bell, unleashing a stream of synthetic birdsong. Barbaros and I stood out of sight of the peephole, listening to the tapping of stilettos getting closer on the tiled floor. A jangling of keys and a series of clicks as the door was unlocked from the inside.

"Carrie!" Azra's forced smile did not reach her eyes. I remembered the last time I had seen her. At the police station after Serkan slashed my tyres. Her cheery grin as she greeted the police officer like an old friend. She appeared to have lost weight. Her skin was pale. Her wild curls tamed into a severe bun.

"Hi Azra," I said.

"*Canım*! It's so good to see you! I have a client arriving any minute, but if you come back in an hour." She took a step back as she began to push the door closed.

"This won't take long." Barbaros pushed past her, striding into her office and sitting on one of the plush armchairs as if it belonged to him.

Legs wide apart, elbows resting on his knees, hands clasped together. His eyes were black as he fixed Azra with his hawk-like gaze.

I had never seen this side of him before.

I perched on the other armchair as Azra took refuge behind her mahogany desk.

"How are you, Carrie?" she smiled nervously at me. "I've been worried about you."

"Why didn't you open a case?" I said, ignoring her.

Azra sat down heavily on her swivel chair. She didn't look at me, running her hands over a few things on her desk, before taking a pair of glasses from a case and putting them on. I noticed that her hands were shaking.

"You didn't receive the court date?" she said, pushing her glasses up the bridge of her nose.

I glared at her. "Azra, we called the family court! We know you didn't open a case!"

Azra stared down at her mahogany desk. The desk where we had shared so many breakfasts, now a barrier between us. She removed her glasses and rubbed her eyes.

"I thought we were friends, "I continued. "How could you do this to me, Azra?"

Azra leaned forward on her desk and held her head in her hands. For a long time, nobody spoke. Somewhere, a dog barked. A snatched conversation from another apartment. Footsteps above us. When she looked up, I was surprised to see her eyes were glistening with tears.

"He threatened me," she said quietly.

"What?"

"Serkan," she continued. "He came to the courthouse with a group of men. There must have been at least ten of them. He was yelling, saying he blamed me for breaking up his family and that he was going to do the same to my family. He said he would make me pay no matter how long it took. They had to be removed by security."

She stared out of the window at the white blanket of sky.

"I filed a complaint," she continued. "Got a restraining order, but he didn't listen. He started showing up at my house. One night I heard a motorbike outside. It was three in the morning, and he was just standing there in the garden. Watching me."

"Why didn't you tell me?" I said.

"He told me to have no contact with you. That if you knew I hadn't opened a case, you would find another lawyer and he would know. The longer it took for you to open a case, the harder it would be for you to win."

"And the more time he had to poison Elif against me," I said.

"I'm so sorry *canım*," she said again. "I feel terrible. But I have kids, you know..."

I sank into the overstuffed armchair as exhaustion flooded my veins. I wanted to go home, crawl into bed, and sleep forever.

We walked together to the door. I turned to Azra. My wild friend. Glass of wine in one hand, cigarette in the other. My brave friend who refused to play by the rules of this patriarchal society. I knew it would be the last time we would ever see each other.

"I'm sorry too," I said, putting my arms around her. "For everything."

When we pulled apart, there were tears in her eyes.

"You know, it may not be possible for you to get Elif from Serkan's house," she said. A smile played around her lips. A glimpse of the old Azra. Clever. Mischievous. Unafraid.

"But if she were by herself, in the street, for example. Or at school..."

She smiled. This time it was genuine.

"There is nothing to stop you from taking her."

"What time does Elif finish school?" Barbaros looked at his watch.

"Half past two. What time is it now?"

"Five past." He grabbed my hand. "Let's go."

Chapter Thirty-Nine

Maralya, Turkey. February 2016.

"Put this on."

Barbaros reached into the back seat for his black hoodie and threw it towards me. I pulled it on, my head colliding with the window as the car veered sharply left. It was enormous. The hood almost covered my eyes. The sleeves drooped several inches from the ends of my arms.

"We have a window of opportunity," said Barbaros, zigzagging in and out of traffic with millimetres to spare.

"If it's not safe today, we won't take her. We'll stay in a hotel and come back tomorrow. We can't fail. If we do, he will know what we are planning, and he won't let her out of his sight." He slammed on the brakes as a car pulled out straight in front of us, my seatbelt locking with a snap as I was thrown forward. I glanced at the driver, keeping the hoodie pulled low over my face. He didn't look familiar.

The market was still in gridlock. Frustration gnawed my stomach as we inched forward. Headscarved women meandered between the stalls, pulling wheeled shopping trolleys, rifling through piles of clothes, and selecting the ripest fruits with expert hands. Babies stared glassy-eyed from their buggies; blanketed against the cold. Vendors touted their wares in repetitive patter."*Bir lira! Bir lira, Bir lira!*"

As we reached the other side, Barbaros pressed his foot to the floor, accelerating through the once-familiar streets. Restaurants I used to eat in, parks, where I had taken the children and my old local supermarket, sped by. Eventually, the buildings, traffic, and roundabouts thinned out and we were surrounded by the fields and tree-lined streets of Kirazlı. Immediately, I was back in my old life. The journey to school. Bruno Mars on the radio. Cem in his booster seat, swaying from side to side.

We turned left at the mosque, past the muddy field with its solitary cow. We reached the crossroads and stopped.

Barbaros pulled into the curb and turned off the ignition. He lit a cigarette and reached for my hand.

In the centre of the school playground stood a circle of women in headscarves and long coats, jiggling from foot to foot and rubbing their hands against the cold. My attention was diverted as the main doors to the single school building were pushed open and a few of the smaller children began to emerge. A little boy of about Cem's age made his way towards the circle of women. I watched as his mother's face brightened in a smile as she crouched down to admire the brightly coloured painting he clutched in his hand. A pang of longing hit me as he wrapped his arms around his mother's neck, stretching on tiptoes to place a kiss on her cheek.

More children began to stream from the open doors. The smaller ones, looking lost in uniforms too big, pulled school bags on wheels and scanned the playground for their mothers. The older ones weighed down with bags and art projects, lolloped awkwardly towards the school gate.

It was her bright pink coat I saw first. Her hair was in bunches, her coat hanging open. I remembered it had a zip that used to stick, making us late for school. I had been meaning to buy her a new one.

She was standing with her back to us, slightly apart from a group of older girls, watching as the skipping rope between them turned in wide circles. The girl in the middle's high ponytail swung as she jumped.

"It's Elif!" I said. "She's over there!"

"Where?"

I pointed. "Right there! In the pink coat."

"Are you sure?"

I nodded. My mouth was dry. My words had disappeared.

"Are you ready?" Barbaros turned to me. I felt his hand tighten around mine.

I glanced at the clock on the dashboard. Two thirty-five. Serkan was late, I thought, before remembering he needed to pick up Cem from his new school in Maralya before making the ten-minute drive to Kirazlı. I prayed that this would buy us some time.

Barbaros started the ignition and swung the car around, slowing to a stop in front of the school gates.

He leaned forward and scanned up and down the street.

"Go!" he said. "Now!"

The cold air hit my skin as I stepped out onto the pavement. Laughter and giddy end-of-school excitement assaulted my ears as I made my way towards the chain-link fence. I pushed my fingers through the cold metal and held on.

"Elif!"

Her head whipped around at the sound of my voice, but she did not see me. "Elif!" I called again, my voice drowned out by the rhythmic whir and slap of the skipping rope as it hit the tarmac. The chanting of girl's voices.

"*Bir, iki, üç…*"

"Elif!" I called again, louder this time. I pushed the hoodie back an inch from my eyes.

She turned around again and froze.

"Mummy?"

I smiled. "It's me, sweetheart!"

Her eyes darted around the playground.

"Baba told me not to go with you."

"Elif, please, I just want to talk. I miss you."

I turned back to the car. Inside, Barbaros was signalling for me to hurry up.

"Can I give you a hug?" I said.

I could see her thinking it over. Weighing up the consequences one at a time. The air was suddenly too heavy, the playground noise too loud. I was painfully aware of the passing of time, valuable seconds slipping away before Serkan arrived.

My hands were numb, the skin, a blueish white where I had been clinging to the fence. I let go and took a step back, scanning the playground as I walked towards the open gate.

The circle of women were still engrossed in their conversation, their heads moving as they nodded and laughed. The little boy was bored now, pulling at his mother's coat, his painting still clutched in his hand.

The skipping rope continued to turn circles in the air, but the chanting had stopped. One of the girls was staring straight at me, her hair parted neatly into two long braids, a mixture of curiosity and suspicion in her eyes.

I took another step forward.

"Please, Elif."

She took a tentative step towards me. Then another. Silently, I willed her to keep walking. She reached the school gate and stopped, her father's words holding her back like an invisible leash.

Glancing around the playground, I took the last few steps through the gate. I crouched down to face her. Confusion, fear, and mistrust stared back at me as I took her hands in mine and rubbed them against the cold. I tried to fasten her coat, but the zip stuck.

"I'm so sorry, Elif," I said as tears sprang to my eyes.

Her small body was stiff, resistant as I put my arms around her, but she did not pull away. I closed my eyes and breathed in the smell of her. Strawberry shampoo and washing powder. For a moment, the cold and noise around us disappeared, and it was only us.

"I'm sorry," I whispered into her hair. "I missed you so much."

She seemed to give up then, her body yielding as she sank into me. Her voice in my ear was little more than a whisper, but it was all I needed to hear.

"I missed you too."

I pulled back to look at her, unable to stop the hot tears that slid down my cheeks, stinging my skin in the cold air. Slowly, the playground shifted back into focus. A rush of noise, sing-song voices, shouts, and laughter. There was another sound. Insistent. Intrusive. Impatient. I spun around to see Barbaros pressing down on the car horn as he motioned frantically towards the playground.

The girl with braids was pointing towards me, the skipping rope lifeless and forgotten on the ground. The circle of women, silent and staring. A teacher, grim-faced, strode across the playground towards us.

She was in my arms. I stood, gripping her tightly as I staggered back towards the car. We fell together into the backseat. I managed to slide the door shut as the car sped away.

"Baba's going to kill me!" Elif burst into tears.

"Shhh." I pulled her towards me, stroking her hair as I enveloped her in my arms. "He can't do anything to you."

We clung together as through the window, the village passed in a blur. Ramshackle houses, wood smoke curling from their chimneys. Orchards of orange trees. A barking dog straining at the end of a chain. As we reached the end of the village and pulled out onto the motorway, my phone buzzed angrily from my bag. I knew who it was before I saw it, but fear still flooded through me as Serkan's face stared from the screen.

Holding my daughter tightly, I put my phone on silent and dropped it back into my bag. I turned to look through the rear windscreen. Hazy sunlight was trying to push through the blanket of white clouds, haloing snow-capped mountains against an eggshell sky.

There was no one behind us.

Chapter Forty

Venice, Italy. June 2016.

I knew the time without having to check. It was the same time. The loneliest hour before the dawn. Still and silent, it pulled me from sleep to join it in its solitude every night without fail.

I rolled onto my back and opened my eyes. A ceiling of thin blue fabric stretched taut above me. Through the diamond of fine mesh, I could see branches, green leaves, and a small, grey patch of sky.

It wasn't long before they started.

What kind of mother leaves her son?

You've made a huge mistake.

What are you going to do now?

The familiar, tight ball of worry contracted in the pit of my stomach as a grim future presented itself; Elif and I. A dismal flat in a strange city. The insurmountable task of starting all over again.

Elif stirred slightly as I unzipped my sleeping bag, turning onto her side with a murmur and a sigh. I unzipped the tent entrance as quietly as I could, and stepped outside, barefoot on the damp grass.

Around me, the tents and caravans of our neighbours stood in eerie silence. At this time of the morning, after the cicadas had ceased singing and before the birds had begun, it was as if I were the only person awake in the whole world.

I pushed my feet into my flip-flops and made my way to the water's edge. Through the early morning mist, faint lights glimmered in the distance.

Venice.

Four days earlier we had arrived, hot and tired after the long drive from Florence, to catch the ferry from Fusina to Venice. The campsite had been an unexpected surprise. Elif and I had by now well and truly caught the camping bug and immediately decided to spend a night or two here on our return.

From the ferry, we had watched as the famous domes and spires of Venice shifted into focus. The calm, empty waters were replaced by buzzing water taxis, competing for river space with slipper-shaped gondolas. The air was rich with Italian as people shouted back and forth.

"Wow! Venice really is sinking!" declared Elif as we stepped off the ferry onto the pavement. The water reached well above our ankles. Flip-flops in our hands, we lifted our small suitcase out of the flood water and waded across the *piazza San Marco*, following the emailed directions through a labyrinth of narrow streets and across tiny bridges to our hotel.

Inside, the reception area lay submerged under several inches of flood water.

"*Buongiorno!*" The man at reception stood behind the desk as if he had been awaiting our arrival.

"*Buongiorno,*" I smiled, presenting my confirmation email.

He tapped at his computer.

"Is it always like this?" I asked, indicating the floor.

"Yes," he replied, a flicker of sadness in his eyes, before recovering and flashing a bright smile.

"But don't worry, tomorrow morning it will all be gone!"

The sky over Venice had turned a deep violet as we set out again to wade barefoot through the floodwater in search of a place to eat. The glowing light from the streetlamps bounced off the water, casting the *Piazza* in a ghostly light. Tourists, some wearing yellow plastic boots, others barefoot like us, laughed as they took photos of each other, shin-deep in water in front of the *Basilica San Marco*.

"This is so much fun!" said Elif as someone behind us let out a small scream. We turned around, stepping aside quickly as a rat swam furiously past.

Clearly used to the water-logged streets, waiters stood in knee-high plastic boots outside the flooded restaurants holding menus and smiling at passers-by as in any other city in the world.

The following morning, exactly as the receptionist had predicted, the water had disappeared, and the streets were dry. The sky was a clear blue and the weather warm as Elif and I set out to explore the floating city.

For the next three days, we lost ourselves in a living, breathing fairy tale. Gothic lamp posts lined the labyrinth-like streets, slipper-like gondolas glided through the water and delicate bridges straddled narrow canals. Not forgetting my promise to Atakan, Elif and I clutched cornettos as we smiled into the camera from the back of a swaying gondola. Around every corner, a scene so beautiful, I found myself reaching for my phone to take yet another photo.

***

On the water's edge, I smiled at the memories as a new day danced tentatively on the horizon. The light was different now. First light. Shimmering across the glass-like water and bathing the famous skyline in an ethereal glow. As I watched the sunrise, a fragile peace settled over me. A stillness. For the first time in as long as I could remember, I stopped thinking. About the past. About the future. About anything.

The voices were silent now. The questions ceased. the accusations stilled. Then, from somewhere inside the silence, came another voice. My voice, although it didn't sound like me. A voice without judgment. Without blame. Without fear.

"It's going to be OK," it said.

Suddenly, everything was as clear as the dawning day.

In taking away my old life, Serkan had unwittingly given me a new one. For the first time in my life, I had nowhere to go, no one to answer to, and nowhere to be. My future stretched in front of me like a blank page.

I could start again.

When I was a little girl, I used to write stories. I would fold pieces of paper in half and staple them together before filling the pages with words and detailed illustrations. A multitude of characters and stories took up residence in my head, and I was frequently told off at school for daydreaming as I stared out of the classroom window. When did I stop daydreaming? I wondered as I gazed across the water. What happened to that little girl and her imagination and her stories? Life had swept me along on a relentless river of marriage, career, children, chores, and bills. My dreams were pushed aside to be periodically taken out and examined, like a precious family heirloom before being put away again. One day I'll write a book, I would tell myself. Waiting for something, although exactly what, I wasn't sure.

The right time?
The right place?
The right story?

It seemed that I had run out of excuses.

The domes and spires of Venice were clearly visible now. The to-ing and fro-ing of scattered birdsong punctuated the silence. A light came on in one of the caravans. The click of a kettle being switched on. The tinny sound of a radio as the world stirred into life.

Getting to my feet, I crossed the dewy grass to the car and pulled open the sliding door to the backseat. Elif's school notebooks were still there, in her backpack, as they were the day we left. Some of the pages were scrawled with her childish handwriting, sentences in pencil, and mathematical problems. Others were filled with sketches she had drawn on our travels. I selected the one with the most empty pages and returned to the water's edge.

"It's going to be OK," said the voice again.

And I knew that it was.

Opening the notebook on the first blank page, I smoothed down the paper with my hand and began to write.

Chapter Forty-One

Bodrum, Turkey. March 2016.

"When are we going to England?"

I was drifting somewhere between wake and sleep, enjoying the warmth of the sun on my face. The sweet, coconut smell of sun cream mingled with wafts of barbequed chicken, and I was surprised to find that I was hungry. I opened my eyes, shielding them from the sun with my hand. Silhouetted above me, her wet hair dripped droplets of saltwater onto my skin.

"To England," Elif persisted. "When are we going?"

I propped myself up on my elbows. Crouched down next to the small portable barbeque we had bought a few days earlier, Barbaros smiled and winked, the embers glowing bright orange as he fanned the flames.

"Who says we are going to England?" I said.

"Baba said if I went with you, you would take me to England, and I'd never see my friends and family again."

She said the words with the brutal honesty of a child, unaware of their gravity as the missing piece of the jigsaw puzzle finally slotted into place.

Cem, recoiling from me as he clung to his father. The downcast eyes and monotone voice.

"*I wanna stay wiz baba.*"

Suddenly, it all made horrible sense.

"Nobody's going to England, sweetie," I said. "We live here. This is our home."

"OK." Elif grinned, kicking up sand, as she turned and ran back towards the sea. A different child to the frightened little girl that had clung to me in the back of the car as we sped away from Maralya two weeks earlier.

Barbaros reached for the tongs, carefully turning the chicken pieces over one by one.

"Spin me around again!" Elif, perched on a Lilo, called from the water.

He stood up and brushed the sand from his knees.

"Spin you around?" Barbaros splashed towards her, grabbing the Lilo as she squealed in delight.

The past two weeks had passed in a blur of happiness. Shopping trips, outings to the cinema and barbeques on the beach. With only the clothes she stood up in, I had taken the opportunity to spoil Elif rotten with a whole new wardrobe. The walls of the pale pink bedroom had been transformed with colourful posters. New books lined the bookcase. Her new Disney princess duvet was buried under an avalanche of stuffed toys.

Along with a brand-new room and a brand-new wardrobe, another necessity for Elif was school.

Akyarlar Primary School consisted of a single one-storey building and around a hundred pupils. Most of them gathered around us in a curious throng, enthralled as Elif and I spoke to each other in English.

Enjoying her instant celebrity status, she was whisked away towards the playground that backed directly onto a secluded stretch of golden beach and an expanse of pristine sea.

"*Hoş geldiniz!*" A woman clutching a pile of books smiled as we made our way through the double doors. She had wild, frizzy hair and kind eyes. Her glasses hung around her neck on a frayed cord.

"Sevda." She smiled warmly as we shook hands, "I'm the principal."

"We just moved to the area," I explained in Turkish. "I need to register my daughter."

"Of course." Sevda smiled again. "Please come with me."

Sevda's office was cluttered in a homely, comforting kind of way. A strong smell of coffee. Floor-to-ceiling shelves crammed with dog-eared books and binders. The walls were plastered with children's paintings.

Dumping the pile of books on the cluttered desk, Sevda motioned for us to sit down.

"Do you have the child's *Kimlik*?" she said. "And the *ikametgah*?"

I glanced at Barbaros. By law in Turkey, everyone must register their address at the town hall and receive a document; the *ikametgah*. For obvious reasons, we had yet to do this.

Barbaros leaned forward in his chair, directing the full force of his charm at Sevda. I watched as she unconsciously batted her eyelashes and tilted her head.

"We have a complicated situation," he said, the huskiness of his voice creating an instant intimacy as he leaned towards her.

Sevda listened as he explained the story, flashing occasional sympathetic glances towards me.

"We are worried Carrie's ex-husband could trace us if we register our address," he explained.

"The information is not publicly available," she replied. "But..."

"...but this is Turkey," continued Barbaros with a smile.

Sevda nodded and smiled back. "I understand your concerns, but unfortunately, we can't register Elif without the *ikametgah*." She turned to me. "I will tell the staff to be extra vigilant. Make sure Elif knows not to leave the school grounds until one of you comes to collect her."

That afternoon, we reluctantly registered our address at the town hall and returned to the school to enrol Elif. Tomorrow would be her first day.

"Beautiful family," said a voice behind me in English. "Your daughter's having so much fun with her dad!"

I looked around to see an elderly woman with short grey hair that poked out in tufts beneath her flowered hat. By her side, a small beige terrier panted in the unseasonable heat.

I opened my mouth to correct her, silenced by a squeal of laughter from Elif as Barbaros upended her from the Lilo, tipping her into the warm shallow water with a splash.

"She is," I said.

"Mine are all grown up now. They're back in the UK with kids of their own. I don't see them as often as I would like, they're always so busy." She looked down at the terrier. "But we're alright, aren't we, Teddy?"

A pang of longing for Alfie hit me as she scratched the top of the dog's head.

"Anyway, enjoy the beach, my dear. Such beautiful weather we've been having. And enjoy every minute with your daughter. They grow up so fast!"

"Thank you," I said.

With a nod and a smile, the woman turned and continued down the beach, pushing her cane into the sand as she walked, the terrier trotting at her heels.

I looked back towards Elif playing in the shallow surf, captivated by the image of us through a stranger's eyes. A glimpse of a future that, a few short weeks ago, would have been unthinkable. Suddenly, everything seemed to be slotting into its rightful place. Had the horrific events of the past few months been steering me towards a different life? A better life? In Bodrum, I could start again in a way that would never have been possible in Maralya. A tentative picture began to take shape in my mind. I would buy an apartment. Get Alfie back. Sort out access to Cem. Barbaros and I would find jobs. For the first time since Christmas, I felt a fragile optimism about the future.

"Are you hungry, *aşkım?*" Barbaros picked up a piece of chicken with the tongs and placed it on a paper plate before adding a generous helping of salad.

"Starving!" I said. Barbaros smiled. "It's so good to see you eating again, my love." He passed me the plate, leaning towards me to place a kiss on my nose.

"Ooh, food!" cried Elif, running towards us. She grabbed a plate and pointed to the biggest piece of chicken. "I want that one!"

I gazed out across the sea. Behind Rabbit Island, a single grey cloud floated in a bright blue sky.

Since taking Elif, I had heard nothing from Serkan. The silence was deafening. My phone calls and messages went unanswered as the whisper of dread grew louder with each passing day.

Like the unseasonably warm weather, I couldn't shake the feeling that this peaceful interlude would be short-lived.

As it turned out, I was right.

Chapter Forty-Two

Bodrum, Turkey. March 2016.

"CARRIE!"

My eyes flew open. Fear pressed down on my chest, holding me paralysed. My heart thumped in my ears as I held my breath. In the semi-darkness, I moved my eyes over the familiar shapes of the room.

Another nightmare? I thought as I forced myself to take slow, deep breaths. It had seemed so real.

Next to me, Barbaros slept. The comforting weight of his arm slung across my stomach, his rhythmic breathing in my ear. It was Saturday; I remembered. We were going to Gümüşlük for a picnic.

"CARRIE! OPEN THIS DOOR!"

I froze. This time there was no mistake. Serkan's voice was quickly followed by the terrible, familiar sound of fists hammering on wood. Next to me, Barbaros rolled onto his back and rubbed his eyes.

"Mummy!"

"Elif, come here!" My voice sounded strange. Thin and disconnected, as if it didn't belong to me. The bedroom door burst open, and I glimpsed the terror in her eyes as she threw herself into the bed beside me.

"OPEN THIS DOOR NOW!"

I wrapped my arms around her, pulling the duvet over her head as if this would somehow protect her from what was happening.

"CARRIE, I KNOW YOU'RE IN THERE!"

Barbaros was on his feet, his phone pressed to his ear as he spoke in a low voice. I couldn't hear what he was saying.

"OPEN THIS DOOR, YOU BITCH!!!"

"The police are on their way," Barbaros said calmly. He lit a cigarette and stared out of the window through a cloud of smoke.

Elif and I clung together under the duvet, my body tensing with every blow to the cheap wooden door as I prayed it wouldn't break. After what felt like an age, the shouting and hammering were joined by the distant wail of a siren, getting louder and louder before coming to an abrupt stop outside. A moment of silence as the day held its breath. The slam of a car door. The static crackle of a radio. Quick footsteps on the concrete steps. The shouting and hammering stopped.

Barbaros stubbed his cigarette out in the ashtray on the nightstand and moved towards the door.

"Come," he said.

"Stay here, sweetie." I kissed the top of Elif's head and prised myself free from her arms. Barbaros and I made our way to the front door, listening to the male voices that echoed in the stairwell. Serkan shouted sporadic insults as several other voices tried to calm him. I moved towards the door and peered through the peephole.

I hadn't seen Serkan since that night. The night I had tried so hard to block out now stood as real as day under the bright lights of the hallway. He was flanked on one side by Kadir and on the other by his cousin Ihsan.

In front of them stood a military police officer, or *Jandarma,* in army fatigues and a blue beret.

In my mind, I had built Serkan up to be a monster of almost fictional proportions. It felt strangely surreal to see him here. In the flesh. Inches from my front door. His presence and noise so at odds with the idyllic world we had created. Our safe bubble now polluted beyond repair. The *Jandarma* rang the doorbell and cleared his throat.

"*Jandarma.*"

Barbaros stepped back behind the door as I took a deep breath and pulled it open. Immediately, Serkan lurched towards me, held back by Kadir and Ihsan. A barrage of insults spewed from his mouth.

"FILTHY WHORE!"

"*OROSPU!*"

"DIRTY BITCH!"

The *Jandarma* cleared his throat and waited for the shouting to stop.

"Caroline, *hanım?*" he said.

"Yes."

"This man is your ex-husband?"

I nodded.

"And the father of the child inside?"

"Yes."

A movement in the stairwell caught my eye, and I looked down, a flood of emotion rushing through me as Cem's face appeared in the shadows. He peered up at me, a flicker of curiosity in his eyes, the hint of a smile before he disappeared down the concrete steps.

"I WANT TO SEE MY DAUGHTER!" bellowed Serkan, waving a crumpled piece of paper towards me.

It was the first time we had seen each other since that night. The night I still hadn't talked about, as if saying the words out loud would somehow make it real. The night I had pushed to the deepest depths of my mind. That crept unchecked into nightmares I couldn't remember, leaving only remnants when I woke, like smoke after a fire.

For a brief second, our eyes met. His expression was hard. Fury simmered behind his eyes. There was no trace of acknowledgement. No hint of remorse or regret. I wondered if he remembered. Or if he had blocked it out, as I had.

The *Jandarma* took the piece of paper from Serkan. "Maybe I should come inside?" he said.

"Of course." I stepped back to let him pass, closing the door as Serkan unleashed another torrent of verbal abuse in my direction.

In the light of the apartment, the *Jandarma* seemed very young, no more than twenty. He passed me the crumpled piece of paper.

"According to this custody order, the child's father has visitation rights from 10 am today, until 5 pm tomorrow," he explained.

"I don't want to go with him."

The bedroom doorway was pushed open and Elif appeared, her eyes red and swollen. I wondered how long she had been there, how much she had seen. She rushed over to me and wrapped her arms around my waist.

"I don't have to go with him, do I, Mummy?"

"Of course not." I stroked her hair and turned back to the *Jandarma*.

"And if I refuse?"

"You need to come to the police station and sign a statement that you are denying him access to the child."

I nodded. "OK."

"You are also within your rights to file a complaint against your ex-husband," he continued, nodding towards the door. "For harassment and threatening behaviour."

I sighed. More statements. More complaints. I wondered when it was all going to end.

From the bedroom window, we watched as the three men were led away. Cem wandered aimlessly between them. He looked so small and lost. I wanted to run downstairs and take him in my arms. Take both my children and run away from this forever.

***

The interview room was cold, the bright sunshine outside failing to penetrate the dark interior. Elif sat next to me, swinging her legs, and staring out of the window as the day continued without us. Through the bars on the window, the branches of an orange tree swayed vibrant green against the bright blue sky.

"Do you understand that you are breaching the terms of the custody agreement if you refuse your ex-husband access to the child?" said the police officer as I scribbled my name at the bottom of yet another statement.

Cem's face flashed into my mind. The playful curiosity and shy smile as he looked up at me from the stairwell. Suddenly, I had an idea.

"He can see her," I said. "On two conditions. We stay here at the police station. And I want to see my son."

Twenty minutes later, Serkan and I sat on benches at opposite ends of the police station yard, separated by a man with a gun. Between us, a khaki-clad soldier sweltered in the heat, assault rifle slung around his neck. Elif and Cem ran around him in circles, first one way, then the other. Their squeals of laughter permeated the air.

"Elif!" called Serkan, standing up and waving his arms. "Elif, come here!"

She turned to me, and I nodded my approval, watching as she walked across the yard towards her father. Alone in the centre, Cem stayed where he was, scuffing his shoes in the dust before turning to me. I waved and smiled. After a quick glance towards Serkan, he made his way towards me and sat down next to me on the stone bench.

There was at once too much and nothing to say.

Cem looked up at the orange tree. Despite the onset of spring, a few solitary oranges remained hidden amongst the branches.

"Would you like one?" I said.

He nodded.

I chose the largest orange, twisted it from its stem and passed it to him.

"Thank you."

I watched in silence as Cem dug his fingernails under the skin, removed the peel and placed it neatly on the bench beside him. His left knee was scuffed, and a dark red scab had formed, pink around the edges where it had started to heal. I wondered who had picked him up when he fell. Who had dabbed the wound and applied a plaster? If they had remembered to kiss it better.

On the other side of the yard, Serkan and Elif sat at opposite ends of their bench. Serkan was leaning towards her, talking animatedly, as if trying to convince her of something. Elif stared down at her lap.

On our bench, Cem and I sat side by side, a comfortable silence settling over our shoulders with the midday sun. Cem turned to me, smiling as he popped another orange segment into his mouth. Two of his bottom teeth were missing.

"I love you," I said. Of all the things to say, it seemed the most important.

He turned his head to the side, squinting in the sun and looking around as if searching for something.

"All the way…" He stretched out his arm, shielding his eyes from the sun as he pointed towards a mountain in the distance.

"All the way to that mountain and back?"

"All the way to the moon and back," I smiled.

"Wow!" he grinned. "That's really far!"

Silence settled back over us as Cem ate his orange, carefully removing the pith from each segment before putting them in his mouth.

"Do you love Mummy?" I said after a few minutes had passed. My voice was barely above a whisper. Quietened by the lump in my throat and the involuntary tears that sprang to my eyes. Afraid, perhaps, of the answer.

On the far side of the yard, Elif had moved closer to Serkan. He put his arms around her, and they hugged politely before she began to walk back towards me. I was relieved to see that she was smiling.

"Everything ok?" I asked as she helped herself to a segment of orange.

She nodded. "Can we go to the beach now?"

"Cem!" called Serkan from across the yard. "*Hadi*! Let's go!"

Cem popped the last segment of orange into his mouth. He stood up and wiped his hands on his knees.

"Bye, sweetie," I said, forcing a smile. My voice was stronger now. "I'll see you soon!"

"See you soon!" he grinned.

He walked away, almost reaching the centre of the yard when he stopped and turned around.

"All the way…" He thought for a minute, looking up at the cloudless sky before stretching his arms as wide as he could.

"All the way to the sun and back!" he said.

Chapter Forty-Three

Bodrum, Turkey. March 2016.

We drove straight to Gümüşlük. Barbaros had barely spoken since the morning's events. He smoked cigarette after cigarette as he stared out towards Rabbit Island across the blue-grey sea. Home was no longer safe for us.

The café was empty, except for a few fishermen nursing glasses of *çay*, backgammon boards spread out on the table between them. Barbaros and I chose a table close to the beach and ordered two glasses of *çay*. On the beach, Elif scoured the sand for shells, regularly stooping to pick one up and examining it carefully, before adding it to her collection.

"We have to move," said Barbaros.

"What? Where?"

"Istanbul," he said. "We'll be safe there."

"No!"

"Carrie, he knows where we live."

My new life was floating away from me again. I reached across the table, clutching his hands as if I could stop it.

"He traced us after we registered Elif at school," I said. "He'll do the same thing again!"

"Not in Istanbul," replied Barbaros. "He can't touch us there. I know people."

"We can't keep running away, Barbaros!"

Barbaros pulled his hands away, sighing heavily as he unwrapped a cube of sugar from its paper and dropped it into his glass. "I just wanted a quiet life," he said. "A normal, quiet, peaceful life. But trouble always finds me."

Dark flecks swirled in the amber liquid as he stirred his *çay* with a silver spoon.

"Tell me about your past," I said softly. "What are you running from, Barbaros?"

A shadow passed across his face, like the shutters closing on a window, or the sun disappearing behind a cloud. Around us, the clatter of dice and the tapping of checkers on backgammon boards mingled with laughter and the tinkling of silver spoons on glass. It was so long before he spoke; I had assumed the conversation closed.

"I've done some bad things, Carrie," he said.

Discomfort squirmed in my gut. I remembered the first night in his apartment. The urge to run and never come back.

"What things?"

He stared into my eyes, prolonging the moment before everything changed.

"I was in jail."

I looked down at the backs of my hands as the information sank in. Gradually. Like water through sand. The temporary accommodation. The lack of personal effects. The melancholy that lived behind his eyes.

"What did you do?" I said, in equal parts wanting and not wanting to know.

Barbaros gazed out past Rabbit Island as if at a distant past. The familiar melancholy settled over him like night.

"I worked for some bad people. Dangerous people," he said. When he looked back at me, the pain in his eyes was unbearable.

"Did you hurt anyone?" I said.

Barbaros shook his head. "I was dealing with the money. They needed an accountant. Someone to fiddle the books."

I nodded.

"I'm sorry I didn't tell you," he said, looking deeply into my eyes. "I wanted to forget. To start again. I wanted you to love me."

For months, Barbaros had been my rock. I had clung to him like a stranded shipwreck survivor as the storm raged all around us. Now it was my turn to be strong.

"Of course, I love you," I said, reaching across the table for his hands. "You're right. It's in the past. It's over. We can start a new life. Together. In Bodrum. I'm not going to let Serkan ruin it again. I'm not afraid of him, Barbaros. Not anymore!"

Barbaros closed his eyes. He lifted my hands to his face, brushing the skin with his lips.

"Carrie, it's not over."

He opened his eyes and looked at me.

"I'm out on twelve years parole. One mistake and I will go back inside. And I will never come out."

Suddenly, it all made sense. His haste to leave Maralya. His reluctance to go to the police. His avoidance of any type of confrontation with Serkan. Barbaros had to stay out of trouble at all costs.

"It's not Serkan I'm afraid of, Carrie," he said softly, looking into my eyes. "I'm scared of myself."

Chapter Forty-Four

Bodrum, Turkey. April 2016.

I watched from the balcony as Barbaros scoured the ground below, stooping to examine a tiny glint of silver in the grass before picking it up and placing it carefully in his palm. He looked up at me and smiled.

Last night, the four silver hearts had danced their circular dance in the centre of the table as the three of us had dinner on the balcony. The air was warm and still. The sky glowed a light, golden peach as the sun set behind the mosque on the hill. There was no indication of the ferocious storm that was to come; pulling me from sleep as the wind howled, and the rain drummed against the windowpane. Pressing myself closer to Barbaros, I had descended back into the depths of oblivion.

This morning, the sky was a bright, cloudless blue, the only trace of the storm, a small puddle of rainwater and two overturned plastic chairs. The silver tea light lay on its side in the centre of the table. Minus its parasol and silver hearts.

"It's all I could find." Barbaros pushed open the front door and showed me the parasol and two of the silver hearts, twisted and misshapen in the palm of his hand.

"Thank you," I said.

"I'll try and find the others later." He pressed his lips to mine. "I have to go to work."

Since Serkan's violent intrusion into our lives, there had been no more talk of leaving Bodrum.

Along with Barbaros's revelations about his past, the topic hovered unspoken over our heads like rain clouds at a wedding. We picked up our lives, shook them off and carried on as if nothing had happened. Barbaros found a job delivering produce to bars and restaurants, and with Elif at school, I was alone during the day for the first time in months.

By midday, I had finished all my chores and another empty afternoon yawned ahead of me. The sun streamed in through the spotless balcony doors. A fly buzzed lazily against the glass. The low gurgle of the washing machine, as our clothes flopped back and forth in a sea of suds. I slid open the balcony doors, settling onto the leather sofa with a cup of coffee as I gazed out over the hill.

The flock had been joined by three newborn lambs. Tails wagging, they skipped and chased each other on wobbly legs against a tinkling backdrop of bells.

Coffee cup halfway to my lips, I froze at the sharp rap of knuckles on the front door.

I held my breath, waiting for his voice. For the nightmare to start again.

Instead, the doorbell chimed several times. There was another knock.

"*Posta!*" came a man's voice.

I padded to the front door and pressed my eye to the peephole.

Distorted by the glass, his head too large for his body, a man in a light blue shirt and navy shorts rocked impatiently back and forth on his heels.

He looked straight at me through the peephole, making me take a step back.

"*Günaydın!*" he said cheerfully as I opened the door, thrusting an official-looking white envelope towards me. I stared at the red Maralya postmark in one corner. The words in block capitals in the other. **AILE MAHKEMESI** (Family Court).

He coughed, startling me out of my trance. "*Imza!*" he said as a pen appeared in my line of vision. He tapped the rectangular box at the bottom of his clipboard with his finger, indicating for me to sign.

Scrawling my signature inside the box, I nodded a brief "*teşekkürler,*" and closed the door.

I took the envelope to the sofa where I turned it over in my hands, examining the postmark and sender's stamp again.

Maralya

Family Court

Was it something to do with the divorce, I wondered. Something to do with Cem?

I pushed my thumbs under the seal and removed the two sheets of white, formal-looking paper, unfolding them as I scanned down the page.

It was my name I saw first. Then Elif's. Gradually, more words came into focus, like a slide under a microscope.

... *was unfaithful to him.*

... *left Maralya with her boyfriend, leaving both children in the care of the plaintiff.*

... *did not contact the children for a full month.*

... *is therefore seeking full custody* ...

It was Serkan's incoherent Facebook rant, re-packaged and written in legalese.

I forced myself back to the beginning and read the letter again, slowly wading my way through the jungle of legal Turkish as the information sank in. Serkan had filed for custody of Elif. I reached the bottom of the page and stopped. The court hearing was in two weeks.

There must be some mistake, I thought, as my eyes drifted back to the top of the page. The letter was dated the 7th of January. He had opened the case almost as soon as I left Maralya. Without an address, the court had nowhere to send it. Until now.

I reached for my phone.

"*Efendim,*" Serkan answered on the first ring as if he had been expecting me.

"I got the letter," I blurted. "From the court. What are you doing, Serkan?"

He hesitated.

"How are you, Carrie?" he said.

"Why are you telling lies about me? Trying to take Elif. You know she wants to live with me."

"Is he there?" he continued, ignoring the question. There was something different in his voice. Something I couldn't put my finger on. "Your new boyfriend."

"He's at work," I said.

"I need to talk to you." His voice was strange.

"Please don't do this, Serkan." I continued. "We can work something out. You can see Elif. I can see Cem. Let's put this all behind us. We need to do what's best for the children."

"No. Not like this. Not over the phone." It was then that I realised what it was. Fear. Serkan was afraid.

"Come to Maralya," he said. "Don't tell him you're coming."

I hesitated.

There was a sigh on the other end of the line.

"I'm not going to hurt you, Carrie." He said. "I just want to talk, that's all. There's something you need to know."

The sun was too hot as it streamed in through the open balcony doors, the ticking of the clock on the kitchen wall too loud.

I stared at the white paper in my hand.

"I'm giving you one more chance," Serkan continued. "Come to Maralya. Saturday at twelve. Manzara."

"OK," I heard myself say.

"Oh, and Carrie," he continued. "Don't get any ideas about taking Elif to England. There's a court order preventing her from leaving the country."

I opened my mouth to speak, but the line went dead.

Chapter Forty-Five

Maralya, Turkey. April 2016

Barbaros glanced left and right as he crossed the road. He lit a cigarette, leaning against a tree as he waited for the *dolmuş* to take him to work.

"Elif!" I stared straight ahead at my reflection until she appeared behind me in the windowpane.

"Get dressed!" I forced a smile. "We're going out!"

"Where are we going?"

Outside, the *dolmuş* appeared, its doors swinging open as it slowed to a stop. I watched as Barbaros dropped his cigarette and ground it into the dirt with his foot.

"Maralya," I said brightly as I turned to face her. "To see Baba and Cem."

Her eyes widened. "Baba?" she said. "But..."

"It's fine," I reassured her. "We're just going to talk, that's all."

"OK." Her voice was tinged with doubt. She turned towards her room.

"And Elif..."

She stopped in her tracks and swivelled back around.

"Don't tell Barbaros, OK?"

Uncertainty flickered in her eyes. Something wasn't right, and she knew it.

"It'll be fun!" I said, trying to keep my voice light. "Road trip! Just you and me!"

Since my conversation with Serkan, discomfort had sat heavy in my stomach like an undigested meal. We were meeting in public, I told myself. In daylight. He couldn't do anything. I glanced at the white envelope in my hand. I had to try.

Outside, the *dolmuş* doors swung shut. I watched as the minibus reached the end of the road, turned a corner, and disappeared out of sight.

***

Süleyman *Bey* was squeezed into his plastic chair, the obligatory bottle of Coca-Cola on the table next to him. I could feel his eyes on me as I climbed into the driver's seat of my car. I clicked my seatbelt into place and took a deep breath. It was the first time I had driven since the panic attack three months earlier.

"Why is he staring at us?" said Elif, as from his plastic chair, Suleyman *Bey* took a swig of his Coca-Cola, keeping his eyes fixed on me.

"I don't know, sweetie."

I took another deep breath and turned the key in the ignition.

Ignoring my thumping heart, I pressed my foot down on the clutch and pushed the car slowly into gear, wincing as the car crunched into reverse. I raised my hand and smiled at Süleyman *Bey*.

He did not smile back.

It was early, and the village was quiet. I felt my confidence slowly returning as I made my way along the empty roads. Past shuttered villas with leafy gardens. Sleeping restaurants. An empty supermarket car park.

I had allowed myself plenty of time. Panic attack time. Pull over time. Pull myself together time.

We left the village and joined the main coast road. I tightened my grip on the steering wheel, sticking to the slow lane as traffic sped past. One kilometre. Two. Three. On my right, the vast blue Aegean, like a reassuring hand on my shoulder. Six kilometres. Seven. Eight.

Kos, silent and staring across the sea.

"Can we stop for a drink?" asked Elif from the backseat after around an hour had passed. "I'm thirsty."

There was a layby ahead. The random combination of fresh oranges and handmade stuffed sheep were piled high on stalls behind an elderly man and woman. I pulled in and parked the car.

"*Hoş geldin!*" The woman smiled from beneath her embroidered headscarf as we approached. Her skin was creased into deep lines that crisscrossed her face like fine mesh, a half-finished sheep on her lap. Elif and I sat down on plastic chairs as the man reached for an orange, sliced it neatly in half and pressed it into the juicer.

Despite the whiz of passing traffic and the occasional blare of a car horn, the layby was surprisingly tranquil. We sat in comfortable silence; the woman stitching the sheep with a needle and thread as the man squeezed fresh orange juice into plastic cups.

It felt strange to be without Barbaros. In equal parts liberating and as if I were missing a limb. Since our escape from Maralya, I had come to rely on him so heavily that it was hard to imagine I had ever done anything for myself. The woman who had held down a job, run a house, driven a car, and paid bills felt like a distant memory. Barbaros came with me everywhere from the supermarket to dropping Elif at school. He disapproved of me having any contact with my friends or family. "Your mental state is so fragile, *Canım,*" he would say. "They might say something to upset you. Or you could accidentally say something to put us in danger."

He would look at me then, his eyes full of love. "Besides, we only need each other."

***

Serkan's motorbike was already parked behind Manzara when we arrived. I parked as far away as possible and turned off the engine. It's a drink, I told myself. One drink. A chance to talk. A chance to change his mind. I stared at his motorbike, remembering how the sound of it used to fill me with dread. The roar of it in the driveway at three in the morning, inevitably followed by his drunken gropings and demands for sex.

It's over, I told myself. He can't do anything to you here.

"Are we going in, Mummy?" said Elif after a few minutes had passed. I unclipped my seatbelt. "Let's go," I said.

We entered the cafe through the back door. The smell of food and the noise and clatter of the kitchen pulled me sharply back to the present after the tranquillity of the drive. I held Elif's hand as we made our way past chattering tables, and swerving waiters balancing trays of wine. The double doors slid open and we stepped outside into the bright sunshine. Immediately his eyes locked with mine.

Serkan was at the same table in the shade of the palm tree where we had made our shaky truce almost a year earlier. Next to him sat Cem, dwarfed by an enormous chocolate milkshake.

"Hi Cem," I smiled, pulling out a chair and sitting down.

"Hi," he replied, his eyes darting quickly towards his father, before he returned to his milkshake and sucked studiously at the straw. Elif perched on a chair next to me as Serkan, ignoring her completely, surveyed me from across the table. He took a sip of beer and wiped the foam from his top lip with the back of his hand.

"Kids, go and play!" he barked without looking at them.

The relief clear on their faces, they slid off their chairs and ran towards the beach, leaving Serkan and me alone. I took the white envelope from my bag and placed it on the table.

"Why are you doing this?" I said.

"The children should be together."

"But we agreed," I said. "I have custody of Elif. You have custody of Cem."

"That was before," he said.

"But Elif wants to live with me. She's happy. She's settled in a great school." I could hear myself gabbling under his expressionless gaze and forced myself to stop. "Of course, they need to see each other," I said. "Cem needs me. Elif needs you. Bodrum isn't so far. We can arrange something. Alternate weekends? Once a month? We can work something out."

"And this is what you have decided?" Serkan said when I had finished.

"Can't we come to an agreement?" I pleaded. "We need to do what's best for them."

"Does he treat you nice?" said Serkan, changing the subject. At the next table, two red-headed children were arguing over the last slice of pizza.

"Oh, give it a rest, you two!" chastised their mother, picking the pizza slice up and tearing it neatly in half.

"Anyway..." Serkan picked up his beer and took another swig. "It's not important. It's a nice plan, Carrie, but it's not what is going to happen."

"What do you mean?"

"You are going to come back here. To Maralya."

I stared at him. At the arrogance that gleamed in his eyes, the imperious set of his jaw.

"Oh! Here she is!" A broad smile spread across Serkan's face as he stood up and waved at someone behind me.

"Carrie, there's someone I'd like you to meet."

My heart sank as it dawned on me. Serkan hadn't brought me here to talk about the children or the custody case. He had met someone, and he had brought me here to gloat. I braced myself. The poor girl probably had no idea what she was walking into. I would stay for a *çay*, make polite conversation and leave.

"Hello dear."

I looked up in surprise as an elderly woman sat down next to me. She looked vaguely familiar. Strands of wispy, grey hair falling out of the half-hearted bun on top of her head. An unhealthy tinge to her skin. A weary smile.

"Carrie, this is Margaret..." began Serkan as the recognition sank in.

It was Margaret Crosby, my former hypochondriac patient from the hospital.

"We know each other," I said. "Margaret used to come to the hospital."

"You were always so kind to me, dear," said Margaret with a watery smile. "That's why when Serkan told me, I wanted to speak to you." She glanced around as if someone might be listening. "To warn you."

"Warn me about what?"

She leaned towards me.

"Barbaros," she whispered.

The laugh escaped me before I could stop it.

"This is ridiculous," I said, standing up to leave. "I came here to talk about the children, not Barbaros. I'm sorry Margaret."

Serkan glared at me. "Just listen to what she has to say."

I looked at the white envelope on the table. I had to try. With a sigh, I sat down as Serkan nodded at Margaret to continue.

"My daughter Laura was with Barbaros before you," she began. "They lived together."

My office. The blonde with the ponytail. Barbaros helping Margaret up from the sofa.

"Thanks, dear."

"Barbaros is a bad man, Carrie," Margaret whispered, leaning towards me. "He was in jail." She fumbled around in her handbag for a tissue and blew her nose.

"I know," I said.

"Do you know what he was in jail for?" said Serkan, narrowing his eyes.

"It doesn't matter," I said. "It's in the past."

"You don't know, do you?" A hint of a smile played at the corners of his mouth. "He hasn't told you."

Margaret leaned towards me, her watery, grey eyes full of concern. "Carrie, Barbaros is dangerous," she said. "Laura was terrified of him."

"Barbaros has never laid a finger on me," I said, looking pointedly at Serkan. Our eyes locked as I thought back to that night. When I had looked into those eyes, searching for a glimmer of the man I married. A spark of recognition. For a brief second, a moment of understanding passed between us. A silent acknowledgement, before he looked away.

"Laura was so scared of Barbaros that she went back to the UK," continued Margaret. "After twelve years here. To get away from him."

On the beach, the children had removed their flip-flops and were laughing as they chased each other in and out of the crashing surf. Above them, a kite dipped and climbed in the cloudless sky, bright yellow like the sun, with a smiling face and a twisting, feathered tail.

"There were others, apparently, before Laura. He targets women with money. Foreign women. He's clever. He plays the long game. When you refuse to buy him what he wants he gets violent. He beat Laura up twice. Put her in hospital." Margaret's watery eyes were far away. "Nearly killed her."

She glanced around as if suddenly remembering where she was. "I should go," she said, standing up. "Laura would kill me if she knew I'd been talking to you."

She turned to me. "Please be careful, dear," she said. "Come back to the hospital. We miss you."

Serkan and I watched in silence as she walked away.

"This is why you brought me here?" I said. "To try and scare me into leaving Barbaros?"

"You will leave Barbaros," Serkan replied, his gaze unwavering.

I stood up and turned towards the beach, shielding my eyes from the sun.

"Elif," I called. "Time to go!"

"You don't have a choice."

"Elif!" I called again, waving my arms.

"I'm going to tell the court what he did," Serkan continued. "That you're living with a dangerous criminal. If you stay with him, you'll lose custody of Elif."

On the beach, Elif was brushing the sand from her legs, pushing her feet into her flip-flops. Silently, I willed her to hurry up.

"And when you leave him..."

Serkan suddenly lurched towards me across the table, grabbing me by the wrist and digging his fingernails into the skin.

"You have no idea who you're dealing with," he hissed. "You don't leave men like Barbaros, Carrie. This is the only place you'll be safe. Here. With me. He can't touch you here."

I pulled my arm away, willing Elif to hurry up as she ran towards me across the sand. In the pale blue sky, the kite dipped and soared, its feathered tail fluttering in the breeze. I remembered the last time we were here, how I had envied the kite its freedom. Now I realised that it was never free at all. Like me, it remained tethered to its owner. All Serkan had to do was pull the strings and I would fall to the ground.

Elif arrived, out of breath from running.

"Are we going?" she said.

"We need to get back," I replied. "It's a long drive."

Cem stood by himself. His dinosaur T-shirt I had bought him in England last summer was too tight for him now, its colour faded by the sun. I crouched down, stroking his cheek as I looked into his dark eyes. This time, he didn't look away.

"All the way to the stars and back," I whispered in his ear.

"You see what kind of person I am?" The chair scraped against the ground as Serkan stood up. "After everything you have done, I am still helping you, Carrie!"

I flailed around for Elif's hand, clutching it a little too tightly, walking a little too fast. A table of pale-skinned tourists, laughing as they raised their glasses. A crying baby. A wasp crawling on a coke can. The air conditioning hit me as we walked through the double doors. A white-shirted waiter balancing a tray of drinks. The clattering of the cash register. A ringing phone. I kept walking, my eyes fixed on the red EXIT sign on the wall.

"Carrie, come back here!" Serkan called after me.

Sunlight bounced off the white steps as we stepped outside. Clutching Elif's hand, I quickened my pace as we walked towards my car. I reached into my bag and fumbled around for my keys.

"I wanted ice cream," said Elif as I opened the back door and lifted her into her seat.

"I know, sweetie," I said, fastening her seatbelt. "We'll stop somewhere on the way, I promise."

I climbed into the driver's seat. At the edge of my vision, the back door to the cafe flew open. The shape of Serkan strode towards me as I jammed my key in the ignition.

"Mummy!" screamed Elif from the back seat.

My door flew open. "I warned you, Carrie!" Serkan sneered as his face loomed towards me. "I told you what would happen. You will lose your kids. You will leave Turkey. Don't ever forget, I control you, Carrie. I own you!"

I recoiled from him, my arms in front of my face as I pressed myself back against my seat.

"You can't escape!" Serkan bellowed. "I own you! You belong to me!"

He took a step back, slamming the door hard. Opened it again and slammed it harder. In the back seat, Elif began to cry.

I fumbled around for the central locking, my fingers finally locating the button as the locks clicked shut. My hands were shaking as I turned the key in the ignition and pushed the car into gear. Serkan was at my window, his features contorted in rage, his fists pounding on the glass as I pulled out onto the road.

In my rear-view mirror, I watched as Cem, in his faded dinosaur t-shirt, got smaller and smaller as I accelerated away from Maralya for the last time.

Chapter Forty-Six

St. Tropez, France. July 2016.

We soared along the coast road, music blasting from the car stereo as Elif and I sang along. On one side, rolling green hills dappled with sunlight, on the other, my old friend the Mediterranean, pulling together and apart like partners in a dance.

The sea view was snatched away as we entered a tunnel, emerging after what seemed like an age, blinking in the bright sunshine.

A small blue sign. A single word in a circle of yellow stars.

France

I don't know what I was expecting, but the innocuous-looking sign wasn't it. No queues. No customs. No passport control. No border guards.

"Welcome to France!" I said cheerfully to Elif in the back seat.

She looked up from her sketchpad and gazed out of the window.

"It looks the same as Italy," she concluded.

After the anti-climax of our arrival, I began to think about where we would spend the night. I glanced up at the blue sign that straddled the motorway.

Nice Mónaco Cannes Cote D'Azure

The names conjured up images of supermodels and movie stars with perfect tans and oversized shades. I imagined myself on a sunlounger next to a swimming pool with a chilled glass of wine.

"Can we go camping again, *please?*" Elif pressed her palms together. "I'm bored with hotels. Camping is so much fun!"

"I think we need some glamour in our lives," I said.

"What's glamour?" asked Elif.

"You'll see," I replied, indicating towards the next exit.

It was like no campsite I had ever seen. Palm trees. Gold lettering on a cream-coloured sign above five gleaming stars. POOL. JACUZZI. SPA.

A wave of air conditioning hit us as we entered the plush reception. Behind the desk sat three immaculate blonde women dressed in white, and a young black man in a white baseball cap, polo shirt, and shorts. They smiled in unison as we entered.

"Good morning, *Madam*," said one of the blondes, smiling to reveal perfect white teeth.

"Do you have availability for tonight?" I said.

"You need to book a minimum of two nights *Madam*," she explained in a strong French accent, placing a price list on the desk in front of me. The prices were surprisingly reasonable. "This includes a pitch for your tent, personal bathroom, outdoor kitchen with a fridge and use of all facilities. Swimming pool, bar, jacuzzi…"

"We'll take it!" I said, placing my passport and credit card on the desk.

After entering our details onto the computer, the blonde passed a set of keys to the young black man in the baseball cap.

"Christian will show you to your pitch."

On cue, Christian smiled. "Follow me, please," he said.

We followed Christian in the car as he weaved his way through the vast campsite on his bicycle. Past the lavish pool area, expensive-looking restaurants, upscale shops, and luxury mobile homes. Eventually, we stopped at a large empty pitch containing a cabin and an outside kitchen area complete with a sink and fridge. Christian unlocked the cabin and invited me to look inside.

"It is OK, *Madam*?"

Inside the cabin was a luxury bathroom complete with a large glass-doored shower, heated towel rail, and several fluffy white towels. Camping, or more accurately, "Glamping," St. Tropez style.

"It's perfect!" I said.

"If you need anything," smiled Christian, climbing back onto his bicycle. "Please do not 'esitate."

After setting up our tent, Elif and I headed straight to the pool. A palm tree-encircled paradise, complete with a jacuzzi and a bar from which I ordered my long-awaited glass of white wine. I took a sip, lay back on my sun lounger, and closed my eyes.

"Is this glamour?" said Elif, fresh from the pool and dripping wet, as she perched on a sun lounger beside me.

"This is definitely glamour," I replied.

Chapter Forty-Seven

Bodrum, Turkey. April 2016.

I watched him sleep, his features twitching and hardening as he dreamed. Distant memories tormenting him from a buried past. The bad boy with a broken heart. I wondered what terrible things he saw.

He stirred under the weight of my gaze and opened his eyes.

"What's wrong?" He reached out and stroked my face with his fingertips.

"What did you do, Barbaros?" I said quietly. "I need to know why you were in jail."

In the darkened room, I felt the mood change.

"I already told you."

"Tell me again."

A heavy sigh. He rolled away from me.

"I thought it didn't matter."

"It matters," I said.

"I was young. I got involved with a bad crowd. I did some bad things. It's over."

"What things?"

A few minutes went by. Eventually, he sat up, covering his face with his hands, and rubbing his temples as if the question were a headache he could make go away.

"Why are you doing this?" he said suddenly, glaring at me. His eyes were black, like shards of flint.

"Why are you trying to destroy what we have? Look at all your problems! Everything we've been through, and I've never once complained! All I do is help you. Support you. Love you. Why can't you do the same for me?"

"Serkan has filed for custody of Elif!" I blurted as tears sprang to my eyes.

He snapped on the bedside lamp and stared at me. "What?"

I pulled open the drawer in the nightstand and felt around inside for the white envelope. I passed it to him, watching in silence as he read.

"The case is next week," I said when he had finished. "He opened the case as soon as we left Maralya, but they didn't have an address to send it to. What am I going to do, Barbaros?"

We sat in silence for a long time. He read the letter again and put it back in the envelope.

"I need to know why you were in jail," I said. "I could lose Elif."

"Who have you been talking to?" he snapped suddenly. There was a hard edge to his voice.

"No one."

"Azra?" he continued. "Your so-called friend who dropped you at the first sign of trouble?"

Azra. Her face flickered like a lighthouse through the fog of my mind. I remembered the fear in her eyes the last time we met. The mahogany desk like a barrier between us. An idea began to form in my brain. A long shot, but it was worth a try.

Barbaros passed the envelope back to me and lay down. "Serkan won't win the case," he said. "Whoever you've been talking to is just trying to scare you. You're Elif's mother. She belongs with you."

He turned off the light, declaring the conversation closed. A few minutes passed in silence as we lay side by side in the dark. Barbaros reached for a cigarette from an open packet on the nightstand and placed it between his lips. He struck a match. The flame flickered briefly, illuminating his face in the dark.

"I still know people," he said, blowing out the flame, and plunging us back into darkness. "I can make people disappear."

Smoke curled and spiralled above us, hanging in the air with his words.

Had he just said what I thought he had?

For the first time, I was afraid of him.

We lay in silence as Barbaros smoked his cigarette and stubbed it out in the ashtray. He rolled over to face me, pulling me towards him, stopping as he felt me resist.

"Are you dangerous?" I whispered in the dark.

He smiled and pulled me close.

"Not for you," he said softly, stroking my hair.

I was powerless to resist. My body yielded, slipping under as the spell took effect. I breathed him in. The smell of his skin. The taste of him. His erratic heartbeat against mine. Hot tears squeezed from my eyes.

I knew what I had to do. And already, I yearned for him.

Afterwards, I watched him sleep. Locked again in a prison of my own making. Held by a single jailer. Stronger than Hope, Pride, Guilt and Shame. Stronger even than Fear.

Love.

Chapter Forty-Eight

Bodrum, Turkey. May 2016

Azra grinned at me from my telephone screen. Glass of wine in one hand, cigarette in the other, yellow paper hat perched on the side of her head. Thoughts swirled around my clouded brain like smoke.

Call her
What if she doesn't answer?
Call again.
She'll probably refuse.
There's only one way to find out.
I felt sick.
I don't want to know.
I stared at the white envelope in my hand.
I need to know.

The clock on the kitchen wall stared down, its slow ticking as oppressive as the early summer heat that streamed in through the open balcony doors.

I flicked the switch on the kettle, threw a tea bag into a mug, and opened the fridge. The clingfilm-covered plate containing my half-eaten breakfast stared back at me in silent judgment. I grabbed the milk for my tea and closed the door.

The sun was blinding on the balcony. I sank onto the leather sofa and took a sip of tea as I stared out across the hill.

There were no sheep today. No shepherd. No scruffy dog. The tree stump stood empty in a sea of swaying blonde grass.

Call her.

I stared at her picture again.

I need to know.

Before I could change my mind, I pressed call and leaned back against the headrest. I closed my eyes. feeling the warmth of the sun on my face as it beat down, turning the insides of my eyelids orange. I listened to the ringing across the miles. A distant call to prayer. Sporadic birdsong. The beating of my own heart.

"Carrie?"

I opened my eyes.

"Azra?"

"*Nasılsın, canım?*" she said, in the vague tone of someone who doesn't really want to know.

"Azra, I need your help. Serkan has filed for custody of Elif..."

"Carrie ..." she began. "I'm happy to recommend someone."

"I don't want you to represent me," I interrupted. "I need you to get some information. About Barbaros."

"Barbaros?"

"He has a criminal record," I continued. "He was in jail."

"What was he in jail for?"

"He says white collar crime. Accounting. Cooking the books. But I think there's more to it."

"Jeez, Carrie."

"Serkan says he's dangerous. He's threatening to tell the court. I could lose custody of Elif."

Azra went silent. "What are you going to do?" she said, eventually.

"I need your help," I explained. "I need you to find out what Barbaros did. What he's capable of."

"That's illegal," she said.

"But it's possible?" I replied. "You know people. You can check."

The backs of my legs slid with sweat against the leather sofa. Somewhere in the distance, a dog barked. A lengthy silence yawned on the line.

"Azra, I'm desperate. I need to know who Barbaros is. Please. I'll never ask for anything from you again."

She gave a heavy sigh.

"Send me his *kimlik* number and date of birth. I'll see what I can do."

I breathed a sigh of relief. "Thank you," I said.

The day crawled by. An hour. Two hours. Three. I opened the fridge and nibbled on a piece of cheese. I drank coffee after coffee until I felt sick. I tried and failed to focus on a film. I sat on the leather sofa and stared out at the empty hill.

It was just before two when my phone rang. Azra, in her party hat, lit up the screen.

"Hello?"

I heard her take a deep breath.

"It's not good news, *canım*," she warned. "It might be better if you're sitting down."

"Tell me."

Another deep breath.

"He's been incarcerated three times. The last sentence was the longest. Ten years. He was released early last year for good behaviour on twelve years parole."

I tightened my grip on my phone.

"Tell me what he did."

Azra spoke slowly, pausing after each offence to allow the ripples to disperse. To sink like stones in a lake before moving on to the next.

"Fraud.

Money laundering.

Blackmail.

Extortion.

Criminal Damage.

Aggravated assault and battery.

Grievous bodily harm.

Accessory to murder."

I leaned back on the leather sofa and closed my eyes as my world disintegrated around me.

"Carrie?" she said after a few moments. "Are you OK?"

Behind my eyelids, I saw Barbaros's face. The melancholy in his eyes. *"I've done some bad things, Carrie."*

"Yes," I managed to say. "Thank you, Azra."

"Carrie, he is dangerous. He's probably killed people, though they couldn't prove it. Witnesses have disappeared. He tied one man to a chair and beat him with a baseball bat. He had twenty-three broken bones. The man was so afraid of Barbaros, he refused to testify. Whole families have been relocated to get away from him. He was involved with some serious individuals. Criminal gangs. Organised crime."

It was too hot on the balcony, the sun too bright. A trickle of sweat ran down my stomach, sticking my t-shirt to my skin.

"You need to leave," said Azra in my ear. "You need to take Elif and leave. As soon as possible."

After we said our goodbyes, I sat on the leather sofa and stared out at the empty hill. I worried about the sheep and hoped their *Nazar* were protecting them from harm.

A slideshow of faces began to play in my mind.

Margaret Crosby, her watery, grey eyes staring into mine. *"He's dangerous Carrie."*

Barbaros, his face illuminated in the dark. *"I can make people disappear."*

Serkan, his lip curled into a sneer. *"I will take your children and drive you out of Turkey."*

It was happening.

Suddenly, I was on my feet. I ran to the bedroom and pulled my suitcase out from under the bed, emptying first my wardrobe, then Elif's. Stuffing in as many of her new toys and books as I could and forcing the zip shut. The case was heavy. I dragged it to the front door and bumped it down the concrete steps one at a time.

From his plastic chair, Süleyman *Bey* watched as I heaved the suitcase into the boot. He did not offer to help.

I climbed into the driver's seat, a flash of Déjà vu hitting me as I closed the door and turned the key in the ignition.

New Year's Eve. My frozen breath in the night air. The silver tea light clutched in my hand.

I still don't know what made me go back. Memories, perhaps? Christmas day. Barbaros and I having dinner on the balcony as the sun set over the hill. The silver hearts turning in slow circles above the flame. In the turmoil my life had become, the silver tea light represented something. Something I was losing with every passing hour. I got out of the car and sprinted back up the concrete steps to the apartment. Watched by Süleyman *Bey*.

The silver tea light was still on the shelf where Barbaros had left it after it was blown from the balcony during the storm. The two remaining hearts hung from the dented parasol, twisted at odd angles.

I grabbed the tea light, scanning the room to make sure there was nothing else I'd forgotten. I turned back towards the door and stopped.

Barbaros stood in the open doorway, his expression, unreadable.

"What are you doing here?" I stuttered.

"I finished early," he smiled. "Thought I'd surprise you."

"I was just going to pick Elif up from school."

He glanced at the tea light in my hand.

"I'll come with you."

"No need." I took a step towards the door. "I won't be long."

He moved to the left, blocking my exit.

"Are you telling me the truth, Carrie?" he said calmly, taking a step towards me. "You wouldn't lie to me, would you?"

I stood rooted to the spot as he took another step towards me.

"Were you leaving me?" His voice was soft, his eyes, kind. "After everything I've done for you? Were you going to run away, Carrie?"

He continued to walk towards me, his eyes never leaving mine, forcing me backwards until I was pressed against the kitchen counter. He took another step, so close I could feel his breath on my face.

"Why is your suitcase in the back of the car?" he whispered.

He glared at me. His eyes were black.

"Barbaros, I know!" I cried. "I know about your past. What you did. Why you were in jail."

"So, you were just going to run away?" he said.

"I was scared."

Barbaros stared at me. His anger simmered just beneath the surface like a snake waiting to strike.

"Scared?" he whispered. "Of me?"

I nodded.

He smiled. "Where did you go?" he said, reaching into his shirt pocket for a cigarette. "Last Saturday? You were out all day."

He lit his cigarette and took a deep drag, narrowing his eyes as he surveyed me through a cloud of smoke.

"I know things about you too, Carrie," he smiled.

Süleyman *Bey*. His watchful gaze as I heaved my suitcase into the boot of the car. His silent stare as I left for Maralya. Suddenly it all made sense.

"I went to Maralya," I said.

"To see your ex-husband?"

"To see my son!"

Barbaros shook his head. He took another drag of his cigarette.

"I tried to warn you," he said, staring down at the floor. "I told you a thousand times to leave it alone, but you wouldn't listen."

When he looked back up, tears glistened in his eyes. "Our relationship was so beautiful," he said. "But you destroyed it, Carrie. Everything has to be different now."

Our eyes locked together as the day stood still. The clock on the kitchen wall ticked loudly as if counting down to something. *"He's dangerous, Carrie,"* warned Azra's voice in my head.

I was late. I imagined Elif, alone in the school playground. Waiting.

"Tamam, anneciğim!"

Barbaros and I both looked towards the open door as a high-pitched voice echoed in the stairwell. *"Merhaba!"* said Fatma, grinning as she appeared on the landing. In one hand, she clutched a bag of groceries as she steered her mother gently towards their door with the other.

It was all the opportunity I needed.

I ran.

"*Özür dilerim,*" I breathed as I pushed past them, flying down the concrete steps two at a time.

"*Canım, iyi misin?*" called Fatma after me before her voice was drowned out.

By the rasp of my ragged breathing in my ears.

By the pounding of my heart in my chest.

By the slap of my flip-flops on the concrete steps.

By the second set of footsteps gaining speed close behind me.

Chapter Forty-Nine

Bodrum, Turkey. May 2016.

Sombre storm clouds gathered behind Kos on the horizon as she rose majestically from the slate-grey sea. Behind me, in the hotel room, Elif slept, starfish-like on starched white hotel sheets. I took another sip of wine.

Having run out on Barbaros with no time to think, the hours since had been filled with nothing but. The adrenaline subsided, leaving a flat emptiness in its wake. A dull ache in my chest at the unanswerable question that played on a loop in my mind.

What was I going to do?

I had driven straight to the school, apologising to Elif for being late and muttering something vague about going on holiday as I ushered her quickly into the back of the car. Her silence and lack of questions were a testament to a lifetime of not asking. The way she didn't ask when I sent her and Cem upstairs at the first twitches of Serkan's temper. The way she didn't ask about the yelling or the sound of breaking glass. Or why we were driving to Azra's in the middle of the night.

The Hotel was small and family-run. The room was basic, but clean, with bare white walls and two neatly made single beds. In the corner was a small kitchen consisting of a kettle, a single-ringed electric hob, and a tiny fridge. The owner, a mild-mannered man called Cetin *Bey*, spent his time in reception as his wife Selma, round-faced and lipstick-smiled, bustled around him. Though we were the only guests, Selma had gamely put out breakfast on the roof terrace, laying out plates of cucumber, olives, cheese, bread, and tomatoes and pretending not to watch from behind the bar as I sipped black coffee and Elif slathered Nutella on thickly sliced bread.

Opposite the hotel was a small supermarket, not unlike the one run by Suleyman *Bey*, with over-stuffed aisles and overpriced food. The man behind the counter had peered at me from over the top of his newspaper that morning as I stocked up on coffee, bread, pasta, and a bottle of red wine.

"Look!" Elif exclaimed as she stopped next to a display of shiny blue cylinders. **Special Offer!** The sign above them declared in large black letters. **Easy-assemble two-person tent**.

Elif picked one up. "Can we go camping, mum? *Please!*"

I had never been camping in my life and had no intention to start, but the smile on her face was enough.

"Great idea!" I replied, taking the tent and adding it to our basket.

My wineglass was empty. I poured another and stared straight ahead at Kos on the horizon.

I had just drained my second glass when my phone lit up with his face. He had called multiple times, several times an hour since I left, but now I was weak. Exhaustion and alcohol had worked their way into my blood, seeping into my brain, washing away my defences and drowning my resolve.

"*Talk to him,*" whispered the voice in my head. "*It's Barbaros. Your Barbaros.*"

I watched like a third party as my fingers reached for my phone. My eyes settled on his face, the weight of longing, heavy in my chest.

"Hello."

"Carrie?" He sounded surprised, caught off guard. A heavy sigh.

"It's so good to hear your voice. I've been so worried."

The lights of Kos blurred behind a wall of tears.

"Carrie, listen to me. This is exactly what Serkan wants. You're playing right into his hands. He's bluffing, Carrie. The courts can't even prove we're together."

From high on the white wall, a pale orange gecko stared down at me with bulging black eyes.

"Come home," he said. "It will be perfect again. You, me and Elif. The way it was before. You can buy an apartment. Get Alfie back. Sort out access to Cem. It's still possible, Carrie. Don't let Serkan destroy what we had."

I closed my eyes and sank into the memory.

Gümüşlük. The sun warm on my skin, the air sweet with the smell of coconut sun cream and barbequed chicken. Barbaros fanning the flames. A wink as his eyes met mine, crinkling up at the corners as he smiled.

Loneliness, red wine, and memories conspired together like allies in a war, pulling me under. I tried to force myself back, paddling against the tide.

"But...those things you did."

A baseball bat.

A man tied to a chair.

Twenty-three broken bones.

"It's in the past," he sighed. "I'm not the same person anymore. I left Istanbul to get away from all that. I just want a normal life. A quiet, peaceful life. With you."

A flicker of lightning lit up the horizon. Behind me in the hotel room, Elif stirred and rolled onto her side.

"I have a child," I said.

"I would never hurt Elif. Or you. I love you, Carrie."

"Tell me about Laura," I said. "She was afraid of you. She left the country to get away from you."

Another sigh. "Laura was crazy," he replied. "She drank. She was jealous. I have no idea where she is now."

I rubbed my temples as a dull throbbing began behind my eyes. Suddenly, I needed to sleep more than anything.

"I need some time," I said.

"Time?"

"I need some time by myself. To think. After the court case, when this is all over. We'll talk, I promise."

There was a low growl of thunder. A slow drumming of raindrops began on the terracotta roof. Another lightning flash lit up the sky, spot-lighting Kos on the horizon like a performer on a stage.

When he finally spoke, it was the voice of a stranger, as cold and as hard as steel.

"Do you think this is a game, Carrie?" he said. "Do you think you can just walk out of my life the way you walked into it? Use me and throw me away like a toy? I saved you! I took care of you! I did everything for you, and this is how you repay me?"

The drumming grew louder, faster. Water began to run in rivulets down the sloping balcony roof, dripping onto the table and into my empty wine glass. I stared at the pink-tinged liquid, unable to move as Barbaros continued.

"Maybe I didn't make myself clear," he said in a voice that chilled the blood in my veins.

"You have until tomorrow morning to change your mind. If not, I will offer Serkan my full support. I will testify in court that everything he says is true. You cheated on him. You left your kids. You will lose custody of Elif."

A crack of thunder split the sky in two as sheet lightning lit up Kos on the horizon.

Suddenly I was stone-cold sober.

"And then I will hunt you down and break every bone in your body."

Chapter Fifty

Bodrum, Turkey. May 2016.

The baseball bat slapped against the palm of his hand with a sickening thwack as he walked around me in slow circles. I tried to speak, but there was something in my mouth. My arms were tied behind my back. Barbaros straddled a chair, placed a cigarette between his lips and struck a match, briefly illuminating his face in the dark.

"I can make people disappear."

He blew out the match, plunging us both into darkness.

Someone was banging on the door.

"Mum!"

Elif was sitting bolt upright in her single bed, her hair plastered to her head with sweat. The sun streamed in through the balcony doors of an unfamiliar hotel room. It was a few seconds before I remembered.

Another knock.

"Shhh." I pressed my finger to my lips, swung my legs out of bed and moved slowly towards the door.

"Efendim?" I said, in a voice that wasn't mine.

"Oda servisi!" came back the cheery reply. "Room service!"

I turned the key and opened the door. Selma's round face beamed at me from behind a pile of freshly laundered towels.

We had overslept. It was already past eleven, and we had missed breakfast on the roof terrace. My head throbbed as I checked my phone for missed calls and messages, but there were none.

"I'm hungry," said Elif with a yawn as she stretched her arms above her head. I flicked the switch on the kettle and spooned instant coffee into a mug, sliced some bread and slathered it with honey. I glanced towards the balcony where my rain-filled wine glass sat alone on the plastic table in a puddle of water. Flashes of last night crept into my mind as I wiped the remnants of rainwater from the plastic table and chairs.

We sat in silence. I sipped my coffee and Elif ate her bread. Kos in the distance watched staunch and silent, like a third guest at our breakfast table.

The weather had cleared. Seagulls soared and dipped in the pale blue sky above a glassy sea. It was as if last night had never happened.

"How long are we going to stay here?" said Elif. Honey drizzled down her chin.

"I don't know, sweetie."

My phone buzzed on the table in front of me. A Pavlovian wave of dread rippled through me at the sight of Serkan's face. Reluctantly, I answered it.

"I've just had a very interesting conversation with your boyfriend." Serkan made no attempt to hide the enjoyment in his voice. "Or should I say, ex-boyfriend?"

I put my coffee cup down, splashing black liquid onto the white saucer "You've really fucked up this time, Carrie."

There was a lengthy silence as he waited for me to respond.

"He wants to help me get custody of Elif," he continued. "He wants to testify against you in court."

Across the road from the hotel, a group of Syrian refugees were huddled together in the shade of a tree. The adults held their hands out as people walked by. The children played a makeshift game of "football," kicking an empty Coke can in the dust.

"I haven't said yes to him yet," continued Serkan. "I'm giving you one more chance to come back to Maralya. This is the only place you will be safe."

I knew he was right. The code of honour among men meant that while I was in Serkan's hometown, Barbaros might leave me alone.

"You don't have a choice, Carrie. You can't escape. Not this time."

Escape

The word hung in the air like an invisible thread between me and the refugees. The only differences between us, our countries of origin, passports, and nationalities, were unfairly stacked in my favour. I looked across the sea at Kos, like a beacon of hope on the horizon.

Could the answer be literally staring me in the face?

"Carrie?" said Serkan again. There was a hard edge of impatience in his voice. "Carrie, are you…"

Cutting him off mid-sentence, I ended the call and placed my phone face-down on the table, taking another sip of coffee as I gazed at Kos across the sea.

***

The German woman smiled at me from across the pool as I looked up from the dog-eared book I had found in reception. It wasn't the kind of thing I normally read. A summer blockbuster, light on plot and heavy on tropes, but it offered an escape, if only for a few hours. I smiled back. The couple had arrived yesterday, stereotypically laying their towels over the sunbeds as Elif and I had breakfast on the roof terrace. Between us, in the oval-shaped swimming pool, Elif floated on an inflatable flamingo, her eyes framed by pink heart-shaped sunglasses.

My phone buzzed a message making my stomach sink.

Marie, my yoga-loving artist friend, smiled at me from the profile picture, her hands pressed together in the prayer pose.

> *Hi, Carrie! I'm in Maralya next week. Let's have lunch! Would love to see you!*

I racked my brains, trying to remember when I had last spoken to Marie. Since leaving Maralya, I had barely had any contact with any of my friends.

> *I'm not in Maralya anymore*

I typed back.

> *A lot of stuff happened, and I had to leave*

Immediately, my phone rang.

"Carrie, what happened? Are you OK?" The kindness in Marie's voice brought tears to my eyes.

I took a deep breath, unsure where to start.

"Not really," I said, biting my lip.

"Mummy, look!" Elif called from the pool as she kicked her back legs, propelling the flamingo forward.

"Was it something to do with Serkan? With the divorce?" Marie continued.

She listened in silence as I relayed the events of the past six months. Had it really only been that long? It felt like a lifetime.

"Shit, Carrie," she said when I had finished. "What are you going to do?"

"I don't know."

"You need to get out of Turkey," she said.

"It's not that easy," I sighed. "Serkan has a court order blocking Elif from leaving the country."

"Shit," said Marie again.

I thought back to last night's storm. Kos lit up against the horizon in the night sky. An idea swirled around my brain, an idea without substance or form, like a childhood memory, or a partly forgotten song, but an idea all the same.

"There's a Greek island opposite here," I said. "I think there's a ferry. It's risky, but less so than an airport."

As soon as they were out of my mouth, my words seemed preposterous, laughable. If we even made it to Kos, where would we go? Was I seriously considering driving across Europe with Elif? I had barely made it to Maralya without having a panic attack.

"Forget it," I said. "It's stupid."

"But what else can you do?" said Marie.

There was another reason. A reason so big, I hadn't allowed myself to think it let alone say it out loud. Cem. To leave Turkey was to leave my son.

"Go back to Maralya," I replied. "Get a job. Buy an apartment." I hesitated as tears stung my eyes. "At least I might get to see Cem."

"But you could lose custody of Elif," continued Marie. "And Serkan will never leave you alone. Not to mention this Barbaros guy. He sounds like a nasty piece of work."

The decision no parent should ever have to make hung over me like a guillotine. Give up one child, or risk losing both.

"Carrie, you have to get out of Turkey," said Marie gently. "You don't have a choice."

"Where would I even go?" I said. The thought of returning to the cold and rain of the UK filled me with gloom. That and the fact that Serkan would easily find us there.

"You can come here!" she said suddenly.

"What?"

"Here. To Spain. You can stay with me while you decide what to do next."

"Really?"

"Of course."

"Thank you," I said.

"Think it over," said Marie. "It's a hard decision, Carrie, but you have to do what's best for you and Elif. You know you are always welcome here."

***

That evening, I sat on the balcony with my laptop as Elif slept.

The seed, now firmly planted, had put down roots and was winding its way through my brain with the tenacity of bindweed. After connecting to the hotel's shaky internet, I began to search for answers to the questions that circled my brain in a relentless loop.

There was a ferry from Bodrum Harbour to Kos every day at 9:30 am. From Kos, we could take the ferry to the Greek mainland and from there, another ferry to Italy.

I poured over the map, following the Italian coast with my finger.

Giovinazzo,

Molfetta,

Bisceglie

I had no idea what any of these places were like, but I liked the names.

It was around midnight that they started. I lay on my single bed as message after message lit up my phone in the dark.

Barbaros

> *I'm in Istanbul. It's not too late. Come.*

Serkan

> *Carrie, you need to come to Maralya immediately. He's dangerous. He has people looking for you.*

Barbaros

> *I found a lawyer. He can help you with the case. He says he can help you get custody of Cem, too. Call me.*

Serkan

> *Call me urgently. Don't trust him. It's not safe.*

Despite my exhaustion, I couldn't sleep. The white walls of the hotel room pressed down on me like a padded cell. A mosquito whined periodically in my ear; its comrades martyred in bloody spatters on the white walls. From the corner of the room, a pale orange gecko watched me with bulging black eyes.

At around three, I kicked off the starched white sheet, made my way to the bathroom and switched on the shower. I pulled my T-shirt over my head and slipped out of my shorts, stopping as I caught sight of my reflection in the mirror. I stared, shocked by my appearance. By the skin stretched tight across my ribs. By my jutting hip bones and concave stomach. By my sunken eyes and hollow cheeks. I couldn't remember the last time I had felt hungry, let alone eaten a proper meal.

After my shower, I wrapped myself in a towel and lay back on my single bed. A stream of *what-ifs* danced above me in the hot, still air.

What if we were stopped and sent back?

What if I were arrested?

What if they took Elif?

In the end, it was just us. Myself and Fear. Fighting silently in the airless air of a hotel room.

What if I got lost or had a panic attack?

What if we were attacked or robbed?

How was I going to start again, alone, in a new country?

I stared up at the white ceiling as a picture of my future began to form in my mind.

An apartment in Maralya. Serkan spread out on the sofa, a self-satisfied glint in his eyes. "You are so lucky to have me, Carrie."

In time, maybe I would learn to ignore the stares and the people whispering behind their hands. The prodigal wife. The one who left her kids and ran away with her boyfriend, returned with her tail between her legs. A life lived under his control. A life in the shadows. Watching my children grow up from afar.

I got out of bed and padded barefoot across the cool floor tiles to the balcony, curling my legs underneath me as I settled into the plastic chair.

The night air was warm and still. Across the sea, the lights of Kos glimmered like an invitation.

It was first light, the early morning call to prayer echoing across the skies when I eventually fell back into bed, instantly descending into the depths of sleep. I dreamed of winding Italian roads, vineyards plump with grapes and fields of sunflowers under clear blue skies.

I awoke with a start, a feeling I had overslept or forgotten something important jerking me from sleep as I sat up. The sun streamed in through the open balcony doors. The curtains fluttered gently in the breeze. Elif was still asleep, flat on her back in her single bed. From the coolness of the air and the quietness of the street outside, I could tell that it was still early.

I reached for my phone on the nightstand and scrolled down until I found the number I was looking for. It was answered immediately.

"Carrie?"

"I've made a decision," I said. "I'm going to come if it's still OK."

"Of course."

The line crackled as the internet connection wavered in and out.

"Stay safe. Keep in touch. Let me know what happens," echoed Marie's voice before the line went dead.

Chapter Fifty-One

Spain. July 2016.

I had heard the song many times before but never really listened to the words. I couldn't remember the singer's name.

I stifled a yawn, arching my aching back and wriggling in my seat as, through the windscreen, another motorway stretched ahead. A straight, grey line neatly slicing through rolling, tree-covered hills beneath a sky-blue sky. I glanced at Elif, fast asleep in the back seat, her sketchpad open on her lap.

We had spent five days in France, staying in campsites along the Mediterranean coast, before joining the *Autopista del Mediterráneo* that morning to begin the last leg of our journey towards the border with Spain.

Sia, her name was. I remembered it now. One of those singers with only one name, like Madonna or Beyonce or Prince. Her voice was quiet, almost lost behind the rhythmic plucking of guitar strings as her words pulled me back to a villa in the sun.

Fruit trees. A hammock strung between them. Chickens pecking and scratching in the dust. The smell of jasmine and honeysuckle. The sound of children's laughter.

A villa filled with silence and fear. Locked doors. Cold tiles. The pounding of fists on wood.

Goosebumps prickled my skin as the tempo increased. A chill shuddered through me despite the warmth of the sun.

The motorway forged ahead towards an unknown future. The roar of traffic, oblivious to the butterflies in the bisected meadow, the rush of cars at odds with the whisper of the breeze in the trees.

I reached forward and turned the radio up, pulling down the sun visor and squinting in the bright sunlight as a blue rectangle appeared in the distance. A single word in a circle of yellow stars.

Somewhere between the driving bass and the soaring harmony, my past and future collided, lodging in my throat and blurring the letters on the blue sign. But I already knew what it said.

España

The tears were flowing freely now, sliding unchecked down my cheeks, as her words told my story. I saw myself pinned against the wall, his hands around my throat. The nothingness in his eyes as he pressed the blade against my skin. Clinging to Elif under the duvet as his fists hammered on the door.

I saw myself in a hotel room, tracing names on a map with my finger as I said them out loud. Driving through Italy with the stereo turned up. Past fields of sunflowers. Through terracotta towns. Along winding coast roads high above the sea.

I cried for the ones I had left behind. For Cem. For Alfie. For Azra and Atakan.

I cried for Serkan and Barbaros. For control and fear disguised as love.

I cried for the person I used to be.

I was stronger than I ever thought possible.

I was titanium.

I was free.

Gripping the steering wheel with both hands, I stared straight ahead as I slid silently across the border into my new life.

Chapter Fifty-Two

Epilogue

The silver hearts do not spin as smoothly as they once did. I have tried my best to straighten out the twisted metal, but they still stumble slightly as they circle above the flame.

Most importantly, they are still able to dance.

It took a long time for Elif and I to rebuild our lives. A long time for the nightmares and panic attacks to stop. A long time before I stopped hearing Serkan's voice in my head. Before I stopped checking over my shoulder when I arrived home late at night.

Her şey zaman, someone once said.

My story happened in Turkey, but it could have happened anywhere. And it does. Every day. In every country around the world.

While I'm aware that domestic violence can affect anyone regardless of gender, as a woman, I am focusing on male violence against women and girls. Here are some sobering statistics.

Male violence against women is the leading cause of premature death for women globally. In 2022, around 48,800 women and girls were killed by their intimate partners or other family members worldwide. Of these around 55% were murdered by their current or former partners.

According to the UK's National Centre for Domestic Violence, one in four women will experience domestic abuse during their lifetime. Between March 2021 and March 2022, there were just over 1.5 million domestic abuse-related crimes recorded by the police in England and Wales. An estimated 76% of domestic abuse incidents are not reported to the police.

People often ask me why I wrote this book. In the beginning, it served as a kind of therapy. A cathartic release of words onto a page. A way of making sense of what happened. I want other women to read my story and know that they are not alone. That there is always a way out. In the end, I just felt that this was a story that needed to be told.

Domestic abuse is complex and multi-faceted. I hope my story goes some way to explaining why women don't "just leave."

So how do we stop the growing pandemic of domestic abuse? I don't claim to have all the answers, but I do believe strongly that education is the key.

We need to educate women and girls about the signs of abuse, not only physical but emotional, sexual and financial. We need to teach our daughters to recognise early red flags, and that threats, coercion, manipulation and damage to property also constitute abuse. That jealousy, possessiveness and control are not love. We need to instil boundaries, self-belief, and self-worth in our children, particularly girls. We need to have open, honest conversations, and remove stigma, blame, and guilt.

We need to raise our sons to see women as fellow human beings, not as objects or possessions to be controlled.

Elif is now a happy teenager, doing regular teenage things. She is my pride and joy.

Last year, Elif and I were reunited with Cem in the UK. We are in regular contact and I hope to see him again very soon.

Atakan and I are and always will be best friends. We lived together in Spain for around a year before he met the love of his life and returned to Istanbul. We went on holiday together earlier this year and are already planning a trip for next year.

Marie remains one of my closest friends.

Serkan has remarried and still lives in Turkey. I have no contact with him except to discuss the children.

I have no contact with Barbaros.

A few years ago, I embarked on a new career as a health and medical writer. I still can't believe I get paid to do what I love every day. I continue to write fiction in my spare time.

Damaged, but not destroyed, Elif and I, like the two remaining hearts, have survived.

One of my favourite quotes is by George Addair: "Everything you ever wanted is on the other side of fear."

I for one, believe him.

The End

About the author

Caroline Orman currently lives in Spain with her daughter, a crazy dog, and a slightly less crazy cat. She works as a freelance health and medical writer and continues to pursue her dream of becoming a full-time fiction writer. She is currently working on her next novel.

Follow Caroline on her website carolineormanauthor.com

Instagram @carolineormanauthor

Facebook Caroline Orman Author

Printed in Dunstable, United Kingdom